THE SAHARA

Landscapes of the Imagination

The Alps by Andrew Beattie
Provence by Martin Garrett
Flanders by André de Vries
The Thames by Mick Sinclair
Catalonia by Michael Eaude
The Basque Country by Paddy Woodworth
Andalucía by John Gill
Patagonia by Chris Moss
The French Riviera by Julian Hale
The Andes by Jason Wilson
The West Country by John Payne
The Cotswolds by Jane Bingham
Siberia by A. J. Haywood
The Ionian Islands and Epirus by Jim Potts
The Loire by Martin Garrett
The Danube by Andrew Beattie
The Sahara by Eamonn Gearon

Landscapes

THE SAHARA
A *Cultural History*

EAMONN GEARON

OXFORD
UNIVERSITY PRESS

OXFORD

UNIVERSITY PRESS

Oxford University Press, Inc., publishes works that further
Oxford University's objective of excellence
in research, scholarship, and education.

Oxford New York
Auckland   Cape Town   Dar es Salaam   Hong Kong   Karachi
Kuala Lumpur   Madrid   Melbourne   Mexico City   Nairobi
New Delhi   Shanghai   Taipei   Toronto

With offices in
Argentina   Austria   Brazil   Chile   Czech Republic   France   Greece
Guatemala   Hungary   Italy   Japan   Poland   Portugal   Singapore
South Korea   Switzerland   Thailand   Turkey   Ukraine   Vietnam

Copyright © 2011 by Eamonn Gearon

Published by Oxford University Press, Inc.
198 Madison Avenue, New York, NY 10016

www.oup.com

Oxford is a registered trademark of Oxford University Press

Co-published in Great Britain by Signal Books

Illustrations: All illustrations Wikipedia Commons, except: Siemens.com, p. 151;
tinariwen.com, p. 240; Michelle Brehm, p. 242

Library of Congress Cataloging-in-Publication Data
Gearon, Eamonn.
The Sahara : a cultural history / Eamonn Gearon.
p. cm. — (Landscapes of the imagination)
Includes bibliographical references and index.
ISBN 978-0-19-986196-5 (hardcover) — ISBN 978-0-19-986195-8 (paperback)
1. Sahara—History. 2. Sahara—Civilization. 3. Sahara—In literature.
I. Title. II. Series: Landscapes of the imagination.
DT333.G37 2011
966—dc23   2011028276

1 3 5 7 9 8 6 4 2

Printed in the United States of America
on acid-free paper

Contents

Preface and Acknowledgments ix

Introduction
A QUICK TOUR OF THE SAHARA xi
Flora and Fauna (xviii)

PART ONE: LANDSCAPES

Chapter One
WHALES IN THE DESERT 3
The Green Sahara (7)

Chapter Two
ROCK ART 11
Iconography and Graffiti (15)

Chapter Three
SAHARAN URBAN 21
Oasis-Towns (24)

PART TWO: HISTORY
Conquests and Empires

Chapter Four
FROM ANCIENT EGYPT TO THE ARAB INVASION 29
Land of the Dead (29); The Phoenicians (32); Persian and Ptolemaic
Dynasties (34); The Romans (39); The Garamantes (41);
Camels (45); Christian North Africa (49); The Vandals (55); The
Armies of Islam (57)

Chapter Five
TRAVELLERS, CHRONICLERS, GEOGRAPHERS 63
Gilded Empires (70); Timbuktu (73)

PART THREE: HISTORY
Exploration, Imperialism and Independence

Chapter Six
EUROPEAN FORAYS: THE AFRICAN ASSOCIATION
AND NAPOLEON 85
Hornemann (94); Egyptomania (97)

Chapter Seven
FURTHER HORIZONS: EXPLORATION AND THE EUROPEAN LAND
GRAB 101
Caillié, Barth and Rohlfs (104); Algeria and Abd al-Qadir (110);
The Scramble for Africa (113)

Chapter Eight
WAR AND PEACE AND WAR 117
Motors, Maps and Planes (121)

Chapter Nine
THE SECOND WORLD WAR 131
Desert Warfare (136)

Chapter Ten
HEAVEN AND HELL: INDEPENDENCE AND SINCE 141
The French Legacy (146)

PART FOUR: IMAGINATION

Chapter Eleven
CLASSICAL INSPIRATION 155
Riddle of the Sphinx (160)

Chapter Twelve
POETIC MUSE   163
"The Brutish Desert": War Poets (169)

Chapter Thirteen
A BRILLIANT PALETTE   173
Fromentin and the Orientalists: "Dangerous Novelties" (176)

Chapter Fourteen
ORIENTAL DELIGHTS, STRANGE WORLDS AND SPY STORIES   185
Tales of the Legion (190); Desert Espionage (192)

Chapter Fifteen
SILVER SCREEN SAHARA   197
Beau Geste (201); Desert Epics (206)

PART FIVE: ENCOUNTERS
Indigenes and Visitors

Chapter Sixteen
MEN WITH A MISSION   211
Professionals (216); Missionaries (219)

Chapter Seventeen
LITERARY TRAVELLERS AND TOURISTS   225
Early Observers (226); Wilfred Thesiger (232); Adventure Tourism
(234)

Chapter Eighteen
PEOPLE OF THE SAHARA   237
The Tuareg (238); Toubou and Sahrawi (241); Two Incomers: Isabelle
Eberhardt and Paul Bowles (244)

FURTHER READING   249
INDEX OF LITERARY & HISTORICAL NAMES   251
INDEX OF PLACES & LANDMARKS   258

For my late father, upon whose knee I first learnt about the Sahara;
My mother, for not telling me how much she worried when I first entered
the Sahara;
And to Osama, Ibn Kelb and Baby, my camels, who made it possible for
me to explore the Sahara, thereby exchanging dreams for memories.

Preface and Acknowledgments

My own relationship with the Sahara stretches back over two decades, and my love of the place grows every year. While I have lived, worked and walked in the Great Desert, I have been lucky to learn many lessons from its inhabitants that I would never have found in any library. Foremost among this knowledge was that gained from the Bedouin, which has allowed me to pursue solo, camel-powered expeditions.

Cecil Beaton put the case neatly in a 1942 diary entry, when he wrote from the Egyptian Sahara, "I see that human existence in the desert has not the proportion of the surroundings." It is hard to imagine a place more replete with history, myths and legends. The Sahara is justly a land of superlatives: the world's largest hot desert, with the highest recorded temperatures on earth; it is driest, wildest, most dangerous in its immensity, most beguiling.

It is also one of the most starkly beautiful places on earth and has long captured the imagination of those who have come into contact with it, from the earliest inhabitants to contemporary tourists. From its prehistory, countless generations have been moved to record their impressions of the Sahara. Thankfully, many committed their thoughts to stone, paper, canvas and film, allowing us to share in these experiences.

The plethora of accounts written by those who spent time in the Sahara means that tough choices have been made in selecting who and what to include and exclude. This is no encyclopaedia but it is at least hoped that it will be of service in guiding readers through the literal and imaginary landscapes of the Sahara, its history, cultures and a portion of the creative work it has inspired.

Those who have passed through the Sahara have been as diverse as the landscapes found there. Innocent traveller, prospector and trader, solo adventurer and conquering soldier, writer, poet and painter, ethnologist, biologist, legionnaire or hermit, each account has its place, enjoying some share of that common thread of the story of the desert that inspired them. Whatever reason one might have for being in the Great Desert, the experience leaves no one untouched. The Sahara does not allow a neutral response; its mystery breathes life into even the stoniest of hearts that confronts the desert's vastness, terrible beauty and immeasurable silence.

Thanks are due to numerous people: writing a book is not as solitary a pursuit as some might imagine: To Oscar Blend, whose keen eyes and red pen made the manuscript make sense; Dr. William Sheward, for material support and wise counsel whenever I visit London; to Eileen Clauson, for similar generosity freely given in New Hampshire; Will and Lucy Beharrell, and the peace of Ramsden; Tom and Candace Powers; Phyllis Nemhauser and all the staff of the Baker-Berry and Sherman Libraries at Dartmouth College, and likewise the staff of the Howe Library, Hanover, NH; my agent, Graham Greene; Michael Dwyer and James Ferguson for the initial commission and subsequent encouragement. Finally, my greatest thanks go to my wife, Laura, whose patience, insight, advice, and unstinting backing made this book possible.

Introduction
A Quick Tour of the Sahara

Before exploring the Sahara's human history, we will be well served by a quick tour of its geographical present. The great desert covers portions of eleven North African nations: Morocco, Algeria, Tunisia, Libya, Egypt, Sudan, Chad, Niger, Mali, Mauritania and the Western Sahara. Depending on the results of a January 2011 referendum, which is giving the southern Sudanese the opportunity to vote for independence from the north, this figure may become twelve.

Perhaps the commonest view of the Sahara, as nothing but a sandy place, is neatly summed up by the nineteenth-century Anglican Archbishop of Dublin, Richard Whately, who is responsible, some would say guilty, of the following speculation: "Why can a man never starve in the Great Desert? Because he can eat the sand which is there." Not content with one groan-inducing pun, Whately went on to ask, "But what brought the sandwiches there? Why, Noah sent Ham, and his descendants mustered and bred."

However much sand the Sahara may contain, it must not be thought of as a monolithic entity, a single mass covered in its entirety by sand dunes. The Sahara has numerous distinct geographies but its name is somewhat misleading. It is Arabic and made up of three consonants, *saad, ha* and *ra*, and short and long a-sound vowels. It means simply desert, so to talk of the "Sahara desert" is something of a tautology.

Most Arabic words are drawn form three-letter roots, like the Sahara's *saad, ha,* and *ra*. From these roots families of words branch out and, once mastered, are a great help to both native and foreign learners of Arabic. For example, the Arabic letters equivalent to k, t, and b come together in various forms to make the words book, office (the place of books), library (the house of books) and the verb to write (to create a book). Likewise, the *s-h-r* root, as well as giving us desert or "desolate place", also gives us a barren region, a waste-land, a shade of dusty red, and verbs for "to wither" and "to inflict sunstroke".

In the same way that the *s-h-r* family of letters has numerous members, so the Sahara is many deserts in one, not one desert. These deserts, some named by their inhabitants, some by invaders and by other foreign visitors, each have a distinct identity while at the same time being identifiably a part of the Great Desert by their situation in the top third of the African continent. A native of southern Algeria lives in a desert that he or she knows as the Ahaggar, or Hoggar, while neighbours to the north live in the Tassili n'Ajjer, which translates from the local Tamazight language as Plateau of the Rivers. The local population of northern Chad know home as the Tibesti after the mountain range, while inhabitants of one of the oases west of the Nile may refer to their homeland as *al-sahara al-gharb*, the desert of the west. In Arabic, Sahara as a proper noun seems to have been used first in the ninth century by the Egyptian historian Ibn Abd-al-Hakam (d. 871), when he referred to a distinct piece of desert to the west of the Fezzan and not just as a general description of a desolate place.

Ignoring the varieties of deserts, it is the multi-coloured waves of sand that capture the popular imagination when thinking about the Sahara. Beloved alike of poets and photographers, the dunes are loathed by the foot traveller, for whom they represent an obstruction that must be crossed with great care. These striking, textured, surreal fields of whipped sand have for millennia formed a notable obstacle to free movement between various parts of the Sahara. But for all their terrible majesty, the dunes only make up about fifteen per cent of the total mass of the Sahara. That is not to say they are paltry affairs.

Saharan scales and distances are vast: anything making up "only" fifteen per cent of the desert's surface will still take up a lot of space. If the area covered by the Sahara's sand dunes was laid over a map of Europe it would cover virtually the whole of France, Germany and Spain: nearly 600,000 square miles. The Great Sand Sea alone, the world's largest unbroken area of dunes, which stretches from northern Egypt and eastern Libya to Sudan, covers an area larger than Ireland and Wales combined.

The Saharan landmass covers a remarkable three-and-a-half million square miles—roughly the same size of the United States, including Alaska and Hawaii. But just as remarkable is how little human life is to be found in it; an estimated population of two-and-a-half million gives it a density of less than one and a half people per square mile. While sailing down the Nile, Rudyard Kipling considered the size of the desert, writing in *Letters of Travel*:

Going up the Nile is like running the gauntlet before Eternity. Till one has seen it, one does not realise the amazing thinness of that little damp trickle of life that steals along undefeated through the jaws of established death. A rifle-shot would cover the widest limits of cultivation, a bow-shot would reach the narrower. Once beyond them a man may carry his next drink with him till he reaches Cape Blanco on the west (where he may signal for one from a passing Union Castle boat) or the Karachi Club on the east. Say four thousand dry miles to the left hand and three thousand to the right.

It is not a place in which to get lost. Whether marooned in a sea of sand or abandoned on an almost featureless plain the size of France, one's options are limited and the likelihood of imminent death is high. An individual stranded without water in the Saharan summer cannot hope to survive for more than two or three days. The descent from thirst to madness is swift. If death comes only after a period of intense agony at least when it does come it is a merciful release. The immense, almost inhuman scale of the desert, combined with its limited water and its often alien faces, some of which might as well belong to other planets, all present an environment that many think would be best avoided at any cost.

Added to this are the extreme temperatures. The difference between the mean temperature of the hottest and coldest month can be as high as 45°F (25°C), with maximum temperatures of 112°F (44°C) often not impossible. Being so arid, the desert is devoid of water's latent heat capacity to keep things warm after the sun sets, making the nights extremely chilly. With such fluctuations in temperature, surface rocks are heated and chilled in quick succession, leading to significant erosion. Cliffs are scored, the sand turned into an instrument of abrasion by the wind. In many places such wind erosion has planed the flat rocks of the *hammada* as smooth as ice. Elsewhere, the sand-laced wind has scored the vertical faces of the cliffs with curious imitations of glacial striation.

Sometimes it is easier, and more comfortable, to explore the Sahara from afar. The first satellite pictures taken of the desert, by NASA in 1981, provided clear evidence of something that anyone who lives or has travelled in the Sahara already knew. The desert was not always as dry as it is today. NASA's photographs showed large and numerous dry riverbeds and wadis that provided clear evidence of a once extensive system of surface water.

Fresh, cold-water oasis

Even nowadays many of the wadis continue to function as they are meant to, periodically filling with water funnelled along the channels after the infrequent rainfall that comes to parts of the desert, albeit often less than annually. Finding the path of least resistance, the rushing water cuts its way through the softest beds of normally parched rock.

Today, the only permanent rivers in the greater Saharan region are on its edges, with the Nile and the Niger marking portions of the desert's border along some of their course. Neither of these great rivers draws water from the desert itself but both rather rely on rainfall from wet highland areas in lands far beyond the Sahara's borders. As the alleged traveller and writer Sir John Mandeville writes in his curious mid-fourteenth-century Anglo-Norman French travelogue, "Egypt is a long country, but it is straight (i.e. strait), that is to say narrow, for they may not enlarge it toward the desert for default of water." Whether or not (although probably not) Sir John ever existed, let alone travelled to the ends of the earth as he claimed, the compiler of his *Travels* was more or less correct in this description of Egypt as a land hemmed in by the Sahara.

A far more reliable source of water are the oases, which appear in depressions where water is able to break through—for instance where there exists some break or fissure in the earth's surface that allows the water to intrude on the land. While both the quantity and quality of the water found in the oases vary greatly, the fact that many of the larger oases have been continually inhabited for millennia gives a good indication of just how immense are the underground aquifers that supply them. The water in some of the aquifers below the Sahara was left behind at the end of the Pleistocene epoch, which lasted from approximately 1.8 million to 12,000 BCE, rightly earning this priceless prehistoric resource the name fossil water. Yet although the centuries-old presence of certain oases demonstrates the enormous capacity of these aquifers, it by no means guarantees that some of them will not lose their water at some point. Indeed, there are many examples of oases becoming extinct, and when the water supply disappears so too must the residents of those oases. Quite simply, without these oases, human habitation in the Sahara would be impossible.

Often thought of as underground lakes, the aquifers that lie beneath the Sahara instead of being recognizable, uniform bodies of water can more accurately be thought of as subterranean regions of saturated stone. It is the exertion of pressure on these wet underground rocks that feeds water up to the surface, like squeezing a sponge, in an unbroken flow. The Sahara is blessed with a number of such aquifers, of which two giant examples are especially noteworthy. The first is the Bas Saharan Basin, an artesian aquifer system that ranges not only under the majority of the Algerian and Tunisian Sahara but also stretches as far as Morocco and Libya, encompassing the entire Grand Erg Oriental region. The second great aquifer is the Nubian Sandstone System, which is located in the Sahara's eastern and north-eastern quarters and is reckoned to cover in excess of 770,000 square miles in the area of north-western Sudan, north-eastern Chad, south-western Libya and most of Egypt. Best estimates suggest that the Nubian Sandstone System contains somewhere in the region of 36,000 cubic miles of groundwater. This single gigantic water system is responsible for supplying the majority of the water needs for all of the countries it lies beneath, with the exception of Egypt, which, as it has done since antiquity, relies on the Nile for most of its water needs.

At the other end of the spectrum, the Sahara contains some of the world's least-visited massifs and mountain ranges, which are among the

The Ahaggar Mountains from Assekrem

most isolated places on earth. One reason for the lack of visitors is that these high places tend to have sprung up in the Sahara's more central, and subsequently less accessible, districts. This is a pity for anyone who enjoys wildernesses because these peaks are among the most rugged and remote locations the world can offer. In northern Nigeria, the Aïr Mountains reach higher than 6,000 feet, and the Ahaggar Mountains in Algeria rise above 9,000 feet. To reach the Sahara's highest peaks, however, one has to travel to the Tibesti Mountains in the emptiest corner of northern Chad. Here, among the lunar peaks, is the Sahara's highest point, Emi Koussi, a forty-mile-wide volcanic cone that reaches a height of 11,302 feet, rising a mile and a half above the otherwise flat sandstone plateau that it dominates.

By far the largest proportion of the Sahara's makeup is dun-coloured rock and stone in various forms, thousands of miles of gravel-strewn plains that can initially seem devoid of life or interest, especially for those who travel over these landscapes at speed. As Sven Lindquist once wrote: "In Sweden, when trying to imagine the desert, I thought of sandy beaches which never reach the water. But it is fairly rare to see beaches in the desert, which is more like an endless schoolyard." These stony regions make up approximately seventy per cent of the Sahara, and consist of everything from plains of coarse gravel to plateaus of stripped rock and wadis.

Water's presence does not necessarily mean that life there is sustainable. In the northernmost part of the Sahara, southern Tunisia is home to the Chott el-Djerid, the desert's largest saltpan or, for the sake of technical accuracy, endorheic basin. The Chott el-Djerid is a highly saline marsh lake that covers more than 2,500 square miles, and which glistens a brilliant, crystalline white. A startling sight, saltpans are found in different parts of the world, but especially in hot deserts. Lacking an outflow, either on the surface or underground through permeable rock, any rain that falls into these basins is permanently trapped there, apart from that which escapes through evaporation thus forming the Fata Morgana or superior mirages of mountain ranges and fairy castles as seemingly real as the rocks beneath one's feet. In high summer, it is also possible to traverse the salt lake on foot or, exercising due caution, in lighter vehicles, thanks to the presence of a semi-hard crust that forms during the period of blistering weather.

The sub-sea level conditions of the Chott el-Djerid are broadly the same in Egypt's Qattara Depression, which marks the Sahara's lowest point in places more than 400 feet below sea level; the depression is an area of 7,000 square miles, mainly saltpans and one-time marshes. Like the Chott el-Djerid, the Qattara Depression's surface is saline and unstable, although there are guides willing to lead interested parties along one or more of the basin's more stable paths. Of the few who do venture into these places, farmers are not among them, the salinity of the soil in both the Chott el-Djerid and the Qattara Depression rendering agriculture impossible. Not even the highly salt tolerant palm tree can cope with the high saline content in the regions' soil.

While in too high a concentration salt kills soil and prevents agriculture, it is vital and is the most precious of all the Sahara's minerals. Rightly praised as a jewel among the desert produce, evidence of its importance can be found in the earliest human records found in the Sahara. To this day, great lengths are gone to in order to extract, process and sell this life-giving commodity, and wealthy empires have flourished in the Sahara just because of the presence of salt and its distant, hungry markets.

Among the most notable of the cities founded on salt are Taoudenni in Mali and Bilma in Niger, both of which have been centres of the salt trade for centuries. Whether through mining or harvesting from saltpans, the cargo was transported to the furthest ends of the Sahara and beyond. At the height of these empires it was not unusual for the annual camel caravans to number in the tens of thousands. Early accounts of such camel trains come from the great Arab travellers and geographers al-Idrisi and Ibn Battuta. Today, camel salt caravans have virtually disappeared, and the most sought after minerals lie somewhat further down in the form of oil and gas.

It is a great irony of modern Saharan travel, that while petrol-powered vehicles provide access to more of the desert to more people than before, they have also largely eliminated the need for camel transport, thus removing the romantic sight of a camel caravan that many travellers still dream of seeing. The greatest of late twentieth-century Saharan explorers are also not so far removed from their centuries-long Arab predecessors. Just as it was once geographers who recorded what they saw of the Sahara, today the majority of exploration is conducted by geologists, commissioned by patrons in the boardrooms of energy companies, sending them out to discover energy beneath the desert floor.

FLORA AND FAUNA

If petroleum engineers are not usually thought of as overly interested in flora and fauna, perhaps they should be. After all, the precious oil and gas found in such quantities below the surface of the Sahara was once living itself. Every species of plant and animal that now dwells in the desert has somehow evolved in order to survive in one of the world's most demanding and unforgiving natural habitats. The camel—of whom more later— is only the most obvious example of an animal whose adaptations allow it to thrive where, for instance, the horse cannot.

Nor is the Sahara as devoid of life as the casual observer might imagine. Hundreds of species of insects live happily within its borders. Each species of ant, fly, moth, spider, centipede, locust and beetle manages to eke out an existence because all have adapted to the particular conditions of desert life. Water is obviously the key to all life, but in hot deserts and away from the oases the rarity, scarcity and unpredictability of rainfall have forced both plants and animals to evolve. In the case of certain species of frog and toad, their spawn can wait years for life-giving rainfall that will cause the swift reanimation of dormant life, with tadpoles sprouting and maturing in double-quick time.

Similarly, certain plant species have developed to allow the seeds to survive for years, and in some cases for decades, until a single shower will see them spring to life: seeds turn into seedlings and then rapidly become fully mature, flowering plants that disperse seeds of their own, which in turn lie waiting for the arrival of rain. A number of plant species support delightful names, including grasses such as the scrubby Cram-cram, which grows in low clumps often near the hardy acacia tree, and the Had, both of which thrive along the Sahara's southern border. More impressive are the Sodom Apple or Calotrope, native to central Saharan regions, a large, woody bush with thick, fleshy leaves and pink flowers, and the pleasant-sounding and succulent Desert Melon, but be warned: the latter is a strong emetic, as any who have been tempted to feast on its ground-hugging fruit will attest.

Of the trees, the date palm is best suited to the desert. Able to survive with limited water and high levels of salinity, it is hardly surprising that the date is so highly praised in the folklore of the region and the Middle East as a whole. Acacia trees found in the desert, primarily but by no means exclusively in more mountainous areas, tend to be survivors of a past time instead of new plants, veterans of the Sahara rather than cadets.

Flora and fauna are both integral to the delicate ecosystem that exists in the Sahara, with the trees and smaller plants providing shelter and sustenance to any number of the animal species and with animals fulfilling their share of the bargain by assisting in the dispersal of seeds. For seed dispersal over the greatest distances, plants can do no better than to be eaten by a bird. Most bird species found in the Sahara are visitors. Crossing from West and Central Africa to take advantage of cooler European summers, they migrate south back across the desert to avoid the harsh northern winter. Although drawn by nature to this annual migration, the journey is long and extremely hard and many thousands of small birds do not survive. The corpses of doves, flycatchers, pigeons, pipits, swallows and thrushes will most often be found in early summer, killed by the heat and failure to find water while en route to Europe.

Many ground-based animals share the common characteristic of outsized ears, which allows them to thrive in the desert. Most famous is the Fennec, a small fox-like rodent. These cartoonish appendages are also prominent on the desert fox, desert hare and desert hedgehog. Apart from providing them with an auditory advantage while hunting insects, the ears also allow for the dispersal of heat, thereby allowing the animals to survive.

Unfortunately for naturalists, the larger the desert mammal the rarer it is and, therefore, the slighter the chance of seeing one. The tracks of increasingly rare Saharan gazelle or antelopes such as the oryx and addax may be found but one can spend a lifetime without seeing the beasts themselves. Conversely, among some of the more plentiful desert reptiles, one must hope that any encounter is not too unexpected, scorpions in particular being attracted to the warm bodies of sleeping people. Hiding is also the specialized hunting technique of the horned viper, which lies in wait for its prey just beneath the sand, its eponymous horns alone visible above the surface. Woe-betide the barefooted wanderer who steps on this denizen of the desert. Its venom might not be lethal but its bite will do more than put one in a bad mood.

Whether gazing down from the peak of a mountain or dune, or looking up from below sea level, the Sahara is a land of enormous geographical variety and some beauty, much of which is unknown or too often overlooked. Travelling at high speed may create the illusion that one has seen a great deal of the desert, but in reality one has seen nothing at all. Of nowhere is this truer than the Sahara, which deserves to be discovered over time.

The long-eared Fennec Fox

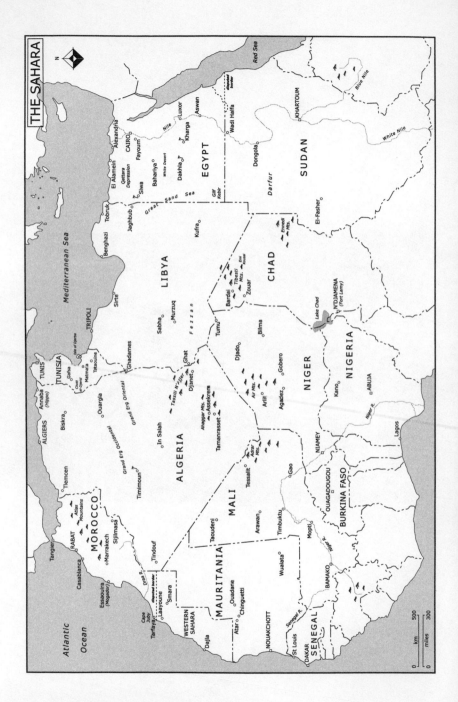

THE SAHARA

Part One

LANDSCAPES

Chapter One

WHALES IN THE DESERT

"And God said, Let the waters under the heaven be gathered together unto one place, and let the dry land appear: and it was so. And God called the dry land Earth; and the gathering together of the waters called the Seas: and God saw that it was good."

Genesis, 1:9-10, King James Version

If asked which words one associated with the Sahara, only the most dedicated surrealist might be expected to offer "whale". "Camel" and "sand" are far more likely choices. But in fact the surrealist would not be entirely wrong—albeit harking back millions of years to the desert's pre-prehistory. This arid expanse hardly seems the ideal habitat for whales but long before the camels moved in (between 3000 and 3500 years ago, making them the most recent mammalian arrival) it was actually teeming with all sorts of marine life. In a period that one can think of as the Sahara's pre-pre-history, a large part of the landmass that would eventually become the largest hot desert on earth lay submerged beneath a vast body of water, the Tethys Sea. Thus, the whale was a resident of what was to become the Sahara.

The sea has long vanished. Today there are only a small number of oases scattered across the northern third of continental Africa which the Sahara covers, mere specks on the map where water allows life in the middle of an otherwise seemingly lifeless and desolate landscape. Yet evidence of the Sahara's watery past can be seen in numerous places, with more fossil discoveries being made every year by marine palaeontologists and archaeologists working in the desert. One of the most impressive sites of fossil remains to be found anywhere in the Sahara also happens to be one of its most accessible, situated as it is less than a hundred miles southwest of Cairo. Wadi al-Hitan, the Valley of the Whales, covers one hundred square miles and contains one of the world's most important collections of fossils of early whales, which is why in 2005 Unesco added it to its list of World Heritage sites.

The majority of the hundreds of fossil remains found in Wadi al-Hitan are examples of the proto-whale known as the Basilosaurus, or "King

Whale skeleton at Wadi al-Hitan

Lizard", which belonged to a long extinct sub-order of whales called Archaeoceti alive and swimming approximately forty million years ago. With an adult Basilosaurus growing up to 69 feet long, they were not only noticeably smaller than today's Blue Whales (up to 115 feet) but also a great deal sleeker, with an elongated body more reminiscent of an inflated eel than a bulbous whale.

Explaining its decision to grant World Heritage status, Unesco explained that "Wadi Al-Hitan is the most important site in the world to demonstrate one of the iconic changes that make up the record of life on Earth: the evolution of the whales." Easily discerned in the fossil record, one can see whales in one of the last stages of their evolution, complete with tiny limbs sticking out from the area of their rear flanks. While complete with moveable joints and toes, these small "legs" are too small to have been of any practical use in supporting the immense body weight of the Basilosaurus. Instead, these vestigial limbs are said by palaeontologists to be evidence of the unusual reverse evolution of whales, wherein they returned to a marine existence having previously been land-based mammals.

It might seem too long ago to be worth considering, but the Sahara's marine past and the sea's retreat is every bit as important as its later, desiccated periods. It is believed that the Tethys Sea evolved out of the mega-marine body known as the Tethys Ocean. This super ocean existed before continental drift had fashioned shorelines into the shapes familiar to us today. The terms Tethys Ocean and Tethys Sea are frequently and frustratingly used interchangeably, in spite of their being at one time distinct bodies of water. This is perhaps forgivable, since many questions related to ancient geology are still, no pun intended, evolving. But the sea is what we are interested in when considering the time when our Egyptian whales died. This "smaller" body of water encompassed the whole of the modern Mediterranean basin, southern Europe, northern Africa and a water bridge that covered Anatolia and the Levant and stretched east through Iran and Iraq, covering contemporary northern India.

Only named in the last decade of the nineteenth century, the Tethys Sea took its name from the Titan goddess, one of those deities who, according to Greek mythology ruled over heaven and earth during the so-called Golden Age, before they were vanquished by the Olympians, that younger generation of upstart gods who made their home on Mount Olympus. As the goddess of fresh water, Tethys was believed to be the source of rivers, springs, streams, fountains and rain clouds. Tethys was thus responsible for nourishing the earth. Referring to "Tethys our mother", Homer, in his eighth-century BCE epic the *Iliad*, places Tethys at the heart of the literary history of the Sahara even before the desert existed. The wife of Oceanus, Tethys was able to draw water from her husband, before passing it on to mankind through underground springs, which appeared in the world as if by magic. Among the forty or so children born to Tethys were such familiar names as Asia, Styx (the river that marks the boundary between earth and the underworld) and a son Nilus, the god of the Nile.

In the 1950s and 1960s, French palaeontologists and geologists working in the deserts of central Niger independently discovered teeth and other fossil remains of another gargantuan prehistoric marine-dwelling animal in the valley of Gadoufaoua, which in the local Tuareg language means "the place where camels fear to go". A fuller picture of this mammoth marine creature was not completed until additional, large-scale discoveries were made in the late 1990s by Paul Sereno from the

University of Chicago and his team. Named *Sarcosuchus imperator* by scientists, the animal is better known by its media tag: Supercroc. A *Sarcosuchus imperator* jawbone discovered by the team measured an impressive six feet on its own. Only distantly related to modern crocodiles, the ancient behemoth, which lived some 110 million years ago, grew up to forty feet long and weighed between eight and ten tonnes. The death knell sounded for Sarcosuchus, Basilosaurus and similar water-dependent mega-fauna between 30 and 26 million years ago, when the Sahara went through a major climatic change, resulting in a more tropical and drier environment.

In order to get to the formation of the Sahara as desert, needs force us to jump forward some 24 million years into the Pleistocene Epoch or "most new age", the older of two epochs in the Quaternary Period, the period through which we are still living. By 1.8 million years ago the outline of the continent of Africa was clearly recognizable. The epoch was characterized by repeated periods of widespread glaciation and thaw, or interglacials, in which violent temperature fluctuations led to the extinction of most species of megafauna, including the sabre-toothed tigers and the mammoth. It also saw the extinction of horses and camels in their home continent of North America. In place of the big beasts, large numbers of smaller animals including mice, birds and cold-blooded species emerged, better suited to the new prevailing conditions. But it was not just small fauna that benefited from the change in the weather, because it was during this time that modern humans evolved, from *Homo erectus*, upright man, into *Homo sapiens*, so-called wise man, just 200,000 years ago.

Our recognizably human ancestors quickly set themselves apart from their predecessors, developing most of those social characteristics one still associates with mankind. No longer content just to eke out an existence, people made the great leap to living in societies. Evidence of early human societies can be found across the Sahara in many forms; in tools and products fashioned by these tools, from the remains of animals killed and skinned to the building of shelters and the digging of graves and the first human burials. As if all of these accomplishments were not enough, it was also during this period that our ancestors in the Sahara, as elsewhere, moved ahead in other, profoundly moving ways by mastering the use of language and in creating works of art.

THE GREEN SAHARA

Having established that whales used to swim in a sea that once covered what is now the Sahara, readers should have no difficulty accepting that at another point in time it was a green and pleasant land. Great fluctuations between wet and dry weather occurred in the Sahara from roughly 10,000 to 4000 BCE, the period rightly known as the Green or Wet Sahara. Indeed, to talk about the "Sahara" is somewhat misleading, as the desert region that now fits this description did not, in a sense, exist at this time.

For thousands of years, landscapes that are today extremely inhospitable used to abound with a rich variety of flora and fauna. Where now there exists a relative paucity of biodiversity there were once well-watered places supporting a large number of productive environments, including rainforests and grassland as well as marshes and other wetlands. Water was so abundant that it offered a home to such marine animals as the hippopotamus, not to mention innumerable species of fish. The savannah was covered in grasses that provided for large mammals such as the elephant, giraffes and gazelle, which were in turn prey for the lions with which they shared the plains. Tibesti, Ennedi and Aïr, today barren and rocky ranges, were instead mountains blanketed in trees—oak, pine, olive and walnut providing fruit for a multitude of animal populations. Indeed, the wealth of flora and fauna that once existed accounts for the massive reserves of oil and gas that are found under the Sahara today. Naturally, this Eden-like Sahara was just as favourable to emerging human societies.

There is plenty of evidence regarding relatively complex human societies during the time of the Green Sahara. The earliest named culture to emerge from the obscurity of pre-history is the Aterian industry, evidence of which stretches from the Atlantic almost to the banks of the River Nile, making it easily the most widespread of North African cultures at this time. It is called an Aterian industry because although the carefully made stone tools from this period share certain common features, it is not appropriate to yoke all those responsible for crafting these tools under one common culture as we might understand the term today. Once confidently said to have emerged around 40,000 BCE, recent finds in Morocco, north of the Sahara, have pushed back the date for Aterian industry to more than 170,000 BCE.

Although one of the Sahara's periodic changes in climate is the most commonly posited reason for the utter disappearance of the Aterian industry around 10,000 years ago, it is also around the same time that the Capsian, an even lesser known culture than the Aterian, emerged. Named after Gafsa, the Tunisian town where it was first identified, the Capsian was a Mesolithic culture that lasted for about four thousand years, dying out in approximately 6,000 BCE, whose influence was confined to parts of Algeria, Tunisia and a small number of sites in ancient Cyrenaica or modern Libya.

Although evidence is limited, what emerges is a picture of a people who had available to them a variety of stone tools and who also managed to domesticate a number of animals. The Capsian diet included auroch, an oversized ancestor of cattle, antelope, hares and snails. While it is clear that Capsians enjoyed a meat-heavy diet, it is less certain what greens they ate for balance.

Capsian culture is noted for the widespread use of ornamentation in tools and containers such as ostrich shells, as well as a fascination with beads and other jewellery made from shells, a fondness they shared with the Aterian industry. But the emotional development of Capsian culture seems to have gone further still, producing many fine early examples of both figurative and abstract rock art. Importantly, Capsian culture also indicates a certain spiritual maturity: their dead were buried, rather than just taken away from where the living fed and slept, and corpses were often painted with red ochre before being interred. Such care clearly suggests a strong faith in some form of afterlife.

Of all the archaeological sites discovered in the Sahara, it is one of the most recently excavated that has proved to be the most exciting. Uncovered in 2000, Gobero, in Niger, is the site of the oldest and largest ancient graveyard in the entire Sahara. So far archaeologists have uncovered the remains of more than 200 individuals and a multitude of objects, including jewellery and animal bones, buried with them. All told, the finds have provided researchers with unprecedented insights into the life of early Saharan peoples who settled in Gobero more than 10,000 years ago. Even more excitingly, archaeologists have discovered that Gobero was home to at least two distinct cultures, one replacing or following the other. The human remains and the extensive artefacts found at the site have offered tantalizing insights into both cultures, which between them ensured the site was more or less continually inhabited for roughly 5000 years. Located on the side of a now disappeared lake, archaeologists have uncovered the remains of 54 species of animal, including elephant, hippo, giraffe, hartebeest, warthog, lion, python and mud turtles.

The earliest settlers at Gobero were of the Kiffian culture, and their remains show men and women who were frequently taller than six feet. The Kiffians are notable for their pottery, which tended to be adorned with delicately wavy lines. Based at Gobero until roughly 6000 BCE, it is thought that they abandoned the site during a periodic dry phase, only to be replaced some time thereafter by the Ténérians. Like the Kiffians, the Ténérians left a great deal of pottery behind them, which betrays their preference for designs made with simpler, straight lines. Between both styles, pots and pottery shards alike demonstrate an interest in the decorative arts with a 10,000-year pedigree, one that likely emerged along the Nile valley before travelling as far west as Mali. Of even more interest than the pots themselves, the craftsmanship demonstrates clear and distinct developments in the skill level of the potters, as well as changes in fashion.

Like the earlier Capsian culture, Kiffians and Ténérians also displayed some sense of spirit in their sensitive treatment of the dead. Burial customs meant that individuals were often laid to rest wearing items of jewellery, including an eleven-year-old girl who was buried with a bracelet on her upper arm that was made from a hippo's tusk. However, a number of the graves excavated have raised more questions than they have provided answers. The most intriguing of these is that of a woman and two children buried side by side in a communal plot. Positioned in such a way that implies they are engaged in a loving embrace, the bodies are thought to be those of a mother and her children. In addition to the tenderness of their proximity, pollen found in the grave suggests to archaeologists that they were laid to rest on a bed of flowers. Although impossible to prove, since none of the bodies bears any sign of violence, and it is assumed they were buried at the same time, it is likely the trio died as the result of a fatal contagion.

Investigations at Gobero and elsewhere are far from complete, and the expectation of further revelations into early Saharan cultures runs high among archaeologists and others. What we do know is that around 2300 BCE the last period of the Green Sahara came to an end. As the monsoons from the south stopped, permanent sources of water dried up.

Human and animal populations were forced to move away or die. In this post-pluvial era, aridity became the new standard, and the Sahara finally took on the parched quality that we are familiar with today.

Chapter Two
ROCK ART

"...We became aware that the valley contained some remarkable sculptures deserving our particular attention... No barbarian could have graven the lines with such astonishing firmness, and given to all the figures the light, natural shape which they exhibit."

Heinrich Barth, *Travels and Discoveries in North and Central Africa*

Everyone who has seen rock art in the Sahara has, in his or her own way, echoed the sentiments of surprise and delight uttered by Heinrich Barth upon his discovery of these examples of prehistoric human creativity. The beauty of these works of art is breathtaking, as is the astounding range and quantity of the works still in existence. Across the Sahara there are tens of thousands of examples of the ancient creative urge brought to life. Of all the evidence available to us regarding ancient human habitation in the Sahara, rock art is the most widespread and dramatic. What more striking sign of the one-time presence of people than a painting on the wall of a cave showing a herd of cattle and the thrill of the hunt?

Even more dramatic than the pictures of cattle and other now domesticated animals are the depictions of bigger beasts, such as elephants, rhinoceroses and crocodiles. In many cases, these have been reproduced on walls and rocky outcrops in something close to scale. To gaze upon the exquisitely detailed, near life-size carving of a giraffe indicates how far conditions in the Sahara have changed over time. The widespread incidence of rock art, including the chosen subject matter, proves that wetter, milder conditions once prevailed in areas that are today uninhabitable, and also that not only was human tenancy in the desert possible but it occurred on a significant scale.

Rock art is broadly divided into one of two types: petroglyphs (engravings or carvings) or pictographs (paintings). The earliest Saharan rock art is between twelve and fourteen thousand years old, although precise dating, as in so many matters prehistoric, is impossible. Also, the vastness of the Sahara militates against any consensus since there is no reason to suppose that while art was flourishing on one side of the continent, artists on the other side were creating works of the same quality or style at the same time. Nor is there any reason to assume that craftsmen thousands of miles apart would concurrently choose the same subject matter or materials.

It is far more likely that items which display some similarity came about as a result of population shifts, for example people migrating after a once reliable water source dried up, or being forced to move with the arrival of a new, more powerful tribe. Less permanent journeys, for instance to seasonal grazing grounds or along trade routes, would also no doubt allow the spread of artistic motifs and techniques. The difficulties of dating and categorizing the work is compounded by the relatively small number of specialists who have been able to visit a majority of the rock art sites, such is the scale of the desert and the distance between many of the places where the best collections are to be found.

There is surprising variety in Saharan parietal or cave wall art, especially if one considers that we remain a long way from successfully interpreting much of the work that is available to us. For every picture that unambiguously shows a human or animal form, any number of suggested interpretations can be forwarded. Theories are affected by, among other

An ancient hunt at Tassili

things, the size and number of the subjects, the colours and detail involved, the medium employed and their location. In broad terms we can say that those works with unambiguous subject matter very often portray animals, that is, food. The human form is another popular choice of subject, while images depicting acts of warfare or violence between men are as rare as pictures of plant life and smaller animals.

This choice of subject matter may simply acknowledge the greater effort and risk involved in hunting large animals so that the greater the risk, and the larger the quantity of meat resulting from the hunt, the higher the esteem in which the beast was held. Even today, in zoos, wildlife-parks and on safaris, people still tend to be far more excited and interested in bigger animals, possibly because of their rarity but also perhaps because of some atavistic memory.

Given how varied scholars' interpretations of Saharan art have been, there is surprising unanimity when it comes to dating rock art. Even after his first encounter with it on examining the engravings at Wadi Telisaghé in 1850, Heinrich Barth recognized that it was not all the same, either in style or age. One of the first Europeans to see rock art in the Sahara, Barth went on to conduct extensive studies of the rock art of the Aïr Mountains in Niger and the Fezzan in Libya. A close observer of detail, Barth deduced that the different styles of the engravings meant the art came from different, prehistoric periods, and also that the presence of large animals suggested that the desert had once enjoyed a very different climate. While such observations may seem obvious to us, when Barth first advanced his untested theories they were radical.

Products of the their time, many nineteenth-century explorers regarded as inconceivable the idea that Africans, by which they meant black Africans, (and non-Christian ones at that) would have been capable of producing such brilliant work. Barth was as guilty of this prejudice as anyone and his conclusions could be completely wrong. Accepting that the works had great merit, Barth remained unconvinced they were created solely from the imagination of local, if long dead, artists. Writing in *Sahara and Sudan* he concluded that, "No barbarian could have graven the lines with such astonishing firmness, and given to all the figures the light, natural shape which they exhibit." He concluded that they must have been "executed by someone who had been in intimate relation with the more advanced people on the coast, perhaps with the Carthaginians."

Modern scholars, in our marginally more enlightened times, more or less agree on there being five very broad divisions in Saharan rock art. The first of these is the Hunter or Bubalus period, named after the *Bubalus antiquus*—a long extinct species of giant buffalo which is widely portrayed in art from this era which stretches between 12,000 and 7000 BCE. The carvings from this phase are distinguished by both the large, almost life-size engravings of the Bubalus and other large savannah-dwelling animals, and the comparably diminutive scale of the few human figures who appear. The total absence of domesticated animals from these rock canvases also indicates an early, non-pastoral epoch, hence its alternative name: the Hunter period.

After this comes a time known variously as the Archaic, Pre-Pastoralist or Roundhead period. Thought to start between 10,000 and 8000 and ending in about 5000 BCE, it takes its Roundhead name from the work of the great, if flawed, French explorer and ethnographer Henri Lhote. One of the first people to conduct extensive studies of Saharan rock art, he came up with the label in the 1950s after noting the presence of numerous strange-looking human figures with large round heads in the Tassili n'Ajjer in south-eastern Algeria. His initial work in recording the carvings was of some importance but it led to his later theories for which unfortunately he is much better remembered—that Martians had inhabited the prehistoric earth.

The Ahaggar and Tassili where Lhote explored are rightly renowned for the magnificent collections they house, the greatest storehouse of ancient rock art on earth, both in quantity and quality. Although these stone canvases were first scored and chipped some 8000 years ago, our knowledge of them was extremely limited until Lhote's work, which is why it is such a pity that he is today largely remembered for his outlandish claims.

Lhote's published findings declared that the admittedly striking and strange, round-headed figures were proof that ancient man once had contact with aliens from outer space. He even named one of the largest and most distinct figures Jabberen, and announced that it was a Martian god. Erik von Daniken who, like Lhote, claims to believe in ancient astronauts, wrote about the round-headed figures in his book *Chariots of the Gods*, citing them as evidence that the earth had been populated by humanoids from outer space. This obviously did nothing for Lhote's reputation. And neither did his failure to realize that a number of heavily stylized, Egyptian-like paintings he "discovered" were hoaxes perpetrated by members of his own research team.

Whether artists from the Roundhead period were recording encounters with aliens or simply being creative, the next artistic period is altogether more straightforwardly named. The Cattle period, also known as the Pastoral period, is variously dated as starting between 7500 and 5000 BCE and ending between 4000 and 2500 BCE and clearly marks the time when Saharans domesticated cattle. If the scale of the herds in these drawings is to be taken literally, it was evidently a time of abundance, when life in the Sahara had never been more comfortable, and when the existence of such food stocks must have contributed to a steep climb in local populations.

From 3000 to as recently as 800 BCE, the Horse and Chariot period marks another profound change in the Saharan landscape, with wheeled vehicles making their mark on the landscape, forging paths from the northern coastal region southwards through the Fezzan to the Sahel and beyond.

The final period is the Camel period, the dates for which, like the preceding periods, are disputed although reckoned to start between 2000 and 400 BCE and stretching to the present day. Like all art, contemporary rock art reflects present-day norms and realities that, in the case of today's parietal art, includes representations of modern inventions such as aeroplanes and modern weaponry as well as human figures and graffiti in Arabic, Berber and Tamasheq, the language of the Tuareg.

ICONOGRAPHY AND GRAFFITI

Establishing a definitive answer to the question of the purpose of rock art is as unlikely as authorities agreeing on its age. One thing is certain; the creation of many of these works of art took a great deal of time and energy, which is suggestive of a relatively highly developed society. In these societies, either time was set aside where everyone was involved in creating art, perhaps after a successful hunt when food was temporarily plentiful, or perhaps there had developed certain individuals in society whose role was making pictures.

One of the most often proposed functions of parietal art is religious. What constitutes religious feeling is naturally subject to interpretation, and with this in mind there is nothing to suggest that the hunting scenes might not be religious icons, both representing the necessity of securing a food supply and offering thanks for any perceived divine assistance received in the chase. It is equally possible, if impossible to prove, that the hunt was itself a religious event, along the same lines as attending those formalized rituals common to any Sunday, or Friday, or Saturday, service.

The figure of a large-breasted female on a cave wall is interpreted without controversy as a symbol of fecundity; perhaps a goddess whom the artist's clan hoped would bless them with healthy children or, for sedentary agriculturists, a good harvest. Similarly, an obviously male figure supplied with an outsized and erect penis might likewise represent a fertility god, or could it just be that it was meant for a spot of fun? There is the hint of a suggestion that certain examples of this megaphallic art may be little more than graffiti, scratches or daubs added later by individuals with a lewd or juvenile sense of humour.

Although in many cases the works are clearly too elaborate for this suspicion to be justified, one certainly senses levity at work in some of the more sexual images. Dr. Bonnet, working for the Paris Natural History Museum in Algeria in the nineteenth century, noted that a number of the engravings' hunters "brazenly display monstrous phalluses... in most cases it is easy to recognize, from the form and the colour of the line, that these organs are later additions to the rest of the figure." In other words, Bonnet saw some of these large erections as little more than early graffiti. There has surely been no time since the emergence of *Homo sapiens* when those distinctive male and female body parts have not been, so to speak, held up as objects of ribald humour.

The overtly sexual illustrations so shocked a number of the Europeans who re-discovered this art that many ignored them altogether in their accounts. However, in 1848 the French traveller Jean-Jacques Ampère published an account of his journeys through Egypt and Nubia, which included comments on engravings he had found around Philae. Apart from lions, elephants and ostriches, he noted some distinctly obscene portrayals of humans. Of all the human figures proudly displaying their sex, those engaged in acts of zoophilia have always provoked the sharpest intakes of breath. Even so, bestiality is surprisingly common in the works of these early artists: the shock of the old, perhaps. It also happens that bestiality in Saharan rock art is more common than in other sites around the world of a similar age. Whether this is because most of these works were destroyed elsewhere in the world or whether Saharans had a particularly keen enthusiasm for coupling with animals, it is impossible to say.

Then there are those images of men copulating with animals far larger than themselves, including giraffes, rhinos and elephants, which certainly raise far more questions than they answer. Whatever the reason for carving these images into a rock face, it was not done lightly. Again, there is nothing to suggest that there is not present here some religious iconography. It is still the case today that hunters in certain tribes will engage in ritual copulation with antelopes they have just killed. Perhaps these images are of great symbolic, rather than literal, importance, votive offerings for human domination over larger and potentially lethal prey. Other forms of bestial activity include engravings of men either urinating or ejaculating into the eyes of rhinos.

Another opinion is that the images are linked to the existence of prehistoric, mythical creatures, a race of giant men whose ritual intercourse with animals was linked to the daily life of mortals. Support for the ritual or shamanistic nature of these curious couplings can also be found in engravings of therianthropes, creatures with both human and animal attributes, most frequently with the head of a dog or a bird. Saharan therianthropes are sometimes shown standing alone but more commonly are depicted copulating with female humans. There are probably as many possible interpretations for these examples of rock art as there are pieces, and the ritual, boastful, humorous explanations all have a possible validity.

Like other parts of the Sahara, the desert in Egypt beyond the oases was once wet enough to support sizeable animal and human populations. In the farthest south-western corner of the country, the Gilf Kebir is a large rocky plateau near the border with Libya and the Sudan. It was here in the 1930s that a British-Hungarian team, including László Almásy, found the so-called Cave of Swimmers, popularized in *The English Patient*. Whether the figures are really swimming or engaged in some other activity such as prostrating themselves before a deity, is not clear. Either way, it is a most evocative corner of the Sahara and the red and ochre paintings are simply awe-inspiring. Archaeologists have determined that bones and cooking pots found in the area date from some 5000 years ago. While this makes this remote culture contemporaneous with ancient Egypt's Nile Valley civilization, the Gilf Kebir settlements were almost certainly distinct from it.

Animals apparently dancing

Today there is grave concern about the continued survival of these prehistoric masterpieces, which face various threats, the most insidious being unscrupulous collectors who scrape or chisel off what chunks of rock they can, taking these broken pieces away with them. It has also been known for cultural vandals to commission locals to perform these vile acts, paying a handful of dollars for priceless artefacts. Whether for financial profit or a magpie-like desire for a personal hoard, the results are the same. Every year, pieces of mankind's ancient bequest, our collective cultural inheritance, are damaged, smashed, and stolen.

Equally culpable are those who think it appropriate to add their own graffiti. Painted or, more ruinously, carved alongside or over the top of the ancient art, the perpetrators of such vandalism presumably see nothing wrong in doing their bit to destroy this repository of Saharan and world culture. Such defacement is not exclusively modern. Cultural vandalism has long accompanied an ascendant ideology underscoring its domination by destroying anything of the old order. The visitor, however, whether moneyed Victorian or twenty-first century package tourist, has no excuse for this behaviour, nor is ignorance an acceptable excuse. Where once tourists threw water onto cave paintings to make the colours brighter, thus enabling a better photograph, today most guides will stop their clients from this terribly damaging practice. But not all of the destruction of rock art is manmade. The elements have played their part with wind erosion no doubt causing most wear and tear over time.

Steps are being taken to educate people about the fragility of these works, but it is an enormous task, whose sphere of activity is continental in scale, and funding for such causes is not easily secured. The problem has attracted enough attention to warrant the involvement of the United Nations, with Unesco World Heritage status being declared for a number of the better-known sites. At the same time, awareness of the problem is increasing, thanks to the work of organizations such as the Trust for African Rock Art, and the efforts, albeit sometimes patchy, of national governments, local agencies and tour companies who all recognize that visitor income depends on the continued existence of the rock art.

Chapter Three

SAHARAN URBAN

A number of Sahara towns have locations that are among the most dramatic, wild and beautiful on earth. Some have been inhabited, without interruption, for thousands of years. Several enjoyed high status in the ancient world, about which Herodotus and others wrote, noting the oracular wisdom imparted there. One was an unrivalled seat of learning in the medieval world, and several were ruled over by kings whose wealth was equal to that of Croesus. Today the majority are simple, unremarkable places, quiet, isolated and frequently forgotten by outsiders. Yet many of these plain and dusty towns have other charms that draw visitors to them. The allure of an ancient name, a place of legend or mystery, is easily more powerful than that of a younger, brassy locale. Timbuktu has nothing to fear from Las Vegas.

Art in the Sahara is not what it was, however. Taste has changed since ancient artists scored and painted the record of their residence. The people who live in the oasis-towns today may still adorn their walls with pictures, but they no longer feature hunting or round-headed aliens. It is more likely that one will come across an Alpine scene, an eight-by-twelve foot photographic image delivered in a roll, as wallpaper. I have seen these pictures—snow-capped peaks and green pastures, or the common variant of a limpid, palm-fringed lagoon—adorning walls in homes, offices and cafés across the desert. Such images are obviously not found solely in the Sahara, but their very incongruity here reminds one of the desert dwellers' love of water and cool places, which many will only ever experience through Chinese-made posters, in themselves a wry nod to globalization.

Although it is hard to talk about a "typical" Saharan town, partly because of a surfeit of clichés, many of them do share common characteristics. Apart from some source of water, heat and dust are the most obvious features. The heat—or cold—will vary according to the season and time of day: the dust is more consistent. Consistent too is the ubiquitous breeze-block architecture, the low-level buildings and the unplanned proliferation of power lines and cars. Inevitable links of geography and climate aside, oasis-towns in the Sahara are notable for their differences rather than their similarities.

For example, Timbuktu, a byword for isolation in the non-Saharan world, was for centuries renowned across the region as a major centre of trade and learning. Founded in the eleventh century, the town in Mali is today a Unesco World Heritage Site, whose mud brick mosques were said to have inspired and informed the architecture of Antoni Gaudí. The priceless collection of 700,000 ancient scrolls and manuscripts kept here rightly make this remote, medium-sized town a place of pilgrimage for scholars and romantically inclined tourists alike.

By contrast, the town of Arlit, in neighbouring Niger, is ugly, industrial and far from romantic. Founded in 1969, the town currently has a population of about 80,000, but it is only really attractive to those working in the uranium mining business. That tourists will, eleven centuries from now, trek to Arlit to stare into vast holes gouged out in open pit mining seems unlikely, although one never can tell. Surrounded by shantytowns that house African labourers, Arlit's fortunes and its population of foreign mining engineers rise and fall in line with world uranium prices. The town made international newspaper headlines in 2003 when western intelligence reports indicated that the Iraqi leader, Saddam Hussein, had been trying to buy significant quantities of uranium from the area.

With a population just over half that of Arlit, the oasis of In Salah in Algeria looks in many ways like a "typical" large oasis, complete with a towering sand dune that each year moves approximately one foot closer to burying the town. Almost exactly in the middle of the Sahara's north-south axis, with more than 200,000 date palms, In Salah was always an agricultural oasis, as well as being on a trade route. Africans and Arabs exchanged slaves and gold for European products here. Although the town sees small numbers of desert tourists, the majority of today's European visitors come to the region for black gold. The centre of Algeria's hugely important energy industry, In Salah finds itself sitting on top of some of the world's biggest oil and gas fields, attracting hundreds of engineers and others involved in its extraction and processing.

On a much smaller scale than Arlit or In Salah, industry is present in many other, otherwise agricultural Saharan oasis-towns. Tessalit, an unremarkable town of a few thousand in the Adrar Mountains in northern Mali, has deposits of gypsum that have pushed the growth of a local plaster industry. Famous for dates, olives and Alexander the Great, Siwa, a town of 20,000 on the edge of the Great Sand Sea, is not the only oasis to host

Goat market, Nouakchott

a water bottling plant, in this case taking un-carbonated Siwa Water to the tables of Cairenes who demand a purity not found in their stretch of the Nile. On the banks of the Nile in Sudan, Dongola, where Kitchener enjoyed a famous victory over the Mahdi's forces in 1896, has also embraced engineering plants, even while it continues to be an important local centre of farming, both agrarian and livestock.

As far from Dongola as it is possible to get in Saharan terms, Nouakchott, the capital of Mauritania, is probably the desert's largest city, with a population between 800,00 and two million, and host to the country's sole university. Such a gap between high and low estimates is mainly due to the large migrant population that comes and goes, from the desert's interior to the shores of the Atlantic. Since becoming the nation's capital upon independence, when it was home to some 9,000, the city has grown massively, if not carefully. Today, any further growth in Nouakchott, a Berber name meaning "place of the winds", faces a unique dual challenge. The sprawling city is hemmed in by both ocean and desert, the Atlantic offering a barrier to any westward expansion, while its eastern borders are steadily being overrun by advancing dunes, a problem that has attracted international attention with, as yet, no permanent solution.

OASIS-TOWNS

Once centres of trans-Saharan trade, many oasis-towns have been stuck in obscurity for centuries now with their inhabitants making what money they can through trading dates, olives and livestock with poorer oases in the area. The old town of Ghadames in Libya is one such place, and another Saharan town designated a World Heritage Site by Unesco. Its ingenious architecture consists of hundreds of whitewashed palm tree trunks, filled in with lime, stretching between the rows of similarly whitewashed houses that face each other, forming a series of dark, cool alleyways that give the impression that the town is actually underground. Hundreds of concrete houses were built by the government in the 1970s that, while better equipped to keep the desert sand out, were inevitably inferior to the old buildings when it came to keeping those inside cool.

As the last town in south-western Algeria before one enters Morocco and/or the Western Sahara, Tindouf enjoys an importance out of all proportion to its natural resources. Algeria's 1977 census found the town's

Ghadames

population to number 6,000. A 2006 estimate puts it at 45,000. These swollen numbers are thanks to an influx of refugees from the Western Sahara who live in seemingly permanent camps, waiting for independence and surviving on aid and water, both of which are brought in by road to this otherwise desiccated spot on the map.

One of these camps, Smara, has its namesake town over the border, in that part of the Western Sahara that is either occupied or integral to Morocco depending on one's position. Only founded in the mid-nineteenth century, and the sole city in former Spanish Sahara to be established by a local ruler, it has been sacked and almost completely destroyed in its short history. Once it gains independence, the Sahrawi government in exile has said that Smara will become the nation's capital city. In the meantime, it has remained firmly in Moroccan hands since they overran and expelled Polisario forces from the city.

Like Smara, the remote oasis of Zouar in northern Chad has been variously besieged and occupied over the past four decades, by both Libyan forces and domestic rebel groups. Although far from the Chadian capital, Zouar's remote location in the Tibesti Mountains, not so far from the Libyan border, means that this otherwise unimportant place not only has an airport but a strong military presence.

Although military considerations might prevent outsiders from visiting certain towns, it is not always the case. The city of Tamanrasset, in the Ahaggar region of Algeria, is one of the Sahara's larger and better-known oases. It is also the centre of the four-nation Joint Military Staff Committee, whose members—Algeria, Mauritania, Mali and Niger—along with outside support, most notably from the US, are working to combat criminal gangs and terrorist activity in the region. The scale of the desert, combined with low population density, is what makes places like Tamanrasset so remote. It is also why illegal pursuits here are so hard to thwart, and why they are in turn so persistent. The French initially settled Tamanrasset, which they named Fort Laperrine, as a bulwark to protect the trans-Saharan routes from banditry.

Long a favourite goal of adventurous tourists, Tamanrasset's population of nearly 80,000 means that the city is large enough to survive even when numbers of foreign visitors are down. Atar in Mauritania, population 25,000, is likewise large enough and, as a district capital, important enough to survive without tourism, especially crucial given that events such as the Paris-Dakar Rally, which used to have a scheduled stopover here, seemed to contribute little cash to the local economy. For relatively nearby Chinguetti, founded in 777, and the smaller twelfth-century town of Ouadane, tourism has become a staple of the local economy. Unfortunately, tourist income is notoriously unpredictable, making the prospect of financial security and planning for growth as remote as the towns themselves.

There are numerous other Saharan settlements that have neither wonderful mud-brick architecture nor bewitching ruins to attract foreigners, and few have the natural resources of Arlit or In Salah, even where these prove to be a curse instead of a blessing. The majority are humdrum towns, lacking pretension or bustle but ideally offering their inhabitants a peaceful agricultural living, or even modest prosperity for those fortunate enough to run or own some small business such as the grocery shop, café or garage. Then again, there are any number of dusty, overlooked and ignored one-donkey towns that lack even these modest offerings. Lucky even to feature on the most detailed map, these hamlets in the Sahara are often literally nothing more than home to a hundred or fewer souls, where the physical horizons may be unlimited but opportunities are entirely absent. Yet none of these places is an unchanging entity. With almost universal access to motor vehicles, steadily improving roads, satellite television and, increasingly, internet connectivity, all oasis-towns are changing as much as the life of those who inhabit them. Perspectives change, and so too do expectations.

Not even in the desert is life frozen in some imaginary past. I remember certain oases without electricity only twenty years ago. Likewise, I recall being startled the first time I heard a mobile telephone ringing in the Great Sand Sea, as the shadow of progress spread reception into the wasteland. It is possible to sympathize with tourists who say they would prefer it if the oasis they are visiting were still lit only by candle-light and oil lamps, but it is telling that one hears such musings as they queue in the oasis' internet café.

Part Two

HISTORY

CONQUESTS AND EMPIRES

Chapter Four

FROM ANCIENT EGYPT TO THE ARAB INVASION

"O Egypt, Egypt, there shall remain of thy religion but vague stories which posterity will refuse to believe, and words graven in stone recounting thy piety… The Divinity shall re-ascend into the heaven. And Egypt shall be a desert, widowed of men and gods."

Hermes Trismegistus, or the Thrice Great; syncretic deity of Hermes and Thoth

LAND OF THE DEAD

The period following the end of the Green Sahara brought suffering to all Egyptians, except those living along the Nile and its delta which avoided the enduring state of barrenness into which the vast majority of the Sahara had been plunged. To be sure, the farmers had to learn how to manage the annual inundation of the river, understanding that its clear flowing bounty was regular but not always predictable. But overall river-based farmers were clearly better off than those who found their soil becoming increasingly thin each year. Indeed, as the Sahara grew drier and non-Nilotic inhabitants learnt that things were literally greener along the river, swelling numbers moved to settle in the more fertile regions and this steep growth in population led directly to the emergence of the Egyptian Empire, an ancient superpower.

As the waters of the Nile were revered for their life-giving powers, so too the ancient Egyptians regarded the sun as worthy of veneration. Rising each morning, the sun's daily path was a metaphor for the journey of life, not only that on earth but the more important journey of the soul after death. Before the Old Kingdom, Egyptians buried their dead in the desert, where the remains would be naturally mummified in the moistureless earth. Also during this period, bodies were interred with their backs to the desert, facing east so that even after burial the dead could witness and recall the daily rebirth that comes with the rising of the sun. The setting of the sun in the west, in the heart of the waterless desert, pointed towards the realm in which one's soul would find its final dwelling for the afterlife.

Egyptian funerary text, in the Land of the Dead

It is by no means a coincidence that all the great Egyptian tombs, whether the Old Kingdom Pyramids at Giza or the Valleys of the Kings and Queens of the New Kingdom, are on the western side of the Nile.

Thus, in the religion of Ancient Egypt, the Sahara was identified as the Land of the Dead, the nightly setting of the sun a profound *memento mori*. The closeness of this relationship between death and the desert is alluded to in the *Pyramid Texts*, a series of spells from the fifth and sixth dynasties that were found carved into the walls and sarcophagi of the pyramids at Sakkara. Reserved for the sole use of the Pharaohs, the *Texts* were intended to ease the progress of the dead into the afterlife and to make that journey a comfortable one. This was also the main function of the incantations that made up the Egyptian *Book of the Dead*, composed after and heavily influenced by the *Pyramid Texts*. The earliest of these culturally and historically invaluable documents date back to 2400 BCE, making them the world's oldest extant religious texts which offer unparalleled insights into the early years of the Egyptian Empire.

The *Book of the Dead* and the *Pyramid Texts* illustrate the ancient kingdom's religious observances and social mores which were refined and reinvented by later generations. For example, simple desert interment was the common pre-dynastic practice that lasted for centuries before formal mummification and elaborate tombs, as can be seen in Spell 662 of the *Pyramid Texts* where the dead king is told to "arise... Cast off your bonds, throw off the sand which is on your face." In the *Book of the Dead* the deceased may converse with the gods, not always to praise them, and the gods are able to respond in kind. The disgruntled soul who finds himself in the Sahara bemoans his fate in Spell 175. Addressing Atum, the prime creator in the ancient Egyptian panoply of gods, the dead man's soul cries out: "O Atum, why is it that I travel to a desert which has no water and no air, and which is deep, dark and unsearchable?" Atum offers the not overly sympathetic response: "Live in it in content!" to which the corpse's soul impatiently responds: "But there is no love-making there!"

The desert to the west of the Nile was also said to be the dwelling place of those gods associated with death, thereby ensuring the closest possible proximity between human burial and divine afterlife. In Spell 175, Atum refers explicitly to the one god who has particular power in the Sahara: "How good is what I have done for Osiris, even more than for all the gods! I have given him the desert." Osiris, who is also known by the honorific Lord of the Western Desert and addressed using the formula "Hail to you who are in the sacred desert of the West!", is of crucial importance not just for his later role as the god of the dead but also because he is, in spite of his divinity, the first character to die in ancient Egyptian religious mythology, having been murdered by his brother Set, or Seth, and resurrected by Isis. For his actions, Set was banished to spend eternity in the Sahara. The patron god of Lower Egypt, Set was also linked to desert winds and storms, becoming the embodiment of evil for the Egyptians.

After the unification of Upper and Lower Egypt, Set continued to be seen as the god of storms but more generally became linked to chaos in any of its forms, including darkness, wars and the desert. For a short period in the nineteenth Dynasty, which spanned the twelfth and thirteenth centuries BCE, Set was revered once again as a great and powerful god who was actually responsible for holding back the desert from the agricultural land of the Delta and Nile Valley. It seems though, by the twentieth

Dynasty, circa 1187 to 1064 BCE, Set had once more been demoted to his more damning role as a force for evil.

In the earliest days of the united Egypt, when the new empire was beginning to expand, the first direction it headed was west, both into the Sahara and along the coast from the delta. While the empire builders were trying to expand their realm to the west, it seems that the tribes in the Sahara were keen to push to the east. Whether aiming for temporary resettlement in the Nile Valley or a more permanent migration away from the desert, clashes between the Egyptians and the Saharan-based tribes were inevitable. In common with virtually all civilizations throughout history, ancient Egypt divided the peoples of the world into two main camps: themselves and everybody else. Accordingly, Egypt referred to everyone who lived in the Sahara more or less parallel to Upper Egypt as *Temehu*, while anyone who inhabited the lands west of the Nile and delta that abutted Lower Egypt were designated *Tehenu*. Both Berber tribes, or more likely associations or alliances of tribes rather than discrete blocks of people, were unlucky to come up against a swelling Egyptian empire, which would eventually control all of the oases of the Western Desert and the Sahara's northern shores west of the delta.

The first therianthropic—or part-man, part-beast—god to be admitted to the Egyptian pantheon was Ash. Originally an indigenous Saharan god and a mirror image of the Egyptian Set, Ash is always depicted with a man's body and animal's head, usually that of one or other of the beasts found in the desert, including lions, vultures, hawks and snakes. Ash occasionally had more than one head at a time. Originally from the fecund oases, Ash was commonly associated with vines and viniculture, which also saw his fame spread to other regions where vines were grown, such as the Delta. Honouring the god, numerous seals from wine jars dating back to the Old Kingdom uncovered at Sakkara by the great Egyptologist Flinders Petrie were found with a common inscription: "I am refreshed by this Ash." This simple sentiment, stated in the form of a prayer of thanks, is one with which wine drinkers up to the present day would no doubt concur.

THE PHOENICIANS
Although famed as a sea-faring race, the Phoenicians also had an enormous impact on the Sahara because of the skills they brought with them.

Although they did not physically colonize the Saharan interior, the knowledge they imported had a far more profound effect than any occupation. Their arrival also marked the introduction of iron into North Africa, which sparked an industrial revolution in the region.

When the Phoenicians first appeared on the North African coast, around 1200 BCE, Saharan populations had diminished considerably with the continuing desiccation of the land. The direct impact of iron working on the desert tribes was initially limited. For one thing, the Sahara now lacked the ready supply of wood essential for the process of smelting. Trans-Saharan communications were never absent from the desert, however, and as iron tools and weapons made their way south across the Sahara so too did knowledge of smelting, which was capitalized on by peoples living in wooded areas to the south of the desert, with evidence of early smelting operations established in Mauritania, Mali and Niger.

Although the Phoenicians were establishing themselves on the coast, building up their capital Carthage (Phoenician: Qart-hadasht or New City), they were not interested in controlling the tribes of the interior. Important as the Phoenicians and Greeks were to life along the Saharan littoral, the desert tribes kept themselves aloof (a state with which the Phoenicians were entirely satisfied). Many of the nomadic Imazighen, or Berbers, from the interior only involved themselves in the settlers' lives when attacking and looting the colonies. As a result, the Saharans were seen as unruly, uncivilized and ungovernable, and they remained a source of danger to Phoenician and Greek settlers alike who had made their homes in the towns along the desert's edge. The fractious Imazighen so badly harried the settlers that the Phoenicians were eventually forced to agree to pay the desert tribes tribute, or protection money, in order to guarantee a quiet life and allow themselves to secure their coastal holdings. Eventually Phoenician growth dictated a change in policy, and they began to extend their reach into the Sahara, building cities, forts and border ditches, which marked the reach of their influence.

The Phoenicians had long been transformed from seasonal traders to a settled presence with colonies all along the coast. No longer did they just come to North Africa on the back of favourable March winds, returning to their eastern Mediterranean homeland in September. Now they were permanent residents, and rulers, with customs that reflected the physical and emotional distance that separated them from Tyre. The fall of Tyre to the Babylonian king Nebuchadnezzar in 573 BCE marked the end of the Phoenician Empire. From this point forth the Phoenicians of North Africa, with no eastern Mediterranean motherland, can properly be thought of as Carthaginians.

As Carthage grew and became more powerful it inevitably looked to pursue trade across the Sahara. By opening up previously unused paths across the desert, the Carthaginians could bypass their Greek rivals on the coast. Yet instead of being drawn from the sea and into the sand themselves, they relied on the locals to execute their trade missions for them. Using the existing Berber population to transport their goods for them, the Carthaginians opened up Saharan markets without having to endure the hardship and dangers that went with the terrain.

The Carthaginians also used Berber and Numidian mercenaries from the Sahara to swell the ranks of their army when necessary. As paid warriors, however, the desert fighters were as likely to take the side of their foes, especially if offered more money. As the Greek writer Polybius tells us, many erstwhile allies fought against Carthage when the Romans eventually vanquished it. Nor was this bloodletting restricted to the fall of Carthage in 146 BCE. Records show there were frequent revolts and uprisings on the part of the Berbers, Numidians, Libyans and others under the Carthaginian yoke. It seems that the most ruthless local officials were most favoured in the capital, but their inequitable rule led to much resistance and periodic violence against government authority.

PERSIAN AND PTOLEMAIC DYNASTIES
In 525 BCE, while the Carthaginians were extending their influence in the desert to the south, in the Sahara's easternmost point the Persian King Cambyses II, son of Cyrus the Great, founder of the Persian Empire, was conquering Egypt. Having crossed the Sinai, Cambyses' army clashed—or did not—with the Egyptians at the Battle of Pelusium, barely twenty miles south-east of the modern Port Said, the entrance to the Suez Canal. Whether or not any fighting actually occurred is a moot point. Herodotus writes that he visited the battlefield seventy-five years later, and that it was still strewn with the bleached skulls of fallen soldiers.

Even so, legend has it that the Battle of Pelusium was distinguished by the fact that no fighting took place. Instead, so the Macedonian Polyaenus notes in his *Stratagems in War*, the Egyptians ran away before an arrow was launched, being unwilling to harm the cats, dogs and ibises that they saw as sacred, and which Cambyses herded towards them. After this ignominious Egyptian defeat, Cambyses and his army marched on the Egyptian capital of Memphis without further opposition and Cambyses declared himself Pharaoh, launching 124 years of Persian rule in Egypt. From a Persian perspective, the ease with which Cambyses managed to conquer Egypt was an auspicious beginning to their North African sojourn.

Cambyses was keen to stamp his authority on the Egyptian Empire over which he now ruled and sought to do this with a number of military expeditions, including into the Sahara south and west of Memphis. Unfortunately for Cambyses, none of these military adventures produced the hoped-for results. Leading an army south to attack Kush in modern Sudan, "against the long-lived Ethiopians" as Herodotus describes them in his *Histories*, Cambyses was determined to secure Egypt's southern border, and so set off to cross the desert in a straight line, instead of following the more circuitous course of the River Nile. Without adequate supply lines in place, his army was soon starving and in need of water.

As Herodotus tells us:

> So long as the earth gave them anything, the soldiers sustained life by eating the grass and herbs; but when they came to the bare sand, a portion of them were guilty of a horrid deed: by tens they cast lots for a man, who was slain to be the food of the others. When Cambyses heard of these doings, alarmed at such cannibalism, he gave up his attack on Ethiopia, and retreating by the way he had come, reached Thebes, after he had lost vast numbers of his soldiers.

If Cambyses thought that cannibalism among the troops was the worst of his problems, he had yet to learn the fate of the force he sent into Egypt's western desert.

While en route to Kush, Cambyses sent 50,000 of his soldiers west into the desert to march against the oasis of the Ammonians, or Siwa, which Herodotus says was known in Greek as "the Island of the Blessed". On what was reckoned to be a seven-day journey across the desert, Cambyses' army got as far as "the town of Oasis", which may be Kharga (although Bahariya is another likely candidate). After they set out from Oasis,

Herodotus writes, "thenceforth nothing is to be heard of them, except what the Ammonians… report. It is certain they neither reached the Ammonians, nor even came back to Egypt. Further than this, the Ammonians relate as follows: That the Persians set forth from Oasis across the sand, and had reached about half way between that place and themselves when, as they were at their midday meal, a wind arose from the South, strong and deadly, bringing with it vast columns of whirling sand, which entirely covered up the troops and caused them wholly to disappear. Thus, according to the Ammonians, did it fare with this army."

The failure of these military campaigns was an embarrassing failure for the new Pharaoh, especially after the early promise of his swift initial conquests. The country was never fully subdued and after just three years Cambyses was forced to head back to Persia, to deal with a pretender to his throne. He never got there, being accidentally killed in 522 BCE on the homeward journey. In spite of their best efforts, Cambyses' successors never entirely quelled the periodic uprisings that occurred, including those launched by the desert tribes.

Persian rule came to an end with the arrival of Alexander of Macedon in 333 BCE. Alexander's conquest of Egypt was carried out with the same relative ease as Cambyses' two hundred years earlier. The local population saw Alexander as a liberator, particularly welcome because he was happy to leave most aspects of domestic, non-military administration in the hands of the Egyptians. Alexander also demonstrated a high regard for Egyptian religious and cultural traditions, which made a favourable impression on local priests and the population at large.

The year after arriving in Egypt, Alexander and a small band of followers marched eight days through the Sahara to Siwa, to consult with the Oracle of Ammon, one of the ancient world's most venerated sources of prophecy and wisdom, which Cambyses' army signally failed to destroy. First-hand reports of the expedition were made by two of Alexander's friends, Callisthenes and Aristobulus of Cassandreia; the former was Alexander's court historian, the latter an architect and military engineer. Unfortunately, these accounts have not survived but the historian Arrian, whose account of Alexander's Saharan expedition is now the best available source, consulted them.

For Alexander, the journey to the Oracle was a shrewd political move that endeared him to his new subjects. It also fulfilled his own personal am-

ALEXANDER A SACERD·APPELLAT·FIL·IOV·HAMM·

Alexander the Great as the god Zeus-Ammon

bition to show himself the equal of Perseus and Hercules, who had similarly consulted the gods. Alexander's mother, Olympias, was the first person to encourage him to identify himself as the son of the Greek god Zeus. (Although it is common for mothers to think well of their children, persuading a boy that he is the son of a god must invite psychological disorders that would require lifetimes of therapy to unravel.)

In keeping with Alexander's supposedly divine mission, the chroniclers were excited to report miracles that accompanied their journey to Ammon. Travelling along the Mediterranean coast to Paraetonium, today the seaside resort of Marsa Matruh, Alexander's party turned south into the desert. Arrian writes that although this route is largely waterless, Alexander's small band enjoyed plentiful rain as they went. While rain is not unknown here, Arrian also records other more remarkable details to demonstrate the divine nature of Alexander's mission. Arrian tells us there were "two crows flying in advance of the army [that] acted as guides to Alexander." Arrian further notes that Ptolemaeus son of Lagos claimed: "two serpents preceded the army uttering speech, and Alexander bade his leaders follow them and trust the divine guidance; and the serpents did actually serve them as guides for the route to the oracle and back again."

Whatever talking beasts might or might not have accompanied Alexander, upon his arrival he was greeted by the priests of the Temple as the new, rightful Pharaoh of Egypt. Satisfied, Alexander henceforth insisted on being referred to by this new title, Zeus-Ammon. Coins from the period depict Alexander as Zeus, complete with ram's horns signifying his divinity. After Alexander's visit, the Oracle of Ammon enjoyed an even more elevated status across the ancient world, with a notable increase in supplicants travelling there in the hope of a consultation with the Oracle.

After Alexander's death in 323 BCE, Ptolemy, a life-long friend and trusted general, seized power in Egypt, taking the title of Pharaoh and establishing the Ptolemaic Dynasty that was to last for the next three hundred years. Ptolemy, whose name is the Greek for "aggressive" or "warlike", crowned himself Ptolemy I Soter, or Ptolemy the Saviour. His male heirs all took the same name, while females in the dynastic line were named either Cleopatra, "father's glory", or Berenice, "bearer of victory".

Not content to control the desert lands they inherited, the Ptolemies were soon extending their control west into Libya and south into the Sudan. While any Egyptian Empire was tied to the Nile, Ptolemy recognized that the oases, too, were of great importance. Strung out through the desert along the trans-Saharan trade routes, not only were they a source of taxation, but they were also useful bases from which to launch raids. As a result, a sizeable garrison was stationed at the oasis of Bahariya and a temple dedicated to Alexander the Great, which was only uncovered in the 1930s, was built.

The elevated status of the Saharan Oracle did not survive the Ptolemies. Almost exactly three hundred years after Alexander's visit to Siwa, Strabo wrote the following about Oracles in Book XVII of his *Geography*: "In ancient times [they were] held in greater esteem than at present. Now they are generally neglected for the Romans are satisfied with the oracles of Sibyl... Hence the oracle of Ammon, which was formerly held in great esteem, is now nearly deserted." This decline in part resulted in a concurrent dropping off in attention paid to the inhabitants of the oases by their ostensible rulers in Memphis.

THE ROMANS

The razing of Carthage in 146 BCE marked not only the end of the third Punic War but also the end of Carthaginian civilization itself. As Polybius wrote in his *Histories*, "Scipio, when he looked upon the city as it was utterly perishing and in the last throes of its complete destruction, is said to have shed tears and wept openly for his enemies... realizing that all cities, nations, and authorities must, like men, meet their doom."

At that time Rome was not interested in establishing colonies in North Africa. Nevertheless it ended up ruling the region, which it seems almost to have acquired by accident, for five centuries. For its first one hundred years in North Africa, Rome did little more than appoint a senator to the region and collect tribute, both done annually. Eventually, belying these humble beginnings, Rome's North African provinces, including Egypt, would be the breadbasket of the empire and consequently the most important of all Roman possessions. Much changed from when Horace described Roman Africa as *Leonum arida nutrix* or dry nurse of lions.

First occupying the Tripolitanian ports that were the hubs of trans-Saharan trade—Sabratha, Oea (Tripoli) and Leptis Magna—Rome took a share of the profits made from any goods that emerged from the desert. Later, after Julius Caesar landed in North Africa to destroy his rival in Rome's civil war, Pompey, and his Numidian allies, Rome pursued more permanent territorial gains. The old kingdoms of Numidia and Maureta-nia, eastern Morocco and the bulk of Algeria were annexed to become the re-titled Roman province of Africa Nova, thereby distinguishing it from Africa Vetus, or Old Africa, which covered north-eastern Algeria and northern Tunisia.

The process of Romanization itself did not begin in earnest until Oc-tavian—who in 27 BCE was styled Augustus, Rome's first emperor—became the undisputed master of Roman Africa in 36 BCE, eight years after the murder of his great-uncle and adoptive father, Julius Caesar. In 30 BCE Octavian also began to rule Egypt, after the defeat and suicide of his fellow triumvir, Antony and Antony's paramour Cleopatra. The event is recorded with understatement in the *Res Gestae Divi Augusti* (the Deeds of the God Augustus), where it is written: "I added Egypt to the empire of the Roman people."

That relative peace prevailed is clear from the small number of Roman soldiers stationed along the desert's borders. With various client rulers in place, as well as soldiers turned farmers, Rome was able to maintain order for much of this period with about 5000 troops. This is not to say that the Romans were not alive to potential threats from the Sahara proper. There are many *ostraka* or potsherds, shards of pottery that record the comings and goings of local tribes, including details such as the tribe's name, the numbers moving, their direction, what livestock they were leading, and a note of any goods being transported.

The Romans also made a number of trips deep into the Sahara which do not appear to have been military but more aimed at exploration and developing friendly relations with desert allies. One of these, led by Sep-timius Flaccus at the end of the first century CE, took four months and the Romans are believed to have reached the Tibesti Mountains. Another expedition, under Julius Maternus, travelled to Agisymba, the place where rhinoceroses gather. While Agisymba has not been definitively identified, Ptolemy's description of high mountains, the journey from the Fezzan and the preponderance of large animals suggests it was in the Lake Chad area.

Rome never tried to conquer the desert tribes, nor were attempts made to garrison the oases of the desert interior. In spite of this, Rome's presence was felt throughout the desert, from Egypt and the Sudan to West Africa and south of the Atlas Mountains. Trade links between Rome and inhabitants of the desert remained numerous and diverse. One major indication of just how widespread they were was the circulation of Roman coins throughout Saharan Africa, which could still be found in the towns of the north-central Sahara as recently as 1900. It is also believed that the most commonly used word for money in much of North Africa, *filoos*, derives from the Latin word *follis*, a common, low denomination bronze Roman coin.

THE GARAMANTES

Although settling in their central-Libyan homeland around 1500 BCE, it is only with Herodotus that our written record of the Garamantes begins, when he writes: "Further inland toward the South, in the part of Libya where wild beasts are found, live the Garamantes, who avoid all intercourse with men, possess no weapons of war, and do not know how to defend themselves." Like the Phoenicians, we do not know what the Garamantes called themselves, so we must rely on their Greek name, which the Romans, and subsequently everyone else, adopted.

We are, however, better able to piece together an understanding of the Garamantes than any number of their neighbours during this time. One of the glories of the Sahara is its rock art, and this provides us with substantial detail about Garamantean culture, and an idea of how far it spread in the central Sahara. Recent archaeological digs have also increased our knowledge, and surprised everyone with how much more substantial and numerous Garamantean towns were than previously thought.

Unlike other Saharan cultures, the Garamantes only moved into the Fezzan, from the Mediterranean basin, after the process of desertification had taken hold. Once there, they developed an innovative hydrological system that allowed them to farm in the Sahara for centuries. As a result, the Garamantes ruled over virtually the entire Fezzan region from their capital, Garama, for close to a thousand years from 600 BCE.

The Garamantes owed their success entirely to tapping the vast aquifers that lie below the limestone desert floor. By digging an elaborate series of tunnels—or rather making their slaves dig these—they could unleash huge quantities of otherwise hidden water. The fifth-century writer and sometime alchemist Olympiodorus of Thebes wrote of the Garamantes' tunnels, *foggaras* in Berber, that they went down as far as 120 feet before releasing free-flowing jets of water. By taking advantage of slave labour and controlling trans-Saharan trade routes, it is thought that the kingdom eventually covered 70,000 square miles.

Having secured access to water, the Garamantes were able to expand their purview through a successful trade network, in which they again capitalized on their desert location. They dominated the whole eastern portion of the desert and acted as middle men between markets to the north and south. According to Strabo and Pliny, the Garamantes also extracted minerals from the Tibesti Mountains, more than 800 miles from Garama. Apart from salt, gold and semi-precious stones, there is little doubt that the Garamantes also engaged in the slave trade. Turning to Herodotus again, he writes unequivocally: "The Garamantes hunt the Aethiopian hole-men, or troglodytes, in four-horse chariots, for these troglodytes are exceedingly swift of foot—more so than any people of whom we have any information. They eat snakes and lizards and other reptiles and speak a language like no other, but squeak like bats."

It is also likely that their growth depended on acquiring ever-larger numbers of slaves. More slaves meant more tunnels dug; greater access to water meant an increase in population. Archaeological digs in Garama, modern Germa, have uncovered an astonishing total of 120,000 graves. From this number of tombs one can extrapolate that the capital and its satellite towns supported a permanent population of not less than 10,000. According to one of the archaeologists responsible, David Mattingly, this was "the first time in history that a non-riverine area of the Sahara… had produced an urban society." The graves also yielded a wealth of Nubian artefacts, suggesting significant contact between the Garamantes and black tribes of the eastern Sahara.

Herodotus' statement about the Garamantes' use of chariots is supported by numerous examples of rock art from across the Fezzan. Featuring teams of between one and four horses, these often-detailed works clearly show that the Garamantes had great equestrian skills by which they controlled trade along the so-called Garamantean Road, also referred to as the Bilma Trail, which passed through their territory. Running from Tripoli, it cuts through the centre of the Fezzan and on south between the Ahaggar and Tibesti mountains, and via the Kouar escarpment in north-eastern Niger, to Bilma, one of the major centres of the Saharan salt trade.

By the time the Romans arrived, the Garamantes proved themselves to be a persistent source of annoyance to the newly arrived superpower.

When Rome's fortunes in North Africa were in the ascendant after the destruction of Carthage, the Garamantes felt more than able to meet them head on. Their role as Saharan traders and brokers aside, the Garamantes had long been known for their frequent and successful raids, which saw them going as far north as Carthage, even at the height of Carthaginian power. In spite of their raids, however, the Garamantes were no keener to conquer and settle in the north than were the Carthaginians or Romans to conquer and settle in the central Sahara.

In time, notably after the Third Punic war, the Romans became less tolerant of Garamantean aggression, and they determined to end the habitual raids. In 20 BCE the Roman proconsul Cornelius Balbus Minor, from Gades, modern Cadiz, was confronted by a revolt among the Saharan tribes, which grew until it stretched the length of Rome's southern border, from Mauretania to Tripolitania. In a brilliant piece of soldiering, Balbus crushed the unrest, marching his army four hundred miles into the desert and capturing the cities of Cydamae, modern Ghadames, and Garama, the capital of Phazzania, from which we take the name Fezzan. As a result of this campaign, Balbus was granted Roman citizenship and was honoured with a triumphal parade in Rome, the first time a foreign-born Roman was afforded such an honour. But in spite of Roman claims that the Garamantes were now absorbed into the Roman Empire, intermittent raids continued. Although the Garamantes were from this time nominally under Roman control, without a garrison in Garama, Roman control always had its limits.

Rome elected to march again on Garama, now employing the latest military advances and attacking for the first time in Roman history with a camel cavalry, which enabled their forces to venture deeper into the desert and faster than previously. The Garamantes knew they were out-manoeuvred, losing the advantage that isolation had once given them.

Regardless, the Garamantes again launched attacks against Roman coastal settlements, prompting Tacitus in his *Annals* to write in 70 CE that they were "ungovernable", adding "the Garamantes [are] a wild race incessantly occupied in robbing their neighbours." As late as 400 CE, the Numidian rebel Gildo recruited a Garamantean army to join him in a war against Rome.

Over time, however, Romano-Garamantean relations improved, in part because of growth in trade between the two, which meant there was

The ruins of Garama

more to be gained from trading than raiding. Even so, the impermanence of peace between Rome and the Garamantes led to the construction of "limes"—defensive borders that marked the limit of Roman territory in North Africa and across the whole of Europe. The most famous of these is Hadrian's Wall, or Limes Britannicus, in the north of England, built to keep the marauding Picts in their place, that is, in Scotland.

Looking south across the Sahara, the Limes Tripolitanus acted not just as a defensive wall but also the point at which the Romans collected taxes on goods coming into their territory. Many records, kept on clay *ostrakas*, have survived, such as those discovered at Gholaia, Libya, stating that there crossed into Roman lands on a certain day "Garamantes bearing barley, four mules and four asses", while another fragment mentions "Garamantes leading four asses."

From the perspective of the Garamantes, the collapse of Roman rule in North Africa marked the end of a valuable trading partner. When the Vandals became the dominant power in the region, their rule did not extend as far as the Fezzan, and while this provided the region with a greater degree of independence than had previously been the case, it also meant economic decline for the Garamantes and other former trading partners of the Romans.

In modern times, Libya's leader Colonel Gaddafi drew inspiration from the Garamantes when he inaugurated the so-called Great Man-made River Project. This engineering feat in the desert, which extracts water at a rate of 230 million cubic feet per day, should be a source of worry for the country's future rather than the blessing it was trumpeted as. Today the land that failed to sustain the Garamantes' water-heavy agricultural economy is green once again, but the underground tunnels lie unused, replaced by the modern means of drilling and pumping water. The ancient city was not finally abandoned until 1937. In the new town water levels continue to drop and at least in the short-term future the inhabitants of modern Germa are unlikely to see a return to the glory days when theirs was the capital of the Garamantes Empire.

CAMELS

"The camel has a single hump;
The dromedary, two;
Or else the other way around.
I'm never sure. Are you?"
            Ogden Nash, "The Camel"

For anyone who has the same problem as Ogden Nash, the dromedary, which one finds in the Sahara, has one hump, the Bactrian has two, and they are both camels. It is hard to imagine a desert scene without a camel caravan crossing it. Trudging along or watering at some palm-ringed oasis, one easily assumes that the desert and the camel have always been together, but they have not. The camel is a recent introduction to the Sahara, almost modern in the history of the desert.

A fixture in every nativity scene and featured in innumerable pictures of Bible stories, the camel has come to represent the quintessential beast of the Middle East. Yet it is not an Arabian or African native. The earliest cameloid fossil remains, which date back fifty million years, are found in North America. About two million years ago, one branch of the family crossed the land bridge that lay where the Bering Straits are now before spreading west through Asia and into Arabia. The major differences between the woolly coated, two-humped Bactrian camel and the leaner, single-humped dromedary reflect the species' adaptation to climatic conditions in which they each now thrive.

Even today, there are notable differences between camels native to the north of the Sahara and those from the south. For example, native Sudanese animals have less hair than their northern cousins, and will suffer from the relative cold of the northern Sahara winters if taken there too quickly without a period of acclimatisation.

In *The Art of Travel*, the Victorian guide that covers everything for the intrepid traveller, the author Francis Galton says that "Camels are only fit for a few countries, and require practised attendants; thorns and rocks lame them, hills sadly impede them, and a wet slippery soil entirely stops them." Although there may be limitations to the climates and terrains in which camels work best, it would be a great injustice to call them lazy. Further, whoever believes that a camel is a horse designed by committee betrays great ignorance of the genius of the animal. No other creature comes close to camels for their ability to live in the extreme conditions of hot deserts, as anyone who has lived or worked with them can attest. It is a constant source of amazement that a camel can travel in the desert without water for ten days, after which it can drink as much as 100 to 150 litres in a single session.

One reason for camels' ability to go for so long without water is the fact that they do not sweat until their temperature gets above 106°F. In addition, they can lose 25 per cent of their body weight through dehydration before there is a serious risk of death through cardiac failure. Most mammals will die after a drop of 15 per cent.

A camel can carry twice the load of an ox, travel at twice its speed and cover greater distances. This is also achieved without the need for a cart, thereby providing access to places where the terrain is impassable to wheeled vehicles. Camels could, of course, also be made to carry carts across rough country; broken down into their constituent parts and strapped to the animals' sides, they would be reassembled once on more suitable tracks. This was still being done in the nineteenth century, as Galton reports: "Mr. Richardson and his party took a boat, divided in four quarters, on camel-back across the Sahara, all the way from the Mediterranean to Lake Tchad [sic]."

The importance of camels to life in the Sahara can perhaps be summed up in the following exchange between Rosita Forbes and one of her guides: "'What is Allah's greatest gift to man?' [the guide asked] me suddenly. I felt this was a test of my faith in Islam, so I promptly replied, 'The Koran.' He looked at me scornfully. 'The camel! If there were no camels here, there would be no dates, no food, nothing!' He paused and added solemnly, 'If there were no camels here, there would be no men!'"

When Herodotus talks about the Berbers' regular trans-Saharan trading networks he was not suggesting this was achieved with camels. Instead, the literary and pictorial evidence from the period shows laden mules and horse-drawn carriages crossing the desert. Camels are notable by their absence from the earliest examples of Saharan rock art.

Exactly when the camel became established in the Sahara remains a matter of speculation, but it is most likely that there were a number of introduction events. And although they were not found across the whole of the Sahara until the first or second century CE, there is evidence of their presence in eastern parts of the desert several centuries earlier. The idea put forward by some writers that the River Nile formed a barrier that halted their spread is debatable, as camels are actually strong swimmers. It is probable that the camel was first introduced into North Africa by Assyrian invaders in the seventh century BCE, but it was not until the early Ptolemaic period in Egypt, around 300 BCE, that they were particularly numerous or widespread.

Once successfully introduced, the camel became indispensable for desert travel, its dominance being guaranteed once its usefulness as a draft animal was grasped. The Romans, enthusiastic developers of innovative military technology, soon understood the potential uses of the camel as a military vehicle. When Julius Caesar defeated the Numidian king Juba in 46 BCE, among the spoils he took were 22 camels. While not a large number of animals, they are important as the first textual record of camels in North Africa. Having first come across camels in Syria and Egypt, the Romans were soon putting them to use against the Garamantes and other tribes who were keen to attack Rome's desert frontiers. Once the Romans took camel-mounted troops into battle, first in 69 CE, the isolation that had previously been the Garamantes' main strategic advantage disappeared, and raiding from the Sahara likewise tailed off.

Dromedary (*left*) and Bactrian camels

As for the camel being an uncomfortable mount, this rather depends how accustomed one is to riding. The author Paul Bowles, a city dweller, did not find riding a camel a comfortable experience. Writing in *Their Heads are Green and Their Hands are Blue: Scenes from the non-Christian World*, he says, "Of course, the proper way to travel in the Sahara is by camel, particularly if you're a good walker, since after about two hours of the camel's motion you are glad to get down and walk for four. Each succeeding day is likely to bring with it a greater percentage of time spent off the camel."

One of Rudyard Kipling's most memorable *Just So Stories*, "How the Camel Got His Hump", begins:

> In the beginning of years, when the world was so new and all the Animals were just beginning to work for Man, there was a Camel, and he lived in the middle of a Howling Desert because he did not want to work; and besides, he was a Howler himself. So he ate sticks and thorns and tamarisks and milkweed and prickles, most 'scruciating idle; and when anybody spoke to him he said "Humph!" Just "Humph!" and no more.

The Ship of the Desert is unique, and should be respected as such. The only animal capable of ferrying people and their produce across the Sahara, through sun and sandstorms, it has been responsible for more significant social change across the desert than any other animal. In spite of this it is too often misrepresented as a recalcitrant and unyielding beast. It is no wonder that Kipling's camel speaks as it does: Humph indeed!

CHRISTIAN NORTH AFRICA

Christianity came to the Sahara at two distinct periods: first under Roman rule, when the empire adopted it as the state religion; secondly, more than 1500 years later, with the arrival of the European invaders. When Christianity was first introduced to the Sahara it spread slowly but steadily. Starting out in the easternmost parts of the desert, which is where the earliest churches are to be found, it was established in Alexandria in about 43 CE under the evangelizing mission of St. Mark. Honoured as the man who introduced Christianity to Africa with his arrival in Egypt, St. Mark is most commonly represented in Christian iconography with a lion in the desert. Not only was he the first Bishop of Alexandria, where he was martyred, but he also saw the first entry of Christianity into the desert.

Among the oases of the Western Desert, Bahariya was an important early centre of Christianity, where St. Bartholomew was sent to preach and to convert the locals. According to the *Synaxarium* of the Coptic tradition, Bartholomew, one of the twelve Apostles, not only preached in Bahariya but was martyred there. In spite of his death, his mission obviously met with great success, Bahariya having its own bishop until the fourteenth century.

Local tradition also states that the headless corpse of St. George was brought to the oasis from Syria for safekeeping. A former senior officer in the Roman Army, the Syrian-born St. George became a Christian martyr in 303 CE, decapitated on the orders of the Emperor Diocletian for refusing to pay tribute to the pagan gods. The traditional date of his death, 23 April, has become his feast day, and he remains one of the most widely venerated saints in both the eastern and western Christian traditions, and the patron of numerous countries from England to Malta, as well as cities from Moscow to Beirut. St. George's patronage also extends to agricultural workers, knights, and those suffering from the plague and syphilis.

While in North Africa at any rate Judaism is sometimes called the religion of the marketplace, Christianity is the religion of the countryside. The Jewish presence in the Sahara revolved around trade, rather than missionary zeal which characterized much later Christian activity there. Just how far-reaching the Jewish presence in the Sahara was is clear from the numbers of Hebrew inscriptions found across the desert. When Biblically literate Victorian explorers first encountered these Hebraic inscriptions on graves from Morocco to Egypt, the more romantically inclined became convinced that the Berbers, Tuareg *et al* were in fact a lost tribe of Israel.

When Christianity arrived in North Africa it benefited from another monotheistic religion—Judaism—already having been established. The Jewish presence meant that the first Christians quickly got across their message of monotheism. They initially focused their proselytizing efforts on the Jewish faithful. By delivering the message that Jesus was in fact the Jewish Messiah, the Promised One whose return was anticipated in Jewish theology, many were persuaded that this faith was not a challenge but rather the fulfilment of their beliefs. Many of those Jews who converted subsequently became harshly critical of their former co-religionists. Evidence for this can be seen in the earliest Christian text found in the Sahara. The second-century *Letter of Barnabas*, likely written by a convert from Alexandria, contains much that is nothing more than an anti-Jewish diatribe, noted more for its virulence than its theology.

The *Letter of Barnabas* also offers a clue to the very early internationalism of Christianity: literacy. Apart from the movement of Jewish merchants, literacy and the written word were of paramount importance among early Christians, with epistles being written, copied and transmitted by land and sea, quickly spreading the message of the new religion throughout the Mediterranean world. If the new religion was slow to dominate the religious landscape of the Sahara, at least those communities of believers that were there had textual foundations, which could be referred to when needed, settling doctrinal disputes and bolstering faith.

A long-standing dispensation from the Roman emperor exempted Jews from military service in the imperial army. They were also unique in being granted an exemption from making sacrifice to the emperor. So, when many early Christians, as Jewish converts, adopted the same exemptions for themselves, they were able to do so because the Roman authorities saw them as a Jewish sub-sect rather than a new religion. Even so, the growth of Christianity in the empire set it on a collision course with Rome. Once Rome understood that Christianity was not another Jewish cult but a distinct missionary faith intent on promoting un-Roman views of belief in a single God rather than the whole gamut of Roman gods—including the emperor—the empire struck back.

The first Christian martyrs in North African were seven men and five women from the hamlet of Scilium (precise location unknown) in modern Tunisia, executed in 180 CE under the proconsul Saturninus. Their fate was sealed when, during their trial for not paying tribute to the emperor, their spokesman Speratus announced, "The Empire of this world I do not recognize; but rather I serve God whom no man has nor can see with human eyes," echoing St. Paul's first epistle to Timothy. A far-from-unfair ruler, Saturninus gave them thirty days' grace to recant. But they did not and so were beheaded. Many more followed, but as the Christian thinker and native Berber Tertullian said of Rome's policy, "the blood of the martyrs is the seed of the Church."

Tertullian (c. 160-c. 220) was also responsible for coining a number of Latin terms central to Church doctrine, including *trinitas*, or the trinity, and the idea of Christian scriptures consisting of two testaments: *vetus testamentum* and *novum testamentum*. Tertullian would probably have been canonized had he not gone over to the heterodox Montanist cause later in life, which propounded, among other heresies, the idea of continuing, direct revelation through believers.

Another important figure was St. Augustine (354-430), and not just for the Church in North Africa. A Numidian Berber, at first sight Augustine is an unlikely Christian hero. The son of a pagan father, he was a sometime pagan intellectual who as a young adult enjoyed life to the full, having a child with his concubine and famously praying, "Grant me chastity and continence, but not yet." In spite of this, Augustine is revered as a Doctor of the Church and admired in the Catholic, Protestant and Eastern Orthodox traditions alike.

Although he grew up with a Christian mother, St. Monica, Augustine's conversion did not occur until he was 32, after reading Athanasius' *Life of St. Anthony*. Having proved himself an able student in Carthage—in spite of loathing and failing to master Greek—Augustine started writing anti-heretical treatises after his conversion while living in a celibate male community in his home town of Thagaste, today's Souk Ahras in Algeria.

His writings received favourable attention from a Church official in Hippo, who summoned Augustine to the city. While there, he was ordained a priest, against his wishes but at the insistence of the local congregation, before eventually being consecrated Bishop of Hippo, just ten years after his conversion. He held this post until his death when the Vandals were besieging the city.

A prolific writer, Augustine left behind more than a hundred works including sermons, books of Biblical commentary and numerous volumes of theology. His most popular work remains the *Confessions*. Written more than 1600 years ago, it is often hailed as the first modern autobiography and a work of startling honesty that includes a sense of the subconscious centuries before Freud and psychoanalysis existed.

More important than references to the Sahara in early Christian literature, the proximity of the desert to those who formulated early Christian theology cannot be ignored. The impact the Church in North Africa had on the development of Christian theology is huge: it is noteworthy, for instance, that Christianity arrived in the Sahara before it reached either Greece or Rome, which would become important centres of Christianity, but not until after it had been planted among the Egyptians, Berbers, Libyans and Numidians, its tenets very much developed by the likes of St. Augustine and his fellow African theologians.

Important in the life of the early Church were the periods of persecution, notably in the third century under the emperors Decius and Diocletian. Extensive and violent, persecution forced many Christians to flee into the desert on either side of the Nile. When, after the proclamation of tolerance, issued under Emperor Constantine I, or Constantine the Great, persecution ceased and the Church grew, many decided to remain in the desert, marking the start of Christian monasticism. Many were drawn to this ascetic life which was described as a life of martyrdom. And the most famous one to adopt this isolated way of life was St. Anthony.

Although not the first monk, St. Anthony is acknowledged as the first to retreat fully into the desert. Before him many monks lived close to their home villages, spending periods in retreat rather than adopting this full-time abdication from society. As St. Anthony's biographer, St. Athanasius, wrote, "For there were not yet so many monasteries in Egypt, and no monk at all knew of the distant desert; but all who wished to give heed to themselves practised the discipline in solitude near their own village."

The "distant desert" had always been considered dangerous, not just because of the presence of wild animals and absence of reliable water supplies, but also as the refuge of outlaws and bandits. In the desert such people were literally outside of the law, yet it was into this desert that St. Anthony decided to move.

Moving sixty miles west of Alexandria to Nitra, today Wadi Natrun, Anthony placed himself far from any existing population centres, hoping that this would provide him with the ideal opportunity for prayer and contemplation. He stayed at Nitra for thirteen years, emphasizing the importance of a life of isolation: "Just as fish die if they remain on dry land so monks, remaining away from their cells, or dwelling with men of the world, lose their determination to persevere in solitary prayer. Therefore, just as the fish should go back to the sea, so must we return to our cells, lest remaining outside we forget to watch ourselves interiorly."

Despite this and other sayings of the Desert Fathers being uttered more than 1700 years ago, their importance in the history of monasticism and, some would say, contemporary relevance, was recognized in the twentieth century by the monk and scholar Thomas Merton. Although his experience of the monastic life did not allow him to live in the Sahara, in *The Wisdom of the Desert* he pays tribute to the Desert Fathers and extols the virtue of the solitary life, believing that we are all essentially solitary beings who can thus benefit from time spent in solitary contemplation.

Over the course of St. Anthony's long life—tradition has it that he died aged 105—the temptations and torments to which the devil subjected him have provided plenty of inspiration for writers and artists. According to St. Athanasius, the devil visited St. Anthony "one night with a multitude of demons, he so cut him with stripes that he lay on the ground speechless from the excessive pain. For he affirmed that the torture had been so excessive that no blows inflicted by man could ever have caused him such torment," adding that "the demons as if breaking the four walls of the dwelling seemed to enter through them, coming in the likeness of beasts and creeping things. And the place was on a sudden filled with the forms of lions, bears, leopards, bulls, serpents, asps, scorpions, and wolves, and each of them was moving according to his nature."

Many artistic representations of the saint's torments were to follow, the earliest extant examples of the genre being tenth-century frescoes from Italy. Throughout the fifteenth and sixteenth centuries artists such

Martin Schongauer's engraving of St. Anthony's torment

as Martin Schongauer, Matthias Grünewald and Hieronymus Bosch focused on the more fantastical elements of the story, producing some genuinely terrifying work. *The Torment of St. Anthony* is the title of the earliest known painting of one of the greatest artists of all time, the personification of Renaissance man, Michelangelo. His *Torment*, painted when he was twelve or thirteen, follows Schongauer's own engraving of the subject, to which the young Michelangelo has added his own landscape as a background, and altered Anthony's expression from sorrow to saintly detachment.

THE VANDALS

Nearly four hundred years after Rome took control of Mauretania, a Vandal army coming from Spain and led by King Geiseric did the same, beginning their own conquest of North Africa. The Vandals' domination of North Africa, and far less successful encounter with the Saharan tribes, was not the longest stay of any foreign invader in the region, but whatever the Vandals lacked in longevity they made up for in drama. The most widely cited account of their journey from Europe to Africa is provided by the Roman historian Procopius who, in his *Wars of Justinian*, recounts that the Vandals crossed the Strait of Gibraltar in 429 at the invitation of the Roman general Boniface. Boniface soon regretted, and rescinded, the invitation; this did nothing to stop the arrival of the Vandals and their supporters. There followed a decade of fighting and conquest that left the Vandals in control of most of the Roman provinces.

Not all cities went willingly; Hippo was a famous example and underwent a lengthy siege in the third month of which St. Augustine died, aged 76. As related in *Sancti Augustini Vita*, the Life of Augustine, by Possidius, who was present during the siege, Augustine's last days were spent praying for the city's inhabitants whose fate, being of the Roman faith, was not likely to be good at the hands of the Arian Vandals. Possidius records that Augustine "repeatedly ordered that the library of the church and all the books should be carefully preserved for future generations." The siege lasted for fourteen months and when they eventually took the city the Vandals indulged in a destructive rampage that saw death and enslavement of the city's inhabitants and its buildings burnt, except for Augustine's church and library. Such was his reputation that the Vandals ensured his church and books were protected and preserved. In this instance at least, the Vandals failed to live up to their reputation for wanton destruction.

In a North African sojourn that lasted almost exactly one century, the Vandals successfully controlled their coastal subjects but not those living in the Sahara. Although Vandal settlements were largely confined to the coast and littoral, this did not keep them safe from the desert tribes. Whereas the Romans, as far as it was in their power, were unwilling to allow independence to the desert tribes, the Vandals did their best to adopt a policy of ignoring them, looking north instead to the Mediterranean. Even before the fall of Hippo, Geiseric had started building a fleet. As soon as it was ready, he launched himself with enthusiasm into a lucrative career of piracy, a calling he pursued until his death in 477.

The pursuit of plunder at sea meant that in the Sahara a number of independent kingdoms soon developed, remote from the heartland of Vandal territory. Those tribes that had retained their nomadic lifestyle also took advantage of the limited law and order exerted on the fringes of the Vandals' empire, launching raids in increasing number through the fourth century. Saharan-based Berbers achieved at least two major victories against Vandal settlements between 496 and 530, and by the end of Vandal rule, the inhabitants of these areas may actually have welcomed the restoration of some strong, central authority.

When Byzantine forces landed in June 533 and attacked the Vandals, Geiseric's decision to destroy all city walls, bar those of Carthage, came back to haunt his successors. Although his decision must have seemed a good idea to him at the time, it brought ruin to his heirs. The armies of Byzantium defeated the Vandals in just six months, and Procopius, apparently feeling the Vandals' glory days were at an end made the withering observation that "of all the nations I know the most effeminate is that of the Vandals."

The surrender of Gelimer at Mount Papua in western Numidia marked the end of the Kingdom of the Vandals and the transition of North Africa into a Roman province again. For the next century, the entire period of Byzantine rule in North Africa, oppression, revolts and insurrections were the touchstones of Berber-Byzantine relations, which only ended with the collapse of the Byzantine Empire in North Africa in 647, vanquished by the arrival of the Arab armies.

Anyone who thought life would be better under the Byzantines than under the Vandals was soon to be disappointed. Raids from out of the Sahara became more frequent than ever, and where Byzantine rule was stronger it was harsher too. For the mass of the population, rule from Byzantium was marked by greater interference in their lives, which included among other things swingeing taxation, to which the local tribes responded by revolting. The Romanized Berbers in particular, who under the Vandals had been treated no worse than anyone else, soon responded to Byzantine accession with open revolt.

Strong as they were, any influence the Vandals exerted over the Saharan tribes was limited. To a large degree this was the result of their self-imposed, if understandable, unwillingness to tackle the recalcitrant desert-dwelling Mauri and Berber. Pursuing desert-based raiders—whose combative life has been formed around guerrilla tactics—deep into the Sahara is not something any sane city- or coast-based power would be keen to do. Once again, the desert proved to be a formidable barrier to full conquest by outsiders, and a safe haven for its own.

THE ARMIES OF ISLAM

In *The Decline and Fall of the Roman Empire*, Edward Gibbon wrote of the Arab armies that swarmed into Africa in the seventh century: "The sands of Barca might be impervious to a Roman legion; but the Arabs were attended by their faithful camels; and the natives of the desert beheld without terror the familiar aspect of the soil and the climate."

The ineluctable Arab invasion, after the introduction of the camel, had the most profound effect on the history of Saharan North Africa. The Arab conquest of the region was far more thorough than anything achieved by the Phoenicians, Romans, Vandals or any other previous invaders—Saharan life and culture were absolutely Arabized. From Roman through Vandal rule, most of the region's denizens would have seen little change in their circumstances: not so under the Arab invaders. Bringing with them not only a new religion but also a language that was indivisible from that religion, the changes were radical, and had an immediate impact on every aspect of existence.

Arriving in Egypt in 639, in just seventy years the Arabs conquered all of North Africa, from the Nile to the Atlantic, with Romano-Byzantine Africa becoming Arab Ifriqiya. As Gibbon says, "When the

Arabs first issued from the desert, they must have been surprised at the ease and rapidity of their own success." Their westward conquest followed the setting sun to al-Maghreb, (literally the West). Their ultimate African goal, Morocco, they called al-Maghreb al-Aqsa (the furthest West), and it was conquered in 682 by the Ummayad Arab general Uqba ibn Nafi, Gibbon's "conqueror of Africa". According to the Andalusian historian Ibn Idhari Al-Marrakushi, writing in his *Book of the Wondrous Story of the History of the Kings of Spain and Morocco*, on reaching the waters of the Atlantic at Rabat, Uqba rode his horse into the ocean, crying out, "Oh God, if the sea had not prevented me, I would have galloped on forever like Alexander the Great, upholding your faith and fighting the unbelievers!"

Uqba also founded the city of Kairouan, Tunisia. Rendered from the Arabic *qayrawan*, or caravan, the city was built on the site of an established campsite coming out of the desert. From here, one could travel north to Carthage and the coast, east to Egypt, west to the Atlas Mountains or south into the Sahara. As well as being the capital of Ifriqiya, Kairouan quickly developed into a centre of learning that was to exert a centuries-long influence on education and law throughout the entire Islamic world. Once Arabic was established as a written language, Islamic laws grew apace; in this, the religious authorities at Kairouan were instrumental.

The Muslim-Arab invaders who took control of the Sahara were distinct from earlier Roman and Byzantine conquerors, arriving as they did at the vanguard of a religiously inspired army. As "people of the book", those Christians already in the Sahara were recognized by the Muslim conquerors as being superior to the pagan tribes, if still inferior to the Muslim faithful. As a result, Christians were initially accorded certain rights and protections not extended to non-Christianized Berbers and others, including freedom of worship.

Of the four main branches of orthodox Sunni Islamic law, two originated in North Africa: the Shaf'ite school from Cairo and the Malikite school from Kairouan. Both received large numbers of aspiring scholars from the Sahara who, once educated, returned home, graduates of Islamic law. These new graduates were highly admired in their oases and often achieved power among their kinsmen because of their learning. Thus, literacy led to religious authority, which in turn often resulted in political

KAIROUAN — *Minaret de la Grande Mosquée*

Edition Laouani

mastery too. The knowledge that the usually young scholars took home meant they could dictate what messages became religious orthodoxy in the Sahara. By the same token, the isolation of Saharan communities meant that any unorthodox interpretations of Islam could also be promulgated and flourish, guided by a heterodox scholar whose position was unassailable by any illiterate, secular authorities.

It should be said that the swift conquest of North Africa was not without local setbacks, retreats and military defeats. Arab armies conducted raids into the Sahara, although at this stage apparently without a sense that they were attempting the systematic conquest of the desert. They met with some stiff local resistance, with a few anti-Arab uprisings persisting for decades. These revolts led one Arab governor to declare despairingly, "The conquest of Ifriqiya is impossible; scarcely has one Berber tribe been exterminated than another takes its place." The Roman term of opprobrium for any non-Roman—barbarian—had now evolved into an Arabic proper name, creating a Berber identity that saw them as a united people, rather than merely disparate desert tribes.

Saharan resistance among the Berbers was substantial, if poorly organized and disunited. Furthermore, many Berber leaders recognized that the future did not lie in resisting this overwhelming force. Chiefs who made peace with the Arabs were usually allowed to keep their realms, if they converted to Islam and paid tribute to their Arab conquerors. The sincerity of conversions made under duress was questionable. Ibn Khaldun wrote that the Berbers were guilty of apostasy twelve times before they converted sincerely. After the Ummayad caliphate was established in the second half of the seventh century, the goal to dominate the Sahara and its troublesome tribes was more clearly defined, with religious and military conquest marching together.

The most serious challenge to Arab regional supremacy at this time was the uprising started in the 680s, by the legendary tribal leader, al-Kahina, the seer. Variously claimed as a Jewess and a Christian and described as a witch or a sorceress, al-Kahina can be likened to a Berber Boudica who, through her bravery and a desire to see her tribe remain free of foreign domination, inspired others in a series of ultimately doomed revolts. Described as a beauty with the gift of prophecy, she put this last skill to good use, sending her sons to her Arab enemies to be raised to become successful commanders of Arab armies, hence attaching some glory to the Berbers from a story that is otherwise characterized by defeat and subjugation.

Al-Kahina herself died fighting the Arabs in around 702, her death in effect marking the end of Berber resistance in the desert. Since then, al-Kahina has been adopted as an inspiration by an array of disparate groups, from the more obvious constituencies of Berber nationalists and Maghrebi feminists to less likely followings such as Arab nationalists and even French colonialists.

The arrival of Islam led to the almost total disappearance of Christianity from the Sahara, which retreated across the Mediterranean to Rome, not making another appearance until the nineteenth century when the European invaders reintroduced it, although without any real impact on the local population. Noting the decline of Christianity, Gibbon wrote plaintively that "The northern coast of Africa is the only land in which the light of the Gospel, after a long and perfect establishment, has been totally extinguished." As for Islam at the time of the Arab invasion, it was still a century away from becoming established in writing, which meant the beliefs of military commanders were what carried the day.

The evolution of a scholarly class entrusted with establishing orthodoxy was only a matter of time, however. Some writers, among them the tenth-century Andalusian-Arab geographer and historian al-Bakri, claim that the more remote desert-dwellers long remained beyond the religious pale. In his *Book of Highways and Kingdoms of North Africa*, al-Bakri reports a tradition of the prophet Muhammad that on Judgment Day the people of the northern Sahara will be led to hell, "as a bride to her groom". Elsewhere, al-Bakri writes that certain apostates had reverted to worshipping a ram god.

Chapter Five

TRAVELLERS, CHRONICLERS, GEOGRAPHERS

"A desolate, extensive, difficult country."
The Sahara as described by al-Muqaddasi (946-c. 1000)

If one were to offer a single observation about the period following the seventh-century Arab invasion of North Africa, one could say it was a time of tumult and uncertainty, as indigenous peoples and newcomers both struggled to adjust to the altered reality of life. Once the Ummayad caliphate had ostensible control of the Sahara, the local Berber tribes more or less recognized the suzerainty of the caliph. This was demonstrated mainly by the payment of a nominal tribute to the office of the caliph. In reality, those living in the Sahara remained largely beyond the control of any distant, central authority—a situation which pre-dated by a long way the Arab invasion and continues into the modern era. Local emirs controlled their own tribes and maintained the formal right to command confederations of kinsmen and armed militiamen in neighbouring oases as far as their territorial remit permitted.

In 750 the Abbasids overthrew the Ummayad dynasty and founded Baghdad as their new capital. The Abbasid ascendancy and attendant founding of Baghdad ushered in the so-called Golden Age of Islam, an unparalleled time of invention and learning which properly lasted until the thirteenth century. Abbasid control of the Sahara was never as great as that of their Ummayad predecessors and our knowledge of events in the Sahara during this period relies on the work of a disparate group of Islamic travellers, chroniclers and geographers. The political history of the Sahara during this period was dynamic. Rising dynasties took control only to be forced to seek client states to support them, this authority in turn being challenged by another young pretender. For example, the Aghlabids, who were once a client state of the Abbasids, and the Fatimids, who overthrew both Aghlabids and Abbasids, concurrently controlled the Maghreb and Ifriqiya, while to the Sahara's north, al-Andalus was taken over by a surviving member of the Ummayad dynasty.

One important source on the Sahara to have survived from the tenth century is Mohammed Abul-Kassem Ibn Hawqal. A native of southern Turkey, Hawqal spent nearly three decades travelling in the Islamic world and beyond before publishing his most famous work, *Surat al-Ardh* (Picture of the Earth) in 977, with an accompanying map of the world that has also survived. Hawqal's cartographical efforts are notable as much for what is missing as what is there. Even though Hawqal himself writes that one of his contemporaries dismissed his map of Egypt as "wholly bad" and that of al-Maghreb as "for the most part inaccurate", they remained an important source of information for later scholars because, although they take no notice of lines of latitude, they accurately record in days the distances between towns and cities.

Writing at the same time as Hawqal was the Jerusalem native, al-Muqaddasi (946-c. 1000) whose geography of the Islamic world, *The Best Divisions for Knowledge of the Regions*, offers a description of the Sahara as

> a desolate, extensive, difficult country. The population is constituted of many races. In their mountains one finds those fruits that occur gener- ally in the mountains of the realm of Islam, but most of the people there do not eat them... In trade among them, gold and silver are not used; however, the Garamantes use salt as a means of exchange.

This last observation remains true to this day for the Garamantes' succes- sors.

In the mid-eleventh century the Fatimid caliphate in Cairo was playing unwilling host to the Banu Hilal and Banu Sulaym, Bedouin con- federations from Arabia. In order to be rid of their unwelcome guests, the Fatimids encouraged them to move west. It was an invitation they willingly accepted. This second Arab invasion had the greatest long-term impact on the cultural identity of the Sahara. Unwilling to adapt to local customs, the Hilalian invaders ensured that wholesale Arabization took place, includ- ing a permanent linguistic shift to Arabic. These neo-colonialists were also responsible for replacing the existing, carefully moderated system of agri- cultural land management familiar to the local nomads which best suited the local situation, destroying irrigation systems and felling trees on an unparalleled scale.

In the *Muqaddimah*, Ibn Khaldun writes: "Places that succumb to the

Arabs are quickly ruined [because] the Arabs are a nation fully accustomed to savagery and the things that cause it." In citing examples of the destruction wrought by the rampant Arab forces he says: "When the Banu Hilal and Banu Sulaym pushed through to Ifriqiya and the Maghreb in the eleventh century and struggled there for 350 years, they attached themselves to the country, and the flat territory in the Maghreb was completely ruined. Formerly, the whole region between the Sudan and the Mediterranean had been settled. This fact is attested by the relics of civilization there, such as monuments, architectural sculpture, and the visible remains of villages and hamlets." The destruction was so absolute that Khaldun likened it to the arrival of "a plague of locusts". Within just a few years, it is estimated that some 200,000 of these Bedouin herdsmen had descended on the region.

Although the practical destruction wrought by the Hilalian invasion was wholly negative, it opened up the region to outside influences that would prove crucial in future Saharan development. The invasion also spawned an oral epic that remains a classic of Arabic poetry. The *Taghribat Bani Hilal* is a fictionalized account of the Hilalian invasion that recounts the journey of the Banu Hilal from Cairo to Tunisia, in search of new pastures. The tale, like all oral traditions, evolved over time, growing in each retelling and watered both by the imagination of those reciting the tale and the urgings of audiences. Still recited by storytellers in Cairo and Algiers today, the poem was declared in 2003 by Unesco to be a "Masterpiece of Mankind" and now features in the organization's Oral and Intangible Heritage of Humanity scheme. So while contemporary writers spoke of the Hilalian invasion as being like the end of the world, 1,000 years later the story of that invasion is reckoned to be a creative work of global consequence.

While the Hilalian invasion was in progress, in Andalusia Abu Ubayd Muhammad al-Bakri (1014-94) was writing the first comprehensive geography of the Sudanic belt, which was in part based upon interviews he conducted with merchants who had been there. Although he personally never travelled to any of the places that he wrote about, al-Bakri's skill as a copyist and editor means that his *Book of Highways and of Kingdoms of North Africa*, first mentioned in 1068, is still important as a source of information regarding the Sahara, even if a number of his claims and descriptions have been called into doubt.

Al-Bakri acknowledged that an important motivation behind his book was to spread the message of Islam. Sadly, this resulted in his not infrequent belittling of non-Muslims, including a two-dimensional portrayal of blacks, in contrast to the frequent aggrandisement of his Muslim heroes. For example, when al-Bakri describes "The city of Ghana [which] consists of two towns," he shows perhaps understandable favour towards the one "inhabited by Muslims... large and possessing 12 mosques in one of which they assemble for the Friday prayer. There are salaried imams and muezzins, as well as jurists and scholars." In contrast, he dismisses the non-Muslim part of the town as "where the sorcerers of these people, men in charge of the religious cult live."

Like al-Bakri, Muhammad al-Idrisi did not spend his time living in the Sahara but still felt able to write a geography of the region. His descriptions remain important, and are more accurate than those of al-Bakri. Born in Ceuta in 1100, al-Idrisi was a cartographer and geographer who spent the majority of his working life under the patronage of the Norman King Roger II of Sicily, who had recruited him after hearing about the North African's reputation as a man of learning. The relationship between the Christian king and the aristocratic Muslim scholar was apparently a close one. In the preface to his most famous work, al-Idrisi says of his patron: "Of all the beings formed by this divine will, the eye may not discern nor the spirit imagine one more accomplished than Roger, King of Sicily, [who] has carried arms victoriously from the rising to the setting sun." While accepting the expediency of flattering a patron, few modern readers would argue that al-Idirisi's endorsement of Roger is inflated.

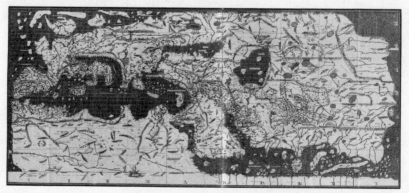

The world, from Ptolemy to al-Idrisi

As for al-Idrisi, it genuinely is hard to overstate his importance in the world of medieval cartography. Working as the permanent secretary of an academy of scholars, al-Idrisi had the task of producing the finest, most extensive work of geography in history. Using existing Muslim and non-Muslim sources and information gleaned from contemporary travellers, the academy took fifteen years to produce *The Delight of One Who Wishes to Traverse the Regions of the World*, more banally referred to as *The Book of Roger*.

Consisting of seventy double-spread page maps, aligned "upside down", that is with south at the top of the page as opposed to the modern north-south orientation, each map came with latitudes marked and distance between towns, as well as a descriptions of these. The book was the marvel of its day and although it has been criticized for not drawing more widely on existing geographers—especially as al-Idrisi claims it was "an exhaustive and detailed investigation"—the work remains peerless. Among the Saharan locations that al-Idrisi mentions is the old capital of the Ghana Empire, near Timbuktu, which he describes as being "the most considerable, the most densely peopled, and the largest trading centre of the Negro countries." One of the most notable geographical features that al-Idrisi successfully plots is the course of the Nile and its source in the African lakes, which Burton and Speke would only "discover" seven centuries later. He was not always so accurate, however. Writing about the River Niger, which he calls, "the Nile of the Negroes", al-Idrisi imagines that it traverses the Sahara from west to east before connecting with the River Nile at some unknown point.

As well as the book, al-Idrisi created a version of his atlas for Roger inscribed on a solid silver disc that measured six feet in diameter, weighed 450 lb and was the first known attempt to produce a true globe. After Roger's death in 1154, his son William the Bad commissioned al-Idrisi to write another book. The resultant work was accorded the gloriously descriptive title *Gardens of Pleasure and Recreation of the Souls*, and although it was said to include more information on various Saharan locations, no trace of the work remains.

Among the otherwise sparse textual records about the Sahara of the twelfth century, we are fortunate that the work of the Jewish traveller Rabbi Benjamin of Tudela, in the Kingdom of Navarre, has survived. Although only a small part of his account, *The Book of Travels* or *Book of Ben-*

jamin, deals with the Sahara, it highlights the difficulties inherent in Saharan travel and the potential trading rewards found at the end of the journey:

> [From Helwan, Egypt] people travel in caravans a journey of 50 days through the great desert called Sahara, to the land of Zawilah [Libya], which is Havilah in the land of Gana [near Sabha, Libya]. In this desert there are mountains of sand, and when the wind rises, it covers the caravans with the sand, and many die from suffocation. Those that escape bring back with them copper, wheat, fruit, all manner of lentils, and salt. And from thence they bring gold, and all kinds of jewels.

Like other writers whom we rely on for our knowledge of the Sahara at this time, Benjamin did not travel extensively in the desert but he obviously spent time talking to those who did, recording their impressions and noting comments from other travel literature extant in his day. By the late Middle Ages, translations of Benjamin's account, originally written in Hebrew, had appeared in numerous languages and were widely consulted across Europe.

Yaqut al-Hamawi, born in 1179, was sold into slavery early in his life. Fortunately, his master recognized his intelligence and educated al-Hamawi before eventually freeing him. Posterity, too, has been rewarded by the actions of al-Hamawi's master; the sometime slave put his education to use in producing the first proper encyclopaedia of the Muslim world. Not only was this a novel way to arrange his material, but al-Hamawi's work, *The Book of Countries*, is just as important for the large number of sources it uses, combining as it does Greek and Arabic scholars on science and cosmology. The book is also full of knowledgeable and descriptive geographies and, like Herodotus, many diversions including the histories and mythologies of the places he visited and ethnographic observations of their peoples. Obviously enamoured with the encyclopaedic form, Yaqut also wrote a *Dictionary of Learned Men*. He died in 1229.

Of all the travellers and scholars from these centuries of—Andalusia aside—European ignorance, the most noted is Ibn Battuta, the greatest traveller of his or any time. Ibn Juzayy, who transcribed and edited

Battuta's work, observed that, "this sheikh is the traveller of his age". In the twentieth century the historian George Kimble wrote: "The Arabs had reserved their best wine until last. After Battuta they can boast few... travellers or writers of repute." Born in Tangier in 1304, by the time of his death in 1368 or 1369 Ibn Battuta had travelled an estimated 75,000 miles in three decades, more than his near contemporary Marco Polo; and unlike Polo, Battuta's accounts of the places he saw are not riddled with falsehood and fantasy. After 24 years away from home, he only stayed for a month before crossing the Sahara to Timbuktu.

His Saharan journeys alone lasted nearly three years. En route to Timbuktu he visited the once famous but latterly abandoned salt-mining oasis of Taghaza in modern day northern Mali. Echoing the thoughts of many travellers in the Sahara before and since, Battuta wrote of this remote spot: "We passed 10 days of discomfort there, because the water is brackish and the place is plagued with flies." He added that it is "haunted by demons... There is no visible road, nothing but sand blown hither and thither by the wind"—which considering how challenging his wanderings had been goes some way to illustrate the region's desolation.

One thing which particularly interested Battuta while he travelled in the Sahara—what he called "a strange thing"—was a blind guide: "Our guide was blind in one eye and diseased in the other, but he knew the route better than anybody else." Battuta would not be the last to make this observation. Blind or virtually sightless guides have been encountered in every part of the Sahara. Even up to the present day travellers have recorded the presence of such individuals, some of whom will sniff the sand before announcing in which direction a party ought to travel or how far they might be from their destination.

Recalling the oasis of "Iwalatan", also spelt Walata, Wualata or Oualata, in south-east Mauritania, Battuta refers to it as "the northernmost province of the negroes". Since the thirteenth century this oasis had grown in importance as the terminus for one of the busiest trans-Saharan routes. Just how extensive trans-Saharan trade was is clear from Battuta's observation that "The garments of its inhabitants... are of fine Egyptian fabrics." Regardless, he was not impressed by the location; even worse, he was deeply offended by the behaviour of the local ruler. In what was clearly a case of cultural misunderstanding, Battuta was annoyed that the sultan's representative would only speak to him via an interpreter, even though they could both speak Arabic. Battuta calls this deliberate rudeness, ignoring the possibility that it might just be the local custom when communicating with the ruler's envoy: "The merchants remained standing in front of [Hussein] while he spoke to them through an interpreter, although they were close to him, to show his contempt for them. It was then that I repented of having come to their country, because of their lack of manners and their contempt for the whites." (Battuta clearly thinks of himself as being among the "whites", distinct from the black locals.)

Battuta's account of Timbuktu disappoints many readers, but at the time of his visit the city was just emerging as an important centre of trade and scholarship. His description of the oasis is most pedestrian, but properly reflects the state of the town at that time: "Thence we went on to Timbuktu, which stands four miles from the river [Niger]." After recording the name of the local ruler and some details of limited interest, Battuta concludes his report by saying: "In this town is the grave of the meritorious poet Abu Ishaq as-Sahili, of Gharnata [Granada], who is known in his own land as at-Tuwayjin [Little Saucepan]." Battuta found Timbuktu to be the unimportant backwater it was then, with little to excite even the greatest traveller and one of the most enquiring minds, of his time. His description is obviously not the stuff that would later drive countless European adventurers and explorers to their death. However, had he returned two hundred years later, Battuta would have found it utterly changed, grown wealthy and filled with the bustle of trade and learning. Within two centuries a dusty oasis near a river had been transformed into the pearl of Saharan destinations. Yet it should be remembered that Timbuktu, whatever place it enjoyed in the European imagination, was only one city among a number of important medieval Saharan empires.

GILDED EMPIRES

"Then I rais'd
My voice and cried, 'Wide Afric, doth thy Sun
Lighten, thy hills enfold a City as fair
As those which starr'd the night o' the elder World?
Or is the rumour of thy Timbuctoo
A dream as frail as those of ancient Time?'"

From Alfred Tennyson, "Timbuktoo" (1829)

If you feel that, until now, the Sahara's north has received an unfair amount of attention over the south you would be right. And the reason is that the Egyptian, Greek and Roman civilizations left behind a far greater body of textual and other material records than their southern Saharan contemporaries. Inevitably, therefore, the northern powers had a greater cultural impact.

The three above-named northern empires also had greater influence in terms of range and duration than any of their counterparts in the south. For one thing, trade along the coastal regions, whether by land or sea, was easier than through the desert. While at no point in the history of the Sahara was the desert a solid barrier between north and south, as the region became increasingly arid the difficulties associated with travel inevitably increased. After the camel was introduced and became firmly established in the region, this situation changed. If knowledge that the arrival of the camel in the Sahara would effect change was not surprising, the speed with which it did so was perhaps more unexpected. The conditions surrounding the increasingly unfavourable climate and progressively complicated cross-desert communications that resulted had long meant that there existed an imbalance in power across the Sahara, which was broadly to the detriment of the south and of benefit to the north.

With camels, men were regularly making their way back and forth across the Sahara, with increasing confidence if not ease, for the journey remained (indeed remains) a demanding one. As they transported ideas and knowledge just as often and as easily as trade goods, large swathes of the desert underwent an economic and intellectual revolution. It is no exaggeration to say that the radical changes that took place across the Sahara from the tenth century did so on the back of camels. The significant economic shifts that resulted from trans-Saharan paths becoming to some extent easier to traverse had political fallouts as well as economic. As goods readily accessible in the south were traded in greater quantities, burgeoning empires there, across the continent's so-called Sudanic belt, soon found themselves exerting greater influence over their northern neighbours.

One of the earliest of these southern Saharan states, whose sway extended beyond its borders, was the Ghana Empire, which initially flourished from roughly 790 until the second half of the eleventh century. Then the empire rose again under the Sosso people, once a part of the collapsed Ghana Empire, before finally ceasing to exist as an independent power

The Great Mosque, Djenné

when it was subsumed into the Mali Empire in 1240. Not to be confused with the modern nation of the same name, at its greatest extent the Ghana Empire covered large areas of contemporary south-eastern Mauritania and western Mali, and it grew strong because of its location and the important commodities that lay within its borders.

The Kingdom of Ghana contained numerous mines with an abundance of gold and salt and several important oasis towns, southern termini of the busiest trans-Saharan trade routes. Then as now, these were two of the most precious commodities under the face of the earth. Once the knowledge of how to mine them was married to control of the export routes across the desert, the kingdom's resultant power was irresistible for nearly three hundred years.

When not mining, levying taxes on those crossing the Sahara, traders and non-commercial travellers alike, was an effortless means of guaranteeing a considerable income for the king. Commenting on the gold wealth of the empire, the eleventh-century Andalusian historian and geographer al-Bakri writes in his *Book of Highways and of Kingdoms of North Africa* that "The King adorns himself like a woman wearing necklaces round his neck and bracelets on his forearms and he puts on a high cap decorated with gold and wrapped in a turban of fine cotton." Al-Bakri illustrates just how much gold the king had at his disposal by writing of the royal dogs: "Round their necks they wear collars of gold and silver, studded with a number of balls of the same metals."

The Ghana Empire was most fortunate to emerge from a region where conditions allowed both horses and camels to prosper. Over time, the empire's rulers developed a strong cavalry, which consolidated their power and imposed authority over weaker neighbouring states.

Although it has been traditional, after Ibn Khaldun, to ascribe the decline of Ghana to an Almoravid invasion, more probably it was due to the discovery of new, equally rich sources of gold elsewhere in the region. Once these were exploited, new kingdoms sprouted and new routes across the desert were opened, leading to Ghana's decline and fall.

The Mali Empire was the most successful post-Ghanaian empire in the region. Emerging as a regional power around 1230, it remained a force until the first half of the seventeenth century and in its heyday was far wealthier than Ghana had ever been. However, like Ghana, the most important reason for both its rise and drawn out collapse was the trans-Saharan trade in gold and other goods.

TIMBUKTU

The Malian kings managed to exploit their gold seams for generations, in the process creating a legendary reputation for affluence. The legend outlasted the reality by many centuries. As well as being noted as a land of unfettered wealth, the empire became a byword for remoteness, with one far-flung oasis town in particular coming to symbolize the otherworldliness of Mali for Europeans, a place that to this day conjures up the romantic image of mysterious city built on gold: Timbuktu. The mythology of Timbuktu, with its almost talismanic name, was the subject of a 1970 article by the traveller and writer Bruce Chatwin in which he asks

> Timbuctoo, Tumbuto, Tombouctou, Tumbyktu, Tumbuktu or Tembuch? It doesn't matter how you spell it. The word is a slogan, a ritual formula, once heard never forgotten. At 11 I knew of Timbuctoo as a mysterious city in the heart of Africa where they ate mice—and served them to visitors. A blurred photograph, in a traveller's account of

Timbuctoo, of a bowl of muddy broth with little pink feet rising to the surface excited me greatly. Naturally, I wrote an unprintable limerick about it. The words "mice in the stew" rhymed with Timbuctoo and for me both are still inextricably associated.

Founded in the eleventh century by Tuareg nomads, the oasis grew into a city and medieval centre of scholarship. Timbuktu's university, which was established in 1327, was by the sixteenth century peerless in the Islamic world, attracting aspiring scholars and established men of learning alike to the three mosque complexes that together made up the university: Djinguereber; Sidi Yahya; and Sankore. Many of the recognized academics who came to Timbuktu brought their personal collections of texts with them, which were added to works commissioned there, thus building up the library until it was one of the largest anywhere in the world. The university's reputation was captured in an Islamic proverb from West Africa that states, "Salt comes from the North, gold from the South, but the word

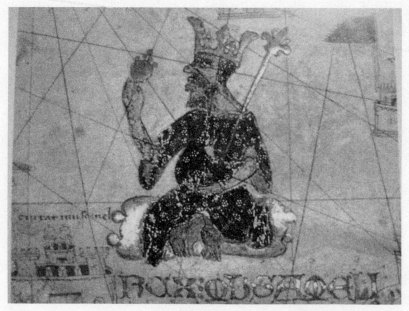

Mansa Musa

of God and the treasures of wisdom come from Timbuktu." Today, although scholars do not gather in the numbers they once did, the city still boasts a unique collection of more than 700,000 manuscripts, mostly in Arabic or Fulani, some of which predate the birth of Islam.

It was the *hajj* performed in 1324 by the tenth Malian emperor, Kankou Musa or Musa I, better known as Mansa Musa, King of Kings, that really brought the Mali Empire to the attention of the wider world beyond its immediate trading partners, and inspired the idea of Timbuktu as the mythical city in the Sahara whose wealth was greater than that of King Midas. By royal decree, all gold in the empire belonged exclusively to Mansa Musa, and trading gold within the empire was illegal, which protected the king's wealth most effectively. This also meant that when the king travelled, he was never short of spending money. The best account of Mansa Musa's *hajj* is by the historian Chihab Addine Abul-Abbas Ahmad ben Fadhlal-Umari, although Ibn Battuta and others also noted Musa's journey.

Born in Damascus in 1301, Chihab al-Umari was destined to follow in his father's footsteps and spend his professional life occupied with a post in the Mameluke civil service in his home city. Yet he was not suited to office life, twice being dismissed from his government position and imprisoned. When he was eventually at liberty to travel, al-Umari made his way to Cairo, arriving a few years after Mansa Musa had been in the city. Writing down stories he heard from Cairo's citizens, he wrote of Mansa Musa:

> This man flooded Cairo with his benefactions. He left no court emir nor holder of a royal office without the gift of a load of gold. The Cairenes made incalculable profits out of him and his suite in buying and selling and giving and taking. They exchanged gold until they depressed its value in Egypt and caused its price to fall.

The fact that the price of gold in Cairo had still failed to recover to its pre-Mansa value twelve years after his visit gives us some idea of the king's profligacy. Al-Umari adds to his account the rather forlorn portrait of Mansa Musa on his return journey, explaining that the king spent so much gold on his way to Mecca—eighty camel-loads according to one source—that by the time he returned to Cairo he was forced to borrow money to complete his journey.

Inevitably the best account to have survived regarding the Mali Empire in its heyday is that of the fourteenth-century Tangerine Ibn Battuta, whose Arabic patronymic intriguingly means "son of a duckling". Ibn Battuta's account of his global travels, *A Gift to Those Who Contemplate the Wonders of Cities and the Marvels of Travelling*, or simply *Travels*, includes a fascinating and lengthy account of the empire, which left him deeply unimpressed. Nevertheless, he stayed for eight months in 1352-3. Of the Malian ruler, Mansa Suleiman, Ibn Battuta concluded that "He is a miserly king and a big gift is not to be expected of him." Possibly drawn to Mali in part because of the legendary wealth and generosity of Suleiman's brother and predecessor Mansa Musa, Ibn Battuta found it impossible to hide his disappointment.

Ibn Battuta was, like many travellers, unfortunate enough to get sick while in the empire's capital city. Unfamiliar food seems to have been the cause, and he writes after eating some local porridge, "All six of us were taken ill and one of us died." Taking medicine given to him by an Egyptian there, Ibn Battuta adds, "I drank it and vomited what I had eaten together with much bile. God spared me from death but I was ill for two months." It is hardly surprising that Ibn Battuta's account of his time in Mali is less than laudatory.

Although sick, Ibn Battuta did manage to rouse himself when a messenger from the *qadi*, the king's representative, arrived with news of gifts from the sultan: "I stood up, supposing them to be robes of honour and money, but there were three rounds of bread, a piece of beef fried in gharti, and a calabash with curdled milk. When I saw it I laughed and was greatly surprised at their feeble intelligence and exaggerated opinion of something contemptible." Two months later, Ibn Battuta notes almost begrudgingly that the king, "gave me a hundred mithqals of gold." He fails to say whether or not he is grateful for this gift of approximately 425 grams of gold, or if his subsequent impression of Mansa Suleiman is any more favourable. In contrast, he writes very favourably about the local black population and even includes their king in this. Ibn Battuta describes them as having "admirable qualities. They are seldom unjust, and have a greater abhorrence of injustice than any other people. Their sultan shows no mercy to any one guilty of the least act of it." He adds that the people take their religion seriously, and "are careful to observe the hours of prayer."

None of this is to say that Ibn Battuta could not find fault. He is most disconcerted that "the women servants, slave-girls and young girls go about in front of everyone naked, without a stitch of clothing on them." Nor does he think much of their dietary habits, which include "the eating of carrion, dogs, and asses". Given the near fatal consequences of eating porridge, it is not surprising that he was so sceptical about these more than out-of-the-ordinary foodstuffs, which would all in any case have been forbidden to an observant Muslim.

Twenty years before Ibn Battuta's visit to Mali, the author of one of the world's greatest books was born in Tunis. Abu Zaid 'Abdul Rahman Ibn Khaldun, or simply Ibn Khaldun, was born in 1332 and died in his mid-seventies in Cairo in 1406. He was the author of the aforementioned *Muqaddimah*, which not only gives an invaluable view of early Muslim universal history, but is also the first book to tackle the philosophy of history and the social sciences—including sociology, demography, historiography and cultural history—not to mention being a medieval forerunner to the study of economics, as we now understand the subject.

If all that is not impressive enough, Ibn Khaldun also expounds on Islamic theology, biology and chemistry. In the introduction to his magnum opus, written in 1377, he explains that the book was to be just the first, introductory volume to a proposed history of the world. Sadly for the world, no further volumes appeared, which is why it is called the *Muqaddimah*, or in Greek the Prolegomena, a critical introduction to a larger work. That said, the *Muqaddimah* is a complete work, with few loose ends.

Like others before him, Ibn Khaldun confuses the Nile with the Niger, writing that certain towns "and Ghana are situated along this Nile". He also notes the fact that "Moroccan merchants travel to their country," before going on to describe the local slave trade, in which his attitude is in step with his era:

> The people of Ghana and Takrur invade their country (to the South), capture them, and sell them to merchants who transport them to the Maghreb. There they constitute the ordinary mass of slaves. Beyond them to the South, there is no civilisation in the proper sense. There are only humans who are closer to dumb animals than to rational beings.

Slavery for Ibn Khaldun is simply a part of the natural order of societies.

A great deal of the work is more generally an explanation of what he sees as the natural order of things in the world, of which slavery is just one aspect. He is especially keen to point out the differences between those who live in the desert and the softer town-dwellers. Writing specifically about the Sahara's inhabitants, Ibn Khaldun explains that

> in other parts, the land is strewn with rocks, and no seeds or herbs grow at all. There, the locals have a very hard time. Instances of such people are the... veiled Sinhaja who live in the desert of the Maghreb on the fringes of the sandy deserts which lie between the Berbers and the Sudanese Negroes. All of them lack all grain and seasonings. Their nourishment and food is milk and meat... In spite of this, the desert people who lack grain and seasonings are found to be healthier in body and better in character than the hill people who have plenty of everything. Their complexions are clearer, their bodies cleaner, their figures more perfect and better, their characters less intemperate, and their minds keener as far as knowledge and perception are concerned... Consequently, the bodies of the urban population are found to be more delicate than those of the inhabitants of the desert who live a hard life.

While Ibn Khaldun was creating his survey, the Mali Empire was entering a period of decline, while the Songhai Empire was becoming a power of its own. One of the greatest West African states of all time, the Songhai Empire flourished from the early fifteenth until the late sixteenth centuries, emerging from its riverside capital at Gao, within the confines of the Mali Empire, in about 1000 CE.

Downstream from Timbuktu and named after the majority Gao ethnic group that lived there, the empire was well placed to make good use of its position as a riverine transport hub, and to challenge the authority of the Mali Empire as that state's power began to wane. It was under the nearly 39-year reign of Sunni Ali at the very end of the fifteenth century that the Songhai Empire really grew with one military victory after another, resulting in control of all trade up and down the River Niger. Shortly after this growth spurt, which transformed Songhai into a region-wide power, another important source visited the area, stopping at Timbuktu—by now in the Songhai rather than Mali Empire—as he went.

The medieval traveller and author of the *Description of Africa*, Leo

Africanus, visited Timbuktu around 1510 with his uncle, who was on a diplomatic mission. As Leo tells us in his introduction, he was born al-Hasan ibn Muhammad al-Wazzan al-Fasi in Granada circa 1494, and moved with his family to Fez. In his mid-twenties, while returning from performing the *hajj* he was taken prisoner by Spanish corsairs. John Pory's English translation from 1600 of the *Description* adds that Leo Africanus "Neither wanted he the best education that all Barbary could afford... So as I may justly say (if the comparison be tolerable) that as Moses was learned in all the wisdom of the Egyptians; so likewise was Leo, in that of the Arabians and Moors." His captors, recognizing their prisoner's superior intellect, made a gift of him to Pope Leo X, and Muhammad al-Wazzan al-Fasi was reinvented as Joannes Leo Africanus.

Once settled in Rome, Leo Africanus or Leo the African was commissioned to produce a description of Africa based on his extensive travels there. The ignorance regarding the interior parts of Africa at the time of writing is hard to imagine today. Maps before this time still featured fanciful descriptions of places and creatures. As the opening paragraph of Leo's *Description* puts it, "That part of inhabited land extending southward, which we call Africa, and the Greeks Libya, is one of the three general parts of the world known to our ancestors; which in very deed was not thoroughly known by them discovered, both because the inlands could not be travelled in regard of huge deserts full of dangerous sands, which being driven by the wind, put travellers in extreme hazard of their lives."

Leo Africanus' description of Timbuktu is extensive, and includes numerous details such as the fact that the "houses here are built in the shape of bells, the walls are stakes or hurdles plastered over with clay and the houses covered with reeds." In addition, while the majority of Europe continued to view Timbuktu as a city isolated from the world, this was not the case in Muslim Andalusia. As Leo explains, "Yet there is a most stately temple to be seen, the walls whereof are made of stone and lime; and a royal palace also built by a most excellent artist from Granada," adding: "And hither do the Barbary merchants bring cloth of Europe."

Of greatest interest to the gold-hungry royal courts of Europe was information about the city's legendary wealth. Regardless of European agendas, Leo pointedly highlights the value placed on learning above gold, noting: "And hither are brought diverse manuscripts or written books out of Barbary, which are sold for more money than any other merchandise.

The coin of Timbuktu is of gold without any stamp or superscription: but in matters of small value they use certain shells brought hither out of the kingdom of Persia." This last point is another indication of how widespread the Songhai Empire's trading networks were, with Persia and the Barbary Coast both being in regular contact with the kingdom in the desert.

If, however, any ruling power from Europe ever considered taking the kingdom by force, a note on the military might that travelled with the emperor would be worth remembering: "He hath always 3,000 horsemen, and a great number of footmen that shoot poisoned arrows, attending upon him. They have often skirmishes with those that refuse to pay tribute, and so many as they take, they sell unto the merchants of Timbuktu."

Pory's translation was a sensation upon its publication, and read avidly for information about the unknown continent. Considering the scarcity of information, the success it enjoyed should not come as a great surprise providing, as it did, much detail otherwise hidden from European scholars, including, for example, the name of the great desert: "But Libya propria, retaineth till this present the name of Libya, and is that part which the Arabians call Sarra, which worde signifieth a desert." Ben Jonson admitted that he had consulted all available sources when, in 1605, he wrote his *Masque of Blackness*, including "Pliny, Solinus, Ptolemy, and… Leo the African."

The Songhai Empire was eventually destroyed in 1591, almost exactly one hundred years after the demise of the Muslim Kingdom of Granada that signalled the end of Muslim empires in Iberia. Songhai fell to a force of Moroccan musketeers, who marched across the Sahara on the orders of Ahmed al-Mansur al-Dhahabi, the Golden Conqueror and head of the Saadi dynasty. The army was commanded by the Spanish-born eunuch and forced childhood convert to Islam, Judar Pasha, who was famed for having a personal bodyguard of eighty Christians. The force consisted of 1500 light cavalry, 2500 arquebusiers (forerunners of modern riflemen) and infantry as well as eight English cannon. For logistical support the caravan had 8000 camels, 1000 packhorses and 1000 stable-hands.

The Moroccan force was confronted at Tondibi, north of Gao, by a much larger Songhai army of 40,000 men and cavalry, raised by the ruler of Songhai, Askia Ishaq II. One thousand cattle also accompanied his force, which were meant to screen the infantry as they advanced against the

Moroccans. Unfortunately for the defenders, the Battle of Tondibi did not go in their favour. As soon as the arquebuses were fired, the unfamiliar noise, smoke and smell of the gunpowder-powered weapons scared the cattle, which turned and stampeded through the defenders' lines. Judar quickly completed his campaign of conquest, sacking the major cities of Gao, Djenné and Timbuktu, and bringing the Songhai Empire to a crashing end.

The Moroccans were disappointed with what gold they found as booty was largely absent. Long gone, the gold trade that had spread far beyond the Sahara dwindled, and so too was ended the great university complex, leaving Timbuktu a shadow of itself, a dusty desert town and a legend. Despite this, news of this paucity of gold failed to reach Europe, and Timbuktu remained the goal of many Saharan explorers into the nineteenth century. Ironically, the prize of 10,000 francs offered by the French Société Géographique for the first person to reach Timbuktu and return with information about the city was worth more than the gold available in the city by the time René Caillié claimed the prize in the 1820s.

The earliest eastern Sudanic Empire from this era to leave a distinct historical trail was Kanem. Occupying much of the Ténéré Desert, Lake Chad's northern shores and the Tibesti Mountains to the north, the Kanem Empire emerged around 700 CE and survived in one form or another through numerous successor states until 1893. The Empire of Bornu was a most important partner state that ensured this longevity, including a period when the two are known by the hyphenated title, Kanem-Bornu.

Ibn Khaldun noted the existence of the Kanem Empire, writing: "To the south of the country of Gawgaw lies the territory of Kanem, a Negro nation. Beyond them are the Wangarah on the border of the Sudanese Nile [actually the Niger] to the North." Founded by the semi-nomadic Tebu-speaking Zaghawa tribe, by the time Yaqubi wrote about them in 890, the kingdom's influence, but not control, stretched as far as the Nile Valley and Kingdom of Nubia. With the growth in influence of Kanem, direct Zaghawa power declined, and they retreated eastward to Darfur. While other Arab geographers contributed occasional details regarding Kanem, the greatest source of information about them is the *Gigram* or *Royal Chronicle*. This document, an official history of the kingdom, was only discovered by chance in 1851 by the explorer Heinrich Barth.

The merger of the Kingdoms of Kanem and Bornu was followed by a period of stability, reform and growth, which lasted until the middle of the seventeenth century. Within the borders of Kanem-Bornu was the important oasis town of Bilma, in the heart of the Ténéré in today's Niger. This small town remains a centre of salt and natron production, and lies on one of the few authentic trans-Saharan trade routes still in use. Some three hundred miles north of Lake Chad, Bilma is remoter even than Timbuktu, the archetype of a lonely place.

From the 1660s until the end of the nineteenth century Bornu was in decline. A number of typical explanations for this include divided leadership and sons who were not fit to take on their fathers' mantles. Unlike its heyday at the turn of the seventeenth century, by the 1870s Bornu was a weak and divided empire, in which slaves were in the majority, controlled in turn by more slaves.

The end was swift, and the empire was overrun by Rabih as-Zubayr, a Sudanese warlord and one-time cavalryman for an irregular Egyptian force fighting in Ethiopia. Rabih's conquest of Bornu allowed him to run a personal empire until his death in a showdown against French forces in April 1900. After his defeat, the French took all of his territories in the west, towards Niger, and the English claimed Bornu.

In the centuries before the fall of Bornu, Europe was still almost wholly ignorant of the Saharan interior, a source of embarrassment for those living in and after the Enlightenment. Something had to be done to banish such ignorance. In European government departments and centres of learning moves were afoot to do just that. Beginning with the creation of learned societies devoted to scientific discovery, and ending with imperial expansion, the relationship between the peoples of the Sahara and Europe was about to change forever.

Part Three

HISTORY

EXPLORATION, IMPERIALISM AND

INDEPENDENCE

Bonaparte in Egypt by Jean-Léon Gérôme

Chapter Six

EUROPEAN FORAYS

THE AFRICAN ASSOCIATION AND NAPOLEON

"I had a passionate desire to examine into [sic] the productions of a
country so little known, and to become experimentally acquainted with
the modes of life and character of the natives."

Mungo Park, *Travels in the Interior of Africa*

Eighteenth-century European knowledge of the majority of the African
continent, including the deserts of North Africa, was limited. More was
known about the Amazon and the Himalayas than the Sahara. Rumours
of golden cities and tales of one-eyed giants did not constitute scientific
knowledge. As a result, meeting on 9 June 1788 in the St. Alban's Tavern,
London, a group of gentlemen banded together in order to start the work
of correcting what they saw as an egregious gap in human understanding.
The minutes of that meeting stated, "Sensible of this stigma, and desirous
of rescuing the age from a charge of ignorance, which, in other respects,
belongs so little to its character, a few individuals, strongly impressed with
a conviction of the practicability and utility of thus enlarging the fund of
human knowledge, have formed the plan of an Association for promoting
the discovery of the interior parts of Africa."

The founders of the African Association were learned men, with
knowledge of the Classics that made them aware of the ties ancient Greece
and Rome enjoyed with North Africa. These great Ancient civilizations,
the inspiration for much European thinking in the late eighteenth century,
had founded cities across the breadth of North Africa as well as having
contact with the tribes of the desert's interior, establishing trade, with
varying degrees of success, along well-established trans-Saharan routes.
That Englishmen living through the Age of Enlightenment knew less
about the Sahara than had their Classical antecedents was an affront to
their dignity.

Serious exploration of the Sahara was impossible, though, while
people relied on a twelfth-century copy of Ptolemy's second-century map,
and for local intelligence they turned to Herodotus and Pliny as much as

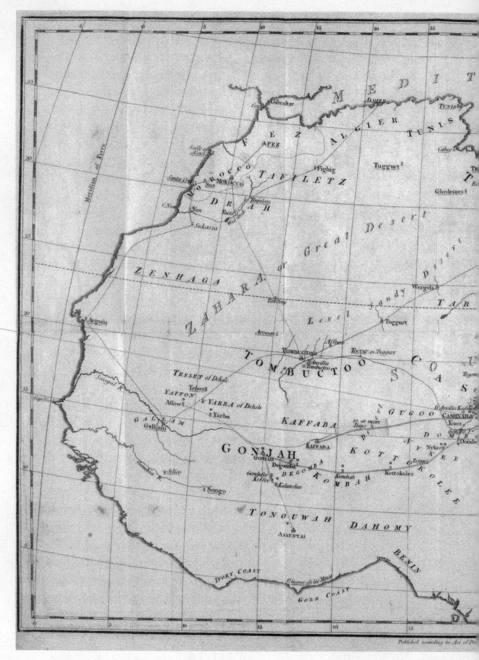

The blank canvas of the Sahara, 1790

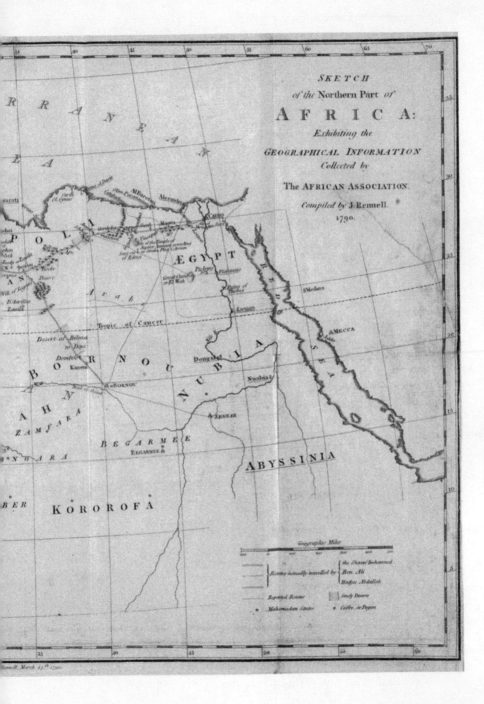

SKETCH
of the Northern Part of
AFRICA:
Exhibiting the
GEOGRAPHICAL INFORMATION
Collected by
The AFRICAN ASSOCIATION.
Compiled by J. Rennell.
1790.

RRANEAN SEA

POLA

ÆGYPT

Cairo

Arab

Tropic of Cancer

Desert of Bilma
to Iban

BORNOU

NUBIA

Dongola

Red Sea

Medina

MECCA
Jidda

Dombeba

Karem

BORNOU

Nubia

ZAMFARA

SENNAR

ZAMFARA

BEGARMEE

N'GARA

BEGARMEE

ABYSSINIA

BER

KOROROFA

Geographic Miles

Routes actually travelled by

the Shereef Imhammed
Ben Ali
Hadjee Abdallah

Reputed Routes   Sandy Deserts

Mahometan States   Caffre, or Pagan

Rennell, March 27th, 1790.

to the most up-to-date volume dealing with Saharan geography: Leo Africanus' 1550 *Description of Africa*. These tomes were hardly sufficient preparation before setting off to "the Interior Parts of Africa". For example, both al-Idrisi and Leo Africanus insisted that the River Niger flowed east to west, emerging into the Atlantic in the area of Senegal and the Gambia, which was wrong. Pliny got it right when he said that the river flowed from west to east, but he then blundered when he said it ended where it entered the Nile. There were also those who believed Ptolemy's view that the Niger was an independent, intra-African river that did not empty out into any sea or ocean at all.

Like the British government, Joseph Banks (1743-1820) and his co-founders of the African Association had various interests that were not limited to exploration. Apart from the avowed pursuit of knowledge for its own sake, the African Association was keen to see an extension of Britain's influence in the world, gained in the first place by leading the Industrial Revolution. In part secured though the services of the Royal Navy, this significant industrial advantage over her European rivals meant unequalled global power for Britain, a position she would not willingly yield. Banks, who accompanied Cook on his first voyage and supplied the expedition's artists and naturalists at his own expense, and who was elected President of the Royal Society upon his return, had his own commercial and humanitarian concerns, which helped him to decide which proposals received by the association ought to be pursued.

To put in context the birth of what was to become one of the most influential societies in the decades ahead, six months earlier *The Times* of London had been launched, and twelve days after the meeting in the tavern, New Hampshire became the ninth state to ratify the Constitution of the emergent United States. It was fitting, therefore, that the first explorer the African Association sent to discover the route of the River Niger and locate Timbuktu should be an American.

During its inaugural evening the association had agreed to employ the services of one Simon Lucas, but his departure from England was delayed because of ill health. Having learnt some Arabic during a three-year period as a slave in Morocco, Lucas was "allotted the passage of the Zahara [sic], from Tripoli to Fezzan". Lucas did eventually make it to Tripoli, but was unable to journey south through the Sahara because of tribal fighting, and so returned to England with little to show for his efforts.

Reckoned to have covered more miles than any other man alive at the time, John Ledyard's (1751-89) credentials as a traveller were impeccable. A native of the pre-revolutionary colony of New England, Ledyard fled from student life in his first year at Dartmouth College, New Hampshire. Leaving with some élan, he cut down a tree and carved a fifty-foot canoe, a skill he learned from the Iroquois, and paddled down the Connecticut river to his grandfather's house. Enlisting in the British Navy, he sailed on HMS *Resolution* with Cook on the captain's third and fatal voyage, during the course of which America declared independence. Following this epic sea-voyage, Ledyard attempted to make an overland crossing of the Russian Empire. Having got as far as Irkutsk, and in spite of the diplomatic efforts of Thomas Jefferson, then US minister to France, Ledyard was arrested as a spy on the personal order of Catherine the Great, and brought back west, being deported over the border into Poland.

Having found admirers on the committee of the association, Ledyard set out for Egypt from London on 30 June 1788. His plan was to spend time securing guides and otherwise preparing for his trans-Saharan trek. Things, inevitably enough, did not go as planned. While in Cairo, Ledyard contracted a stomach bug and decided to treat himself with sulphuric acid, a then common treatment for such stomach ailments. Unfortunately for the association, and even more so for Ledyard, he overdosed on his medicine, died in the Egyptian capital in January 1789 and was buried in an unknown grave next to the River Nile.

Although he had already traversed great portions of the globe, no one had asked whether Ledyard was really the best-qualified candidate for the Saharan mission. He did not speak Arabic and had never travelled in desert lands. Almost universal ignorance in London also meant that nobody wondered why, if he was searching for Timbuktu, Ledyard should start his journey from the opposite corner of the Sahara. It is ironic that while these undoubtedly brave explorers were setting off from the port cities of North Africa, European kinsmen had already established about thirty forts along the West African coastline, just a few hundred miles from most Saharan gold mines.

The African Association, we have seen, hoped to discover the course of the River Niger and reach Timbuktu. While the city had been the intellectual and cultural centre of the Mali Empire, the gold actually came from elsewhere—a fact that would be immaterial had the association's sole intention been to plumb the region's intellectual treasures. If that had indeed been its goal, it is unlikely, however, that it would have attracted the patronage of so many merchants. And if trade interests were paramount for the merchants, so was humanitarianism for more religiously inclined souls. It was only the year before the association's founding in 1788 that William Wilberforce formed the Committee for the Abolition of the Slave Trade leading to a twenty-year battle in and out of the courts and culminating in the end of the slave trade in the British Empire, under the terms of the 1807 Slave Trade Act.

To understand the close relationship between business and exploration, it is worth noting that even the German explorer Heinrich Barth (1821-65)—often cited as the most scientific of nineteenth-century Saharan travellers-cum-scholars—was funded mainly by a group of British merchants. This is not to suggest that Barth's reputation for scholarship is not justified. The journals he wrote about his extensive journeys and the people and places he saw are often the only first-hand sources that exist from this period.

And so it was, undaunted by Ledyard's death, that the association sanctioned more intrepid adventurers. An Irishman who had served in the British Army, Major Daniel Houghton (c. 1740-91), was an ideal candidate, as the records of the African Association say, "as well from his knowledge of the Negro Nations in the neighbourhood of the Gambia, among whom he has travelled, as from the ardor [sic] of his mind and the strength of his Constitution, appears to the Committee to be qualities for the business which he proposes to undertake." It was certainly in Houghton's favour that he had spent time overseas, living both in Morocco and for four years on Goree Island off the coast of Senegal at Dakar, where he had learnt local languages. At the time of his appointment, money was of more pressing interest than extending his knowledge since the former soldier was down on his luck—unemployed and penniless with a wife and family to support.

Working for the glory of the association and fame and riches for himself, Houghton set off for the Gambia in 1790, having kitted himself out with second-hand clothes and equipment that the association had earlier bought for Lucas, which he gave back upon his return. Houghton carried with him a list of 54 questions that he was to ask anyone he met on his journey who had visited the land of the Hausa or Timbuktu. The decision to change the starting point of this expedition took into consideration Houghton's experience of the general area, and immediately put him more than 1500 miles closer to the Niger than Lucas or Ledyard ever got.

Although warmly received upon his arrival by the King of Barra at the mouth of the River Gambia—the king remembering Houghton from his time on Goree Island—once he left the monarch's sphere of influence Houghton frequently encountered the problem of suspicious locals. Many of these were already engaged in trade and were naturally keen to protect their interests. Whatever the alien, white stranger claimed to be interested in, the locals were sure that Houghton's arrival did not bode well for them. Travelling slowly up river, he managed to survive a strenuous year moving further inland than any European before him before eventually dying near the village of Simbing in modern-day Mali. He had got to within 500 miles of Timbuktu and was just 200 miles short of the River Niger.

The next "Geographical Missionary", as the association now called its adventurers, to be dispatched was to become its most famous. From Selkirkshire, Scotland, at the time of his commission Mungo Park (1771-1806) was penurious (seemingly a prerequisite for selection by the association) and hopeful of making a fortune for himself through his Saharan explorations. A determined and physically robust character, with the practical advantage of being a doctor, Park was resourceful where he was unskilled. Lacking Arabic, he travelled with an Arabic grammar for reference; for non-verbal sparring he kept handy a brace of shotguns and a pair of pistols.

Initially following Houghton's path along the Gambia river, Park too wrote that he came into contact with distrustful and hostile local rulers. One of these, a Moorish chieftain, had Park incarcerated for four months until he effected a pre-dawn escape on horseback. Lesser characters would now have had enough adventure and returned home. But not Park who, although now completely alone and with nothing more than some spare clothes, pressed on with his mission to find the River Niger.

Park not only avoided recapture but also managed to live off his wits, guile and the generosity of locals who fed him. He relied especially, he writes, on the kindness of the women he met. Goodness knows what impression the bedraggled Scot must have made on those he encountered: an unimaginably bizarre beggar emerging from out of the bush. After three weeks living on the run in this fashion, Park eventually reached "the great object of my mission, the long sought-for majestic Niger, glittering in the morning sun, as broad as the Thames at Westminster, and flowing slowly to the eastward."

Fever ridden, Park got back to London, via Antigua, and was given a rapturous—in suitably Victorian style—welcome home. In spite of not having reached Timbuktu, Park had settled the question regarding the direction in which the Niger flowed. More importantly, as the first European to reach the Niger and return alive, the association decided he was "permitted to publish, for his own emolument, under the Sanction and Patronage of this Association, a detailed account of his Travels in the interior of Africa, the incidents that occurred to him and the observations which occurred to him during the course of his Journey." His book, *Travels into the Interior Districts of Africa*, was a huge success and much-translated, earning him about £1000. His story also boosted membership of the association and inspired numerous future expeditions to the Niger and Saharan interior.

Returning to Scotland, Park married, started practising medicine and became bored, writing to Banks at the association that "a country surgeon is at best but a laborious employment." Park set off for Africa again in 1805, this time as the head of a large government-sponsored attempt to develop friendly relations and trading rights along the Niger. Bureaucratic delays in London before the start of the journey meant that the forty-strong party of Europeans and their African porters and guides were caught in the rainy season shortly after they set out. Rather than sitting out the rains (the only sensible thing to do), a frustrated and misguided Park forced the expedition into a march-or-die type mission. Naturally, one by one, they died, from fever, from wild animal attacks and by drowning. In a testament to his strength and vainglorious self-belief, Park was among the last of the Europeans to die. Following the umpteenth attack by natives, his boat overturned, drowning him and his companions in the river which had, eight years earlier, brought him fame and fortune.

Park's adventures remained a source of inspiration through the nineteenth and indeed twentieth century, for one thing inspiring the outrageously ribald and entertaining *Water Music*. Published in 1981, this was the debut novel of Tom Coraghessan, or T. C., Boyle. The story opens with Park in Africa during his first mission but it is after his return to

REISEN

in

CENTRAL-AFRICA

von

Mungo Park bis auf
Dr. Barth u. Dr. Vogel.

ERSTER BAND.

London and his hero's welcome that the story really takes off, when we meet the story's fictional anti-hero, Ned Rise. A pimp, thief and all-round ne'er-do-well, Rise is the quintessence of a man without prospects but plenty of plans. Partly the story of travellers in a foreign land, it also cleverly highlights the clash of civilizations between the desert-dwelling Moors and the sub-Saharan black-African tribes, both of whom are as alien to one another as the Scottish explorer is to them both.

HORNEMANN

While Park was on his first African trip, the Association had secured another willing and impoverished recruit to their cause, one Friedrich, or Frederick, Hornemann (1772-1801), from Lower Saxony, who was recommended to Banks by a German friend. Perhaps learning from previous mistakes, the association sent Hornemann to the University of Göttingen, funding his Arabic studies before dispatching him. First, Hornemann had to cross France, which was then at war with England. That he did so safely, armed with a letter of passage which Banks had secured from the authorities in Paris, gives one an indication both of Banks' impeccable contacts and his determination.

Arriving in Cairo in September 1797, Hornemann planned to cross the Sahara along the route that the ill-fated Ledyard had planned. While there he continued learning Arabic, becoming proficient enough to become the first of the Association's men to travel in disguise, as a local trader. In this unremarkable guise of a man from some distant Islamic land, he joined a caravan that was formed to cross the desert. Whether a Christian in disguise or an innocent Muslim trader, there was safety in numbers in the lawless Sahara.

Unfortunately for Hornemann, the caravan's departure from Cairo for Bornu was delayed because of a local outbreak of plague. Just when the threat of the epidemic passed, events of global importance transpired to thwart his departure as Napoleon invaded Egypt. Without the permission of the de facto authorities, Hornemann's preparations would come to nothing. Yet, as Jules Verne wrote in his *Great Navigators of the Eighteenth Century*, the situation was resolved when Hornemann was presented "to Napoleon Buonaparte [sic], who was then in command of the French forces in Egypt. From him he received a cordial welcome, and Buonaparte placed all the resources of his country at his service." Once again it seemed that the French authorities were more interested in advancing than standing in the way of exploration.

The African Association was delighted by their latest protégé, and put their faith in his abilities, not least his passing for an Arab in hostile territory. Indeed, so confident were they in Hornemann's capabilities that they did not pursue enquiries for some time after communications from him ceased. In his last letter to arrive in London, Hornemann had written, "My intention is, respecting that I am the first Traveller in this part of the world going so far, not to stay longer than till the month of September at Bornou [sic] [Chad], but to go to Kashna with that great Caravan, which is always in time travelling form Bornou to Soudan." It appears that Hornemann's disguise held up well, and he managed to travel undetected, albeit accompanied by another German as his interpreter, a Muslim convert called Joseph Freudenburg, Hornemann's Arabic not being adequately fluent.

From Cairo Hornemann and Freudenburg travelled via the oases of Siwa and Aujila to Murzuq, before heading north to Tripoli on the coast. While in Tripoli, Hornemann sent his journals back to London before retracing his steps to Murzuq and continuing south from there to Bornu, where he may have got within sight of Lake Chad. On leaving Bornu, he turned west, getting as far as Bokani, in modern Nigeria, just short of the Niger. There he died some time later of dysentery, a more peaceful if no less unpleasant end than the violent deaths met by many of his fellow explorers.

The Lutheran minister's son was highly regarded by the locals, who thought him a distinguished Muslim holy man. Partly because of his crossing of the Sahara, the first from the north to the east by a European since Roman times, and also because of his journals, which were the first truly scientific study of the region, Hornemann must be regarded as the most successful "Geographical Missionary" sponsored by the Association. News of his death would not reach the African Association in London until 1819, nineteen years after they received his notebooks sent from Tripoli.

If the agents of the African Association failed to reach Timbuktu or trace the length of the Niger, the impact of their endeavours was still great, not least encouraging other explorers to follow in their footsteps. The invasion by Napoleon exposed Europeans, for the first time since the Roman Empire, to the art and culture of Ancient Egypt, which triggered a decades-long wave of scientific and cultural interest in all things Egyptian, guiding architects and fashionable society among others in the footsteps of the ancients. Regardless of the impact of French culture on Egypt, most notably the introduction of the French administrative and judicial systems, it was not nearly so great as the impact Egyptian culture had on the whole of Western Europe.

Napoleon's July 1798 invasion of Egypt, nine years after the start of the French Revolution, represented a collision of two civilizations, one new, dynamic, inexperienced and immature, the other, ancient, traditional and conservative. According to al-Jabarti (1753-1825), an Egyptian chronicler whose non-European perspective is very valuable, he and his countrymen initially assumed that the French invasion was a continuation of the Crusades. Only later did he alter his judgment, seeing it as a cultural rather than a religious attack.

After the French invasion, Hornemann wrote to the African Association justifying his decision to travel in disguise, observing that

> To travel as a Christian will, perhaps, be impracticable for at least five years to come, for it is incredible how deep and strong an impression the expedition of the French has made on the minds of the pilgrims to and from Mecca: dispersed to their several homes they will carry an aggravated prejudice against Christians far and wide, and to the very heart of Africa.

Al-Jabarti's own reaction to the invasion was to retreat into a more conservative mode of behaviour, returning to what he saw as traditional practices. An educated man, al-Jabarti's views were not those of the people, and while he admitted to being intrigued by many aspects of European culture, which he was encountering for the first time, he also believed that resisting the invaders was the right thing to do. Al-Jabarti was convinced that in fomenting *jihad*, Egypt might witness a return to the earliest days of Islam, when Islamic victories were numerous and defeats unknown.

Although militarily the invasion and partial occupation of Egypt was little short of disastrous for the French, who were expelled by British and Ottoman forces just three years after their arrival, Napoleon's scheme was far grander than a simple military one. Travelling with him from France was a team of 167 scholars, Enlightenment savants who represented many branches of art and science including archaeology and botany. Their studies were recorded by a team of artists and engravers on a scale never before assembled for a military campaign, and the breadth of their research was impressive and its impact on Europe, when published, huge. Napoleon—himself something of an intellectual—always spoke highly of the world of academe, declaring that "The real conquests, those that leave behind no regrets, are those made over ignorance."

EGYPTOMANIA

Although al-Jabarti's Arabic account was the first into print after the invasion, it did not gain a wide audience until it appeared in translation. For European readers the first bestselling account of the invasion was Dominique Vivant, Baron de Denon's, *Voyage dans la basse et haute Egypte*, published in 1802 and which appeared in English the next year. Of even greater impact, however, was the monumental and perennially impressive multi-authored *Description de l'Egypte*, the first volume of which came out in 1809, with the complete 23-volume collection, including twelve volumes of plates and one of maps, finally being published in 1829. Between them these two works more than any other revealed the wonders of Egypt to audiences in Europe and America, launching Egyptology as an academic field and precipitating the more populist embrace of all things Egyptian in an explosion of what became known as Egyptomania.

Nascent Egyptomania was clear from Napoleon's decision to travel with his band of savants. For Napoleon, the creation of an Institute of Egypt and the cataloguing of the country were almost as important as military conquest, at which he ultimately failed. When the *Description* came to be produced, Count Siméon wrote in the Preface, "A great number of designers, painters, able printers, artisans, and almost 400 engravers have been occupied, with admirable steadfastness, in the execution of this monument that unites the souvenirs of ancient Egypt with the glory of modern France."

While it is appropriate to acknowledge the Egyptian influence in the heights of artistic creation, the opera *Aïda* for example, it is also important to note that Egyptian style also enjoyed a far wider reach. When the Crystal Palace exhibition halls were built in 1854, the Egyptian Court created by the designer Owen Jones was one of the most popular re-creations of foreign settings. In the thirty years after it opened, the Egyptian

Court received approximately two million visitors annually. Egyptian themes also became common in advertising, selling everything from cigarettes to bed linen. Egyptian motifs were prevalent in fiction too, and for the burgeoning middle class there were any number of Egyptian-inspired designs in such household items as dinner services.

One of the oddest phenomena of the day was the vogue for mummy parties, in which the host bought a mummy that the guests would then unwrap. The idea of re-animating a mummy with electricity also inspired Edgar Allan Poe to write a satire on the subject. Published in *American Review* in 1845, "Some Words with a Mummy" relates a conversation between a group of educated American men, keen to prove the superiority of their culture, and an Egyptian mummy that the men shock back to life with electricity. In the course of the conversation it becomes clear that modern civilization does not surpass ancient knowledge, except in the production of cough drops, which the mummy is forced to concede he did not have in his day.

The rediscovery of Egyptian culture received a characteristically unique interpretation upon reaching America. A new nation, the United States was still developing an original national identity of its own, and if one of the world's first nation states could help in this task, it was to be welcomed. The American doctor, occultist and writer Paschal Beverly Randolph encapsulated this view of Egypt when he wrote in 1863, "For America, read Africa; for the United States, Egypt."

The importance of the Egyptian Revival in architecture can most obviously be seen in the decision that the national monument to George Washington would be an obelisk. The design was selected in a competition in 1836. The winning entry, by Robert Mills, sometimes referred to as America's first trained architect, for an Egyptian-style monument was what the judges thought most fitting to honour the first president and Father of the Country. Mills' original design also called for an Egyptian winged-sun motif above the monument's main entrance, but this was later dropped in favour of the less ornate and less costly design we see today. Upon completion in 1884, more than thirty years after building work started, the 555-foot Washington Monument was the tallest structure in the world; it remains the world's tallest obelisk.

Modern creations or purloined originals, obelisks remain the most obvious ancient Egyptian monumental structures, partly because of the

Obelisk plundered by Caligula, in Vatican City

prominent position they enjoy in cities where they were erected. The earliest obelisk to be removed from Egypt for re-erection in Europe is in St. Peter's Square, Vatican City, and did not come to the city in the nineteenth century, but in 37 CE on the instructions of the Emperor Caligula. While a cross now crowns the Vatican obelisk, the monument was once topped by a metal ball, which was said to contain the ashes of Julius Caesar. The Cleopatra's Needles on the bank of the Thames in London and in New York's Central Park are a pair originally from Heliopolis, via Alexandria, and were unveiled to great public acclaim in 1878 and 1881 respectively. The Luxor Obelisk in Paris was erected in 1836 by King Louis-Philippe in Place de la Concorde, on the spot where a guillotine operated during the French Revolution. This obelisk's former home for 3300 years was the entrance to the temple in Luxor.

More contemporary creations that demonstrate an abiding love of Egyptian styles would include the glass pyramids erected in the main courtyard of the Louvre museum, designed by the Chinese-American architect I. M. Pei, in 1989. Considering Napoleon's role in Egypt, and the fact that there are more than 50,000 items in the museum's Egyptian collection, the striking glass pyramids can hardly be said to be wholly out of place. The large main pyramid and its three smaller satellites were controversial at the time of their construction, not a difficulty encountered by the larger, more affected Luxor hotel and casino in Las Vegas which failed to ruffle any feathers when it opened in 1993. One supposes that whereas the feeling in Paris was that such a modern design was not in keeping with the French and Italian classical and Renaissance architectural styles making up the Louvre, the same was not true of the post-modern brashness of the Luxor Las Vegas, which does seem to fit rather comfortably in its environment.

Far less ostentatious in size or construction material, the so-called Rosetta stone uncovered by workmen digging in the Nile Delta in July 1799 remains the most important ancient relic exported from Egypt. Shipped back to London in 1802 aboard the captured French frigate *l'Egptienne*, renamed HMS *Egyptienne*, the stone shows the same text in three languages: Egyptian hieroglyphic, Egyptian Demotic and classical Greek. Translation of the Greek was straightforward but the Egyptian languages proved more taxing, with two scholars, Thomas Young and Jean-François Champollion, working for years on the puzzle and finally completing the translation in 1824. Breaking the code of the ancient Egyptian texts allowed a flood of translations to be made of as many other Egyptian texts as scholars could manage, a task that remains incomplete today.

Between them the African Association and Napoleon's army of scholars had made an impressive start to achieving their shared missions of exploration and discovery, and although neither completed their self-imposed task, far more important was the impact on those who followed them. For the rest of the nineteenth century the Sahara became the plaything of Britain and France—European rivals who watched each other so carefully that they almost totally overlooked the local populations who, it would become clear, had their own ideas about these foreign interlopers.

Chapter Seven

FURTHER HORIZONS

EXPLORATION AND THE EUROPEAN LAND GRAB

"And if we may regret that the liberty of the Bedouins of the desert has been destroyed, we must not forget that these same Bedouins were a nation of robbers."

Frederick Engels, after the 1847 capture of the Algerian
resistance leader, Abd el-Qadir

If eighteenth-century exploration marked Europe's first forays in the Sahara since ancient times, the following century was concerned with extending those footholds to the furthest horizons. Spurred on by the reports and achievements of the African Association's explorers, subsequent generations produced similar justifications for their Saharan expeditions: the discovery and opening of new markets; the pursuit of scientific knowledge and a need to overcome geographical ignorance; the missionary imperative; and a growing sense of imperial entitlement to other people's lands. None of these was mutually exclusive: geographical discovery, trade and missionary activities frequently complemented one another. Of the litany of validations offered only imperial entitlement was inherently detrimental to local interests.

Some who believed the European cultural model was inherently superior to all others used the theory of evolution, as propounded by Charles Darwin, Alfred Wallace and others, to prove this. While the theory was itself both a revolutionary and blameless work of science, it did produce in some readers a powerful sense of their natural superiority over foreign places, typically those populated by people of a different colour who did not have modern weapons. The pursuit of pure science or honest trade was commendable, but such potentially laudable goals had always been subject to the demands of more covetous appetites.

The passing of the Slave Trade Act by parliament banned, but did not stop, the slave trade in the British Empire. The act only made the trade in slaves illegal, not the institution of slavery *per se*: slavery itself did not become illegal until the 1833 Slavery Abolition Act. In the case of the

United States, similar legislation was not passed until 1865. While the Royal Navy patrolled the seas, looking for any of the many ships breaking the law, they were naturally unable to do anything about the overland transportation of slaves. According to one source, each year between 1800 and 1860 approximately 10,000 slaves crossed the Sahara. Upon reaching the north coast, they would be sold at the slave markets that were a feature of most port cities, the largest of which was in Tripoli. The slaves were then shipped by their new owners to various parts of the Ottoman Empire, which still included the Balkans at this time, and beyond.

Although to modern eyes the abolition of slavery was a wholly good thing, those Africans, Arabs and Europeans alike who had made a living through it now had to find other commodities in which to trade, and this often meant finding and opening new markets. As a result there was a new impetus to explore the African interior, until then among the least-known places on earth. Suddenly the task of penetrating the Sahara and sub-Saharan Africa became an obvious and urgent endeavour. It was in this atmosphere that the major intra-Saharan expeditions of the nineteenth century took place.

One of the most important of these was a five-year mission sponsored by the British government that set out from England in 1822. The expedition's leader was Walter Oudney (1790-1824), a Scottish doctor, sometime naval surgeon and naturalist. Travelling with him were Hugh Clapperton (1788-1827), like Oudney a Scottish-born naval officer, and Dixon Denham (1786-1828), a British Army officer from London who had fought against Napoleon in Spain and at the Battle of Waterloo.

The mission proposed by the government was to accurately determine and map the course of the River Niger, which at least since Park's journey was known to run eastwards. If it seems strange that two of three officers on this Sahara mission were navy men, it should be remembered that they were given the task of charting a waterway and establishing how much and what parts of it were navigable. Perhaps it also makes sense, then, that the officers were accompanied by a shipbuilder, William Hillman, who was in charge of the expedition's stores.

Having sailed to Tripoli, the expedition entered the Sahara, the officers on horseback accompanied by 32 camels, a pair of mules and a couple of dogs. Notably, they did not travel in disguise, as certain explorers both before and after did. Such an open display of their foreignness emphasized not just that they were well-armed, but also underlined the new-found confidence Europeans felt in pressing forward into the Sahara. As Clapperton proudly wrote in his journal, "[we] were the first English travellers in Africa who had resisted the persuasion that a disguise was necessary, and who had determined to travel in our real characters as Britons and Christians, and to wear, on all occasions, our English dresses; nor had we, at any future period, occasion to regret that we had done so." As events transpired, it became clear that the greatest threat to the men's safety came not from angry native tribesmen but from among themselves.

Whatever else the Bornou (sic) Mission, as it was called, became known for it was sadly not for any collaborative spirit among its main participants. Oudney, Clapperton and Denham were men of wildly differing temperaments. The authorities in London had not thought it important to consult the men about their travelling together, and none of the three relished the prospect when ordered to do so, each wanting to be in charge of his own destiny. They failed to reach an equitable division between the civil and military aspects of the mission, and disliked taking orders from one another.

The further into the Sahara they travelled the worse the feuding became. At one stage Denham made the almost certainly unsubstantiated allegation that Clapperton was conducting a homosexual relationship with—heaven forbid!—one of their native servants. The increasingly acrimonious disputes meant that Denham and Clapperton stopped talking to one another, only communicating via official letters, sent back and forth from their respective tents. These missives would be hilarious if found in a novel, rather than during a dangerous mission in a harsh and alien environment. One letter from Clapperton, dated "Tents, Jan 1st, 1823", signals his unwillingness to take orders from Denham, a naval officer, whose jurisdiction over him he did not accept: "Sir, I thought my previous refusal would have prevented a repetition of your orders." Clapperton goes on to explain why he will continue to ignore any further orders, signing off, "I have the honour to be Sir, Your most Obedient humble Servant, Hugh Clapperton." Their first New Year in the Sahara was not to be ushered in to the strains of *Auld Lang Syne*.

Against all odds and in the face of the complete collapse of any rapport between the officers, the mission was a greater success than it had any right to be. Having made a successful north-south crossing of the Sahara, they discovered a large lake on the desert's southern shores. In spite of Denham's hope to see it named Lake Waterloo, it was to become known as Lake Chad, from a word in the local Bornu language, *tsade*, which means a large body of water; so "Lake Lake" was christened.

Oudney died shortly after this, halfway between Lake Chad and Kano, Nigeria, where he was heading with Clapperton. Clapperton pressed on alone to the Sokoto, a tributary of the Niger from which he was now just five days distant. But in Sokoto—the newly established capital of the Fulani's so-called Sokoto caliphate—the sultan forbade him to go any further. For one thing, the local rulers were still active in the slave trade and were fearful of any British interference in this lucrative business. Unable to find a guide willing to break ranks with the ruler's orders, he was forced to retrace his steps to Lake Chad.

While Clapperton was absent, Denham had unsuccessfully attempted to circumnavigate Lake Chad, and had instead headed back to Tripoli. Clapperton too made the journey back to the coast, arriving in Tripoli in January 1825 and then returned to England to make his reports to the government and the African Association, which remained, until its incorporation into the newly formed Royal Geographical Society in 1831, a significant force in Saharan exploration.

CAILLIÉ, BARTH AND ROHLFS

Among the early solo explorers of the Sahara, René-Auguste Caillié (1799-1838) holds a special place as the first European to reach Timbuktu and return alive. Before him, the fate of the few western travellers who made it to the city, dying or being killed on the return journey, resulted in a paucity of information regarding Timbuktu, which served to highlight the city's extreme isolation in the desert over which these pioneering explorers roamed.

By his own admission, Caillié was inspired to a life of exploration after reading *Robinson Crusoe*, Daniel Defoe's novel about a shipwrecked sailor on a desert island. Such are the seemingly small events that unveil kismet. Caillié started his trans-Saharan journey from Freetown, travelling through Conakry, Guinea and onto Tieme and the upper reaches of the Senegal river. During the four months he spent there he suffered from a more typically naval affliction, scurvy: an inauspicious start to his adventure. Once recovered, Caillié set out alone for Timbuktu, travelling in trading canoes

Timbuktu in 1828, from Caillié's book

along the Senegal and Niger rivers. En route, a further bout of illness saw him stranded for a further five months.

Unlike Clapperton, Oudney and Denham's larger, better-equipped and altogether fractious expedition, Caillié travelled in disguise, claiming to be an Egyptian Arab on his way home from Senegal, where he said he had been taken by the French. Having recovered from his second lengthy spell of sickness, he journeyed on to Kabara, Timbuktu's port town on the Niger, from where he crossed the final five miles overland to Timbuktu. Caillié arrived at the "lost" city on 20 April 1828, realizing the dream of countless explorers eleven months after leaving Freetown.

Caillié's account of his arrival at Timbuktu is, naturally enough, filled with the joy at his safe arrival, achieving a target that had occupied him for years. He records the moment thus:

At length, we arrived safely at Timbuktu, just as the sun was touching the horizon. I now saw this capital of the Soudan, to reach which had so long been the object of my wishes. On entering this mysterious city, which is an object of curiosity and research to the civilised nations of Europe, I experienced an indescribable satisfaction. I never before felt a similar emotion and my transport was extreme. I was obliged, however, to restrain my feelings, and to God alone did I confide my joy.

Having got over his initial euphoria, Caillié, an honest observer, goes on to describe the rather commonplace surroundings of the desert town: "I looked around and found that the sight before me, did not answer my expectations. I had formed a totally different idea of the grandeur and wealth of Timbuktu. The city presented, at first view, nothing but a mass of ill-looking houses, built of earth." It was clear to Caillié that the legends about a city of gold were just that. Nearly three centuries after the city's heyday, Timbuktu was essentially a great disappointment.

After spending two weeks in Timbuktu, Caillié started on his return journey, travelling north across the Sahara in the company of a slave caravan, and over the Atlas Mountains to Tangier. Returning home to France by boat, Caillié was given a hero's welcome, a state pension and the Légion d'Honneur. Yet Caillié's account of Timbuktu was so out of kilter with the prevailing view of the armchair experts who had obviously never been there themselves that they accused him of lying about ever having reached the city. Fortunately for Caillié, the Société Géographique of Paris accepted the veracity of his account, and awarded him the 10,000-franc prize money which they had offered to the first person to visit the city and come back to tell the tale. If people did not like the reality of Timbuktu's humble position in the early nineteenth century, Caillié could hardly be blamed for that. The legend of Timbuktu and its limitless quantities of gold may have been tarnished by Caillié's account, but the knowledge he brought back was more important than just another out-of-date European fantasy about the Dark Continent.

Heinrich Barth's (1821-65) wanderings in the Sahara, which covered a five-year period from 1850, were undertaken, like those of his countryman Hornemann before him, on behalf of British interests. With a talent for languages and a keen eye for detail, Barth's detailed five-volume account of his Saharan expeditions, *Travels and Explorations in North and Central*

View over Timbuktu, an illustration from Barth's *Travels and Explorations in North and Central Africa*

Africa, remains an essential reference to this day. Like Caillié, Barth believed that a successful mission demanded proper planning, however long this took. Focusing in particular on his Arabic, by the time he ventured into the desert he was more than comfortable in his chosen disguise of a travelling holy man. Testament to the efficacy of this cover is the fact that, according to his own account, people he met often wanted to receive a blessing from him.

Although a more sympathetic scientist-traveller than many of his fellow Europeans, Barth did not shy away from recording his displeasure at certain local customs. He is rendered almost apoplectic when recording one particular annoyance during the course of a more than nine-month sojourn in Timbuktu. One can imagine him spluttering over his notebook as he wrote, "I was disgusted by the custom which prevails in the houses like that in which I was lodged, of using the terrace as a sort of closet; and I had great difficulty in preventing my guide, Ammer el Walati, who still stayed with me and made the terrace his usual residence, from indulging in this filthy practice." He would have been much happier in the days of indoor plumbing.

From early on, European merchants saw the benefits of new Saharan markets, and were keen to secure exclusive trading rights to these with whatever local leaders they could. This was precisely the mission they paid Barth to conduct, and which he did after overcoming certain personal reservations. Barth reports the eagerness of the Sultan of Sokoto in agreeing to guarantee the security of any British traders who were to come into his domain. This promise was made, as Barth notes, even though the sultan's control over his territory was limited, as was his ability to fulfil any such promise.

Another mid-nineteenth-century German inspired to explore the Sahara was Friedrich Gerhard Rohlfs (1831-96). From Bremen, Rohlfs was the most indefatigable of this group of Saharan scholarly wanderers; family expectations saw him first studying medicine then joining the French Foreign Legion once he was a qualified doctor. It was Rohlfs' time in the legion that made him want to discover more of the desert. He achieved an important step towards fulfilling this dream when he became a physician in Morocco, in the army of the Alaouite ruler Sultan Muhammad IV, also being made chief of sanitation for the sultan's harem, a job not to be sniffed at.

As well as converting to Islam, Rohlfs made good use of this period to improve his knowledge of the Sahara and his language skills, becoming fluent in Arabic. Eventually setting off as an explorer in his own right, he was attacked in southern Morocco and left for dead. His medical training saved his life, as he was able to treat his injuries, which included the near severing of one of his legs. Undeterred, once recovered from the attack, Rohlfs resumed his career as a Saharan explorer, making a number of truly remarkable journeys.

Setting out in 1865, and following a route similar to that taken by the earlier Bornu Mission, Rohlfs successfully made the gruelling trek from Tripoli to Lake Chad, before continuing on to the Niger river. Following the course of the river, he eventually emerged into the Gulf of Guinea after a journey that lasted two years. Later expeditions took him to the far east of the Sahara and the Libyan Desert including Siwa and the even remoter oasis of Kufra, hitherto unseen by Europeans. In February 1874, while in the Libyan Desert in Egypt, Rohlfs recorded that he and his travelling companions experienced two days of very rare rainfall roughly sixty miles south-west of the oasis of Dakhla, and so named the spot Regenfeld, or

Rain-field—as unlikely a name as one might imagine in one of the Sahara's driest spots.

His reach and the extent of the observations he recorded as he travelled had no equal, a fact acknowledged by the Royal Geographical Society in 1868 when it presented him with one of its most prestigious awards, the Patron's Medal. Rohlfs spent more than thirty years in Africa, engaged in many groundbreaking journeys, not just in the north of the continent (beyond the Sahara his travels took him from Abyssinia to Zanzibar). At the Brussels Conference of 1876, organized by Belgium's King Leopold II to discuss Europe's "civilizing" mission for Africa, Rohlfs represented German interests, having established himself as one of Bismarck's most trusted confidants in matters of African imperialism.

Gustav Nachtigal (1834-85), the son of a Lutheran pastor, was another German medical man who became an army doctor and later explorer of the Sahara from 1862, when he first arrived in Algeria. Nachtigal moved to Algeria in the hope that the dry air would provide a cure for his tuberculosis. Like Rohlfs before him, he eventually became an employee of the state, in Nachtigal's case a court physician to Muhammad III as-Sadiq, Bey of Tunis. While still employed by the Tunisian government, Nachtigal took part in a year-long military campaign against tribes from the Saharan south of the country which were hostile to the government.

Later, with help from Rohlfs, Nachtigal received a commission from Wilhelm I of Prussia to travel to the Sultanate of Bornu. Travelling first to the oasis of Murzuk in south-western Libya, Nachtigal made a nearly 500-mile diversion across barren desert to become the first European to reach the Tibesti Mountains in southern Libya and northern Chad. After exploring the desolate peaks, he made his way to Kukawa, capital of Bornu, where he was granted an audience with the sultan. From here, disguised as a Muslim pilgrim, Nachtigal continued south to Lake Chad.

With seemingly boundless energy, and his tuberculosis apparently no longer troubling him, Nachtigal next turned east and journeyed through the independent Saharan states of Wadai, Darfur and Kordofan, emerging from the desert on the Nile. Arriving in Khartoum, Nachtigal had chalked up another first for himself in the annals of Saharan travel by being the first European to traverse the route between Lake Chad and the White Nile, a demanding course that had defeated previous attempted crossings. Nachtigal kept a methodical and involved account of everything he encountered, from notes on local customs and dress to the weather, wildlife and geology. Nachtigal also produced detailed maps, which would prove of inestimable value to subsequent European ventures in the Sahara, not all of which were to travel as peacefully as his.

In all, this epic journey took Nachtigal five years and resulted in the publication of a three-volume account, *Sahara and Sudan*. Upon publication, he was made a number of offers, before accepting the post of consul-general to Tunisia from the German government in 1884. He later became imperial commissioner to West Africa. In this latter role he was responsible for promoting German political and commercial interests in the region. He took to his new government job with enthusiasm; during his tenure he signed treaties with the indigenous leaders of both Togoland and Cameroon, which made the former a German colony and the latter a German protectorate.

One of the more sympathetic travellers of his time, Nachtigal could generally be relied upon to give an objective account of what he found. When he encountered generosity, kindness or intelligence among the local populations he was happy to document it, lacking the ingrained racial prejudice of many of his fellow Europeans. For a man who survived so many dangerous journeys across the length and breadth of the Sahara, it is a strange twist of fate that he died at sea while heading home to Germany. He was first buried at Grand-Bassem, Ivory Coast, before his remains were later ceremonially re-interred at Douala, Cameroon.

ALGERIA AND ABD AL-QADIR

Going back a few years, to 1830, four years before Nachtigal was born, the French had invaded Algeria, renaming it "French Algeria", and were soon forced into a bloody war of conquest. The year before the French invasion, Victor Hugo published a collection of verse called *Les Orientales*, sometimes translated as *Orientalia*. In part inspired by the Greek War of Independence against Ottoman rule, Hugo's Orient was out of necessity an imagined East, he never having travelled to North Africa. In the prologue he wrote, "In Louis XIV's time one was a Hellenist, now one is an Orientalist... For empires as for literatures, perhaps it will not be too long before the Orient is called upon to play a role in the Occident." The reaction of the author of *Les Misérables* and other works that defended the rights and liberty of the common man to the invasion of Algeria is perhaps puzzling. Later known as a great anti-imperialist, Hugo said of French involvement in Algeria: "Strange but true, what France lacks in Algiers is a little more barbarism. The Turks acted more quickly, more surely and made more progress: they were better at cutting off heads." Although he later showed a great antipathy to the death penalty, even pleading in 1880 for the lives of captured Kabyle tribesmen who had fought against the French in Algeria, it is not clear if his political ambition forced him to make such seemingly hypocritical remarks, or whether they were simply the curse of a writer whose output overtook him.

Abd al-Qadir, Abd el-Kader or Abdel Kader as his name is also spelt, was the leader of native resistance to the French invasion of Algeria until his capture in 1847 and exile, first to France and later to Damascus. Born the son of a Sufi sheikh near Mascara, close to Oran, Abd al-Qadir's campaign of guerrilla warfare against the French was marked both by the numerous victories he scored against superior numbers, and for the tactical truces struck between the two sides, which only ever lasted until the reality of new circumstances dictated the need for renewed military action. Some-

Abd al-Qadir leads Algerian resistance to the French invasion what unusually for a native rebel leader at this time, Abd al-Qadir enjoyed widespread popular support among those sections of the popular press in America and Britain that were critical of French aggression. His colourful nickname, the "Napoleon of the Arabs", only served to reinforce the general anti-French sentiment.

In a startlingly close retelling of the story of Jugurtha's resistance to the Roman invasion and conquest of North Africa, Abd al-Qadir was forced to flee to Morocco, having failed to gain the support of the Kabyle Berbers. Also like Jugurtha, upon reaching Morocco Abd al-Qadir was refused sanctuary, which ultimately forced him to surrender to the French. The parallel to the story of Jugurtha was not lost on the journalists of the day. Writing in *Bentley's Miscellany* a year before Abd al-Qadir's surrender, Everard Clive came out in support of the modern-day Jugurtha when he wrote, "Nearly 2,000 years have passed away since Rome, then in her full career of conquest… sent her Consuls to attack Jugurtha, King of Numidia, in the region where France now sends her Dukes and Marshals to strive against Abd-el-Kader."

It was not just the newspapermen that celebrated and embellished his legend. The resistance leader was eulogized in verse by no lesser a poet than Robert Browning in "Through the Metidja to Abd-El-Kadr", and William Makepeace Thackeray in his "Abdel-Kader at Toulon". The timbre of these poems is clear from just a little of Thackeray's panegyric, which opens:

No more, thou lithe and long-winged hawk, of desert-life for thee;
No more across the sultry sands shalt thou go swooping free:
Blunt iron talons, idle-beak, with spurning of thy chain,
Shatter against thy cage the wing thou ne'er may'st spread again.

A difficult legend to overturn, even in exile Abd al-Qadir received adulation from western sources. In 1860, while in exile in Damascus, he became known as the Protector of Christians after intervening to shield Damascene Christians during the massacres then taking place against them. As the Methodist Bishop John Philip Newman wrote in his book *From Dan to Beersheba*, "there was one humane Mohammedan who attempted to stay the massacre, and whose home afforded shelter to the defenceless. Abd-el-Kader, with 300 Algerian soldiers, who had followed their celebrated chief into exile, stood as a wall of brass against the fanaticism and fury of the murderers."

THE SCRAMBLE FOR AFRICA

Back in North Africa, Spain had occupied at least one Moroccan coastal city since the fifteenth century but it was not until 1830 that the French took an interest in the Saharan regions of that country. France and Spain finally agreed upon a mutually acceptable division of the country in the 1912 Treaty of Fez, typically without consulting the Moroccans. In 1881 Tunisia became a French protectorate and in 1882 Britain occupied Egypt and the Sudan. The Sudan was then abandoned in the face of resistance from the self-proclaimed Mahdi Muhammad ibn-Abdalla and his forces, before eventually being fully reoccupied in 1899, after a military campaign led by Lord Kitchener, when it was renamed the Anglo-Egyptian Sudan.

Before Kitchener's action in the Sudan, however, a meeting took place in Europe in 1886 that was to radically alter the fate of Africa, including the whole of the Sahara. The Conference of Berlin was organized so that European nations with commercial interests in Africa could decide exactly where their and other competing national interests lay. In this way the European governments hoped they might avoid war between each other as they further encroached upon the Dark Continent. By the end of the conference, in an act of hubris almost unparalleled in human history, the entire continent of Africa had been divided up between the European imperial powers. The agreement was entered into, according to the document's final wording, "in a spirit of good and mutual accord, to regulate the conditions most favourable to the development of trade and civilization in certain regions of Africa," but without the presence of, or consultation with, a single African ruler. Africa for the Europeans was the order of the day.

After the signing of the General Act of the Berlin Conference, the speed with which the continent was physically divided up between erstwhile European rivals was truly remarkable. The so-called Scramble for Africa took place at great speed between 1880 and 1900. Against a background of national expansion and at the cost of very few European lives, it is perhaps unsurprising that cultural products of the period tended to be pro-empire, jingoistic and one-sided. Before the Scramble, a term coined in 1884 by a journalist with *The Times*, the European presence in the desert was fairly limited. In the northern half of the Sahara, the countries in which European powers began to take an interest were all technically Ottoman lands, rather than nation states. In some cases any semblance of Ottoman control was nominal at best and it is easier to think in terms of slices of the Ottoman Empire, known at this time as "the sick man of Europe", being snatched away from Constantinople, rather than there taking place the wholesale conquest of independent countries. Even if the results were ultimately the same, the distinction is important and worth highlighting.

The formal agreement reached in Berlin was an enormous alteration in terms of European intervention; from what has been called "informal imperialism" based on economic and military control to the formalization of the process and direct rule by the governments of Europe. From a European perspective, which was the only one under consideration at the time, such a formalization of their relationship to one another in Africa would prevent wars. It would be much better to focus expansionist inclinations against less well-armed and distant peoples than one's militarily competent neighbours, as the concerned parties were to discover between 1914 and 1918.

In many cases, European nations seemed to be interested in grabbing any land they could, simply to deprive their rivals, and the race for the Sahara was just as bitter as it was elsewhere in Africa. Under the terms of the General Act, Spain was awarded the "Spanish Sahara", today's Western Sahara, where the locals continue to fight for independence, now against the independent Kingdom of Morocco.

By 1890 France controlled the majority of Saharan land, to which the then British prime minister Lord Salisbury, affecting sublime insouciance, said it was nothing more than, "light soil in which the Gallic cock can scratch". In response, Jules Cambon, governor-general of Algeria said, "Very well, we will scratch in this sand. We will lay railway-lines, we will put up telegraph-poles, we will make the artesian water-tables gush to the surface, and in the oases we will hear the Gallic cock crowing his most melodious and happiest fanfare from the rooftops of the Kasbah."

French forces went on to appropriate Mali in 1892, as well as occupying parts of Niger and Chad during the 1890s, taking full control of Chad in 1900. During the same period the French claimed administrative control over Mauritania in a policy that went by the innocuous-sounding title of "peaceful penetration".

The last slice of the Sahara to be swallowed by Europe was "Italian North Africa", that is Libya, which did not become a colony until 1912, after the Italian invasion of the previous year. So, just two years before the start of the Great War the Sahara was entirely a European political entity without any native independence, although there were still some resistance movements fighting on, notably in Libya. As a result, for a small number of adventurous Europeans and Americans, the Sahara was about to become the latest playground for the leisured, offering visitors a little taste of the East, albeit a taste that the occupiers had started to sanitize, outfitting the ports and oases with western amenities.

Omar Mukhtar (*second left*) meets with occupying Italian forces, Libya, 1929

Chapter Eight

WAR AND PEACE AND WAR

Ex Africa semper aliquid novi.
(Out of Africa there is always something new.)
Pliny the Elder

Whereas in 1800 the majority of the northern Sahara was part of the Ottoman Empire, and the southern Sahara and Sahel were ruled by various independent states, by 1900 every one of the modern Saharan nations, north and south, were to a greater or lesser extent under European control, with France claiming the largest portion of the desert. It was not until 1848, eighteen years after the French invasion of Algeria, that it was officially declared French territory. Resistance to occupation, which had been especially stiff until the capture of Abd al-Qadir, gradually tailed off. In 1900 French Algeria was granted administrative and financial autonomy and placed under a governor-general. Ten years later, resistance to occupation had effectively ceased.

In 1881, using a Tunisian raid into French Algeria as the excuse to launch a counter-invasion, a 36,000-strong French force marched on Tunisia. With the country swiftly occupied, Muhammad III as-Sadiq, Bey of Tunis, had no choice but to sign the Treaty of Bardo, which made Tunisia a French protectorate. Determined to carve out far larger claims in North Africa, three French military expeditions were sent out in 1898: the Voulet-Chanoine Mission headed east from Senegal, the Foureau-Lamy Expedition moved south from Algeria and the Gentil Mission set out from the Middle Congo to meet up with the other two. Working in concert, by 1900 the missions had successfully conquered the whole of the Chad Basin and united French territories across the Sahara from West Africa to the border with Sudan and north to the Mediterranean, incorporating the modern Saharan countries of Mauritania, Mali, Niger, Chad, Algeria and Tunisia.

To the east of France's massive Saharan territories, the British were in control of Egypt since occupying it, and Egyptian Sudan, from 1882. The rebellion in the Sudan led by Muhammad ibn Abdalla, the Mad Mahdi, forced the withdrawal of Anglo-Egyptian forces in 1885, after which he established an independent theocracy there. Britain retook the whole of the country in 1898, after a military campaign led by Lord Kitchener. Although technically the British were only present in Egypt in an advisory capacity, in light of the time and energy spent in regaining it Britain decided to maintain formal control in the Sudan. To satisfy the convoluted imperial politics of previous agreements with the Egyptians, this led to the formation of the Anglo-Egyptian Condominium in 1899, under which the Egyptians would appoint a British governor-general to rule the Sudan on behalf of the Egyptian khedive, who was in reality also under British control.

In 1900 Libya and Morocco were both just managing to hang on to their independence from European control. The three Ottoman *wilayats*—semi-autonomous states—of Tripolitania, Cyrenaica and Fezzan would not become united as Libya until the 1911 Italian invasion, which Rome claimed was aimed at freeing the North Africans from Ottoman oppression. Attempts by Morocco to develop closer links with Europe and the US, begun in the mid-nineteenth century, only really led to greater interference by France and Spain. Although France and Spain recognized Moroccan independence at the 1880 Conference of Madrid, two crises in

Imperial guns keeping order in the desert

the first decade of the twentieth century, prompted by a rise in Anglo-German tensions, led to Morocco being carved up into French and Spanish protectorates at the 1911 Treaty of Fez.

War, meanwhile, was just beginning in Libya. Although greatly outnumbered by regular Italian troops with the latest arms, resistance from Ottoman Turkish troops was fiercer than the Italians were expecting, forcing the invaders to increase their troops from 20,000 to 100,000. The Italian-Turkish war is notable for the first use of aerial bombing as a weapon of war when, on 1 November 1911, Lieutenant Giulio Gavotti, flying at 600 feet, dropped four hand grenades on a Turkish camp. Although Gavotti did not kill or injure anyone in the attack, his actions earned him a small, if dubious, footnote in the history of warfare.

Even though the 1923 Treaty of Lausanne ceded the provinces of Tripolitania, Fezzan and Cyrenaica to Italy, Bedouin attacks against the invaders grew in number and vigour after that date. The fight dragged on for twenty years, during which time the Italians held the cities but rarely had effective control in the rest of the country.

Born in a small village near Tobruk, Omar Mukhtar, the man who would become the most famous Libyan resistance leader, was an unlikely national hero. Before the Italian invasion he taught the Quran to children in the local school. After the invasion he became known as the Lion of the Desert. Mukhtar owed his success against Italy's superior numbers to avoiding large-scale, direct confrontation with the enemy, and his knowledge of local geography. Leading small bands on raids against Italian outposts and their lines of communication, Mukhtar was also adaptable, developing new tactics whenever the Italians changed their own strategy. Mukhtar was eventually captured by Italian troops in September 1931. His trial was swift and he was hanged in front of thousands of his countrymen in a concentration camp at Suluq, which was built for resistance fighters. When, before his execution, Mukhtar was asked if had any last words, the teacher-turned-national hero replied with a verse from the Quran: "From Allah we have come, and to Allah we shall return."

Eighty years after his death, Omar Mukhtar's legend is still strong in Libya. His image is ubiquitous, appearing on the Libyan ten-dinar banknote and on car bumper stickers. In June 2009 the theatrically inclined Muammar Gaddafi wore a photograph of Mukhtar as an Italian prisoner on his lapel when he met Italian prime minister Silvio Berlusconi.

It is striking that the guerrilla resistance led by Omar Mukhtar lasted five times as long as the First World War, although the impact of that conflict in the region was minimal because there were virtually no German colonies in Saharan Africa. Getting to North Africa was a different matter, as Edith Wharton noted: "In 1918, owing to the watchfulness of German submarines in the Straits and along the northwest coast of Africa, the trip by sea from Marseilles to Casablanca, ordinarily so easy, was not to be made without much discomfort and loss of time." How inconvenient war can be to one's travel plans!

The armed opposition to the Italian invasion continued in the desert regions of Libya throughout the Great War, and in Egypt's Western Desert the Sanussi periodically harried British troops. In response, the British were forced to deploy the newly created Imperial Camel Corps and the Light Car Patrols in offensive engagements and reconnaissance missions against the religiously-inspired Sanussi. Today this minor piece of soldiering on the fringes of the larger conflict is almost entirely forgotten, but thankfully not entirely. For one thing, there is a small bronze memorial to the Imperial Camel Corps in Victoria Gardens on the Embankment in London. The statue features a soldier atop his war-camel and on the plinth is inscribed, "To the Glorious and Immortal Memory of the Officers, NCO's and Men of the Imperial Camel Corps—British, Australian, New Zealand, Indian—who fell in action or died of wounds and disease in Egypt, Sinai, and Palestine, 1916, 1917, 1918."

T. E. Lawrence was also in Egypt for a part of the First World War, before Arabia. Based in Cairo with the Arab Bureau, it is curious to note that Lawrence spent more time in Egypt than he did in Arabia, working in the Cairo Intelligence Department, a unit of British intelligence formed after a suggestion by Sir Mark Sykes, whose name was later attached to the Sykes-Picot Agreement. Lawrence spent his time preparing maps and writing the daily intelligence bulletins for, as he put it, "the edification of 28 generals". A life-long lover of desert places, before the war Lawrence spent time working on an archaeological dig close to the Nile and although he never wrote a great deal about this time, it certainly contributed to his reputation for being able to work in harsh conditions. The Arab Bureau was also responsible for running a network of agents in the Sahara, who were supplying information about the Sanussi and gun-running operations in the Western Desert.

Tied to Lawrence by friendship, the poet, novelist and translator Robert Graves spent the first half of 1926 in Egypt, teaching English literature at Cairo University. When Graves wrote to Lawrence for advice about his forthcoming move to Egypt, Lawrence replied that "Egypt, being so near Europe, is not a savage country," which he followed up by advising Graves to "Roam about—Palestine. The Saharan oases… Wilfred Jennings Bramley's buildings in the Western Desert." It was not a happy time for Graves, and he and his family and his mistress, who all travelled to Egypt together, left again after six months.

Short though it was, Graves' Egyptian interlude inspired his most famous short story, *The Shout*. Set in a mental asylum, Graves said the idea for the story came to him "while I was walking in the desert near Heliopolis in Egypt and came upon a stony stretch where I stopped to pick up a few mis-shapen pebbles; what virtue was in them I do not know, but I somehow had the story from them." Graves ventured into the Sahara a number of times fostering his life-long fascination with Egyptian, and Greek, mythology.

MOTORS, MAPS AND PLANES

"People condemn the motor-car as unromantic. I am afraid this is natural, for no one can become fond of a thing he does not really understand, and the ordinary person understands a camel, if in concept only, because it is an animal like himself."

Ralph Bagnold, *Libyan Sands: Travels in a Dead World* (1935)

From the first upright steps of homo sapiens to the birth of motor transport, the greatest speed people had experienced was on the back of a galloping horse. For most, their maximum speed was limited to however fast they could propel themselves. The development of the motorcar radically changed this. With the arrival of motorcars, large areas of the Sahara were accessible for the first time. The arrival of the car did not, however, herald the end of camels or cameleers.

Even as some said camels would become obsolete in the face of motorized transport, some of the most adventurous camel-powered desert exploration was taking place. In the winter of 1920 the Oxford-educated Egyptian diplomat and politician, two-time Olympian and grandson of the last admiral of the Egyptian fleet, Ahmed Hassanein Bey, set off for the oasis of Kufra, in the heart of the Libyan Desert. Accompanied by the English travel writer Rosita Forbes, the small band crossed the Sahara from Ajdabiya, near the Gulf of Sirte, without a car in sight.

Forbes' account of the journey, *Kufara: the Secret of the Sahara*, was rightly criticized for not giving sufficient credit to Hassanein for his central role in the expedition. Yet she did dedicate the book to him, the father of Egyptian exploration: "To Ahmed Mohammed Bey Hassanein. In memory of hours grave and gay, battles desperate or humorous, of success and failure in the Libyan deserts." Walking through the winter, the coolest and so best time for Saharan exploration, the pair and their retinue headed south towards the famously closed oasis.

Apart from its geographical isolation, the oasis had stood aloof from outsiders since becoming home to the Sanussi brotherhood in the 1890s. Hostile to all foreign occupation of the Sahara, the Sanussi clashed at various times with the French, Italians and British. Part of Forbes' motivation for making the journey was because it was forbidden. As she says, "For a year I had worked and plotted to reach Kufara because the thought of this holy oasis, nucleus of the greatest Islamic confraternity, rigidly guarded from every stranger, the centre of the mighty influence against which every European Power has battled in turn, stirred my imagination."

The book charts their four-month round trip of more than a thousand miles to Kufra and back via Jaghbub and Siwa, and contains all the requisite elements for a gripping yarn including fractious camels and disgruntled guides. Forbes remembers with fondness the journey's privations and expresses a common desire to return to the magical: "Some time, somehow, I knew not where or when, but most assuredly when Allah willed, I should come back to the deserts and the strange, uncharted tracks would bear my camels south again."

Although Forbes was the first non-Arab woman to visit the Sanussi's home oasis, she was not the first European to do so. The German explorer Gerhard Rohlfs and the botanist Paul Friedrich August Ascherson travelled there from Dakhla in the winter of 1873. En route, they came across Abu Ballas, Pottery Hill, so-called because of the remains of hundreds of smashed pots that litter the desert there. The legend is told that the oasis of Dakhla suffered regular raids from the west, an area of completely waterless desert. The raiders were only able to attack Dakhla if they kept a supply of water on their path through the wilderness. After one raid some Dakhla inhabitants followed the raiders. Although they failed to catch them, they did find the raiders' water-filled pots, and smashed them all. The raids stopped, the raiders presumably dying the next time they approached Dakhla and finding their vital supplies gone.

Writing about the trip that he and Forbes made, Hassanein said that the journey "only whetted my appetite for more", which is why he set out again, in 1922, on a longer, more perilous journey. On his second expedition Hassanein skirted the Great Sand Sea, which stretches across the Egypto-Libyan border, before heading south through Darfur to al-Obeid in the Sudan. This impressive trek took Hassanein eight months and covered 2300 miles. In the process he discovered Jebel Arkenu and Jebel Uweinat in the extreme south-western corner of Egypt, the so-called lost oases of the title of the book he later wrote about the trip. If the scale of Hassanein's journey was not impressive enough, he also discovered the exceptional collection of rock art that occurs in the isolated Gilf Kebir, Great Barrier, region that straddles Egypt, Libya and the Sudan.

Writing in the *Geographical Journal*, Hassanein outlined the hard daily routine of a camel-powered expedition: "Twelve to thirteen hours of walking, [that] if conditions have been good, bring us to the end of the day's trek, though sometimes we cannot go on so long. The order is given to halt, the camels, with grunts of satisfaction, kneel to have their loads removed… The men of the caravan are not slow to prepare and eat the evening meal, to feed the camels and then to dispose themselves for sleep. But I must compare my six watches and wind them, record the photographs and geological specimens taken and collected during the day, change the cinema films in the darkness, and write up my diaries." For this journey Hassanein was awarded the Royal Geographical Society's Founder's Medal in 1924.

Even as Hassanein was presenting his findings in London, the Sahara was opening up for cars as well as aircraft, which offered a completely new perspective on the great desert. With technological developments allowing aircraft to cover greater distances, trans-Saharan journeys became possible which did not even require the traveller to set foot in the desert at all, unless things went badly wrong.

Among the pioneers of aerial trans-Saharan routes was Captain René Wauthier, a Frenchman who in the early 1930s flew across the Sahara on numerous occasions, including to Lake Chad and Agadez via Tamanrasset and In-Guezzam. Wauthier's experiences at the vanguard of desert flying were retold in *Air Adventure: Paris-Sahara-Timbuctoo* by the American occultist, asylum inmate and one-time cannibal, William Seabrook. Notorious in his day, Seabrook wrote about flying when the experience was still a novel one and the glamour of flight still made heroes out of flyers. Conversely, however, its newness meant that risks were still acute.

Seabrook was not embarrassed to admit that in his case much of the danger was caused by his own lack of preparedness. As he recalls:

> It was only when the sandstorm rose up from the Great Sahara, ripped us down out of the pretty sky, and taught us that it could make skeletons out of airplanes as easily as camels, that we really began to get acquainted with the desert, or to take it or ourselves seriously. In fact the whole adventure had been cooked up so casually, so suddenly, and had moved so quickly in time and space, that it had been impossible from the first, for me at least, to focus on its reality.

Flying with primitive navigational equipment and weak radios, disaster stalked every flight, and success seemed little more than good luck.

The most famous pioneer of trans-Saharan flight was Antoine de Saint-Exupéry. Most famous today for *The Little Prince*, his fable for children and adults, Saint-Exupéry was nonetheless a noted pilot, opening up aerial routes over the desert for the burgeoning international postal system. Saint-Exupéry writes most movingly about the Sahara in *Wind, Sand and Stars* (in French, *Terre des homes*), particularly about his and his navigator André Prévot's crash and near-death experience five days after Christmas Day 1935 during a long flight in bad weather.

With a cash prize of 150,000 francs for the fastest flight time from Paris to Saigon it is scarcely surprising that they took risks. On crashing, Saint-Exupéry and Prévot knew that, even if a search party were sent, they were not likely to be found and Saint-Exupéry, thinking about what he had been taught about the desert, observes:

> In the Sahara humidity is a constant 40 per cent, but here it drops to 18 per cent. And life evaporates like a haze. Bedouin tribesmen, travellers and colonial officials all teach that a man can last for nineteen hours

without water. After twenty hours his eyes flood with light, and it is the beginning of the end: thirst's onslaught is devastating.

With this grim knowledge in mind, the men decided to try to walk out of the desert. But here too they were faced with a troubling dilemma. Not knowing where they were, in which direction should they head? After four days a Bedouin found them and led them to safety: "The Arab simply looked at us. He placed his hands firmly on our shoulders, and we obeyed him. We lay down upon the sand. There are no races here, nor any languages, nor any discord… There is this poor nomad who has placed his archangelic hands on our shoulders… All other pleasures seem trivial to those of us who have known the joy of a rescue in the Sahara."

The crash also features in *The Little Prince*. Translated into 180 languages, the book has sold more than eighty million copies worldwide, the best-selling French-language book of all time. With line drawings by Saint-Exupéry, it tells the tale of a little prince who comes from asteroid number B216 which, he explains, is the size of a house. The tale's narrator is an airman who has crashed in the desert where he meets the Little Prince.

The novel brilliantly encapsulates Saint-Exupéry's experiences of the desert both before and after his rescue, with the airman worried about his impending death and the Little Prince focused rather on the joy of friendship. "'My friend the fox –' the little prince said to me. 'My dear little man, this is no longer a matter that has anything to do with the fox!' 'Why not?' 'Because I am about to die of thirst…' He did not follow my reasoning, and he answered me: 'It is a good thing to have a friend, even if one is about to die. I, for instance, am very glad to have a fox as a friend.'"

Despite a lucky escape from death in the desert, Saint-Exupéry eventually died while flying. Flying reconnaissance missions for Free French Forces, on the evening of 31 July 1944, having taken off from Corsica on his final mission to collect intelligence on German troop movements in the Rhone Valley, Saint-Exupéry failed to return to base. In spite of the mystery that surrounded his s death, or perhaps in part because of it, his reputation in France was assured and his memory honoured with a memorial plaque in the Paris Pantheon. Tom Wolfe also acknowledges the place of the pioneering pilot, describing Saint-Exupéry in *The Right Stuff* as "A saint in short, true to his name, flying up here at the right hand of God. The good Saint-Ex! And he was not the only one. He was merely

Saint-Exupéry

the one who put it into words most beautifully and anointed himself before the altar of the right stuff."

There is a lonely memorial to Saint-Exupéry in the desert outside the city of Tarfaya, formerly Cape Juby, near the border with Western Sahara. Saint-Exupéry was the manager of the Cape Juby airfield, which marked a stopover for the Aéropostale flights plying the Toulouse-Dakar route. As he wrote in *Wind, Sand, and Stars*, "And yet we loved the desert... If at first it is merely emptiness and silence, that is because it does not open itself to transient lovers." It was a remote spot, far from the sort of civilization of city-life he enjoyed when he had the opportunity, and Saint-Exupéry came to appreciate the loneliness of his posting, as he said later: "But I know solitude. Three years in the desert have taught me its taste."

Literature by those who explored Saharan *terra firma* is plentiful and rich, perhaps because they felt the thrill of covering ground which for millennia had lain untouched. Throughout the 1920s and 1930s Ralph Bagnold spent his free time driving in the desert. Although told by older desert-hands that it was impossible to drive there, especially in the dunes,

Bagnold decided to find out if this was true for himself. His education was a practical one, taking his Ford Model T on ever-longer trips into the Sahara until he felt ready to tackle the seemingly impassable Great Sand Sea.

As in many fields of endeavour, the more Bagnold learnt the more he knew he had to learn. Well aware of the size of the challenge he and his fellow travellers had set, Bagnold wrote in *Libyan Sands: Travel in a Dead World*, "the fact is that we were a little afraid of the desert… because it was so different from all experience… It lures the foolish onwards by its good firm surface, as several would-be sportsmen have found to their cost… It is most disconcerting, after one has set a course for some known feature on the map, to find, when the correct mileage thither shows up on the speedometer face, that the place one is aiming at is simply not there."

In the course of his driving experiments Bagnold devised a number of useful tools, including the sun compass. This car-mounted device allowed navigation by dead reckoning without a vehicle's metal body interfering with bearings, as it would with a regular compass. Another Bagnold invention was the sand mat, used then as now under a car's tyres to give it traction, thus freeing a vehicle stuck in sand. His most ingenious invention, though, was a closed-loop system linked to a car radiator, which captured escaping water vapour and sent it back into the radiator, greatly reducing the amount of water that had to be carried for the vehicle.

Bagnold also worked out how to drive over soft sand, simply by letting out some of the air in a car's tyres. In addition to his desert driving experiments, in the second year of the Second World War Bagnold published the specialist text, *The Physics of Blown Sand*, which remains the best single-volume work describing in practical terms the formation and movement of sand dunes. Writing in the *Geographical Journal*, Major Bill Kennedy Shaw, one of Bagnold's fellow explorers, explained: "Broadly speaking, desert sand may be divided into three types: (1) That in which no car will stick. (2) That through which it is often possible to force a way by keeping up speed and by intelligent use of the slopes of the ground. (3) That in which any tyre yet made will bog." Most were of the opinion that the Great Sand Sea only contained the third type.

Bagnold's main foreign rival during the halcyon days of motorized desert exploration, was the Austro-Hungarian count László Almásy. Given the nickname Abu Ramla, Father of the Sand, by the Bedouin, Almásy was, like Bagnold, an explorer and innovator with a love of cars and the desert. One of his most famous expeditions saw Almásy and three British friends travel to the Gilf Kebir region in 1932. Using cars and an aeroplane, the team, which included Sir Robert Clayton, Patrick Clayton (no relation) and Commander Penderel, surveyed a large area of the desert, first scouting suitable locations from the air then exploring them on the ground. Michael Ondaatje gave a highly fictionalized account of Almásy in his 1992 novel *The English Patient*, yet fictional or otherwise, Ondaatje captures the camaraderie that existed among the desert dreamers, his Almásy explaining: "Just the Bedouin and us, crisscrossing the Forty Days' Road. There were rivers of desert tribes, the most beautiful humans I've ever met in my life. We were German, English, Hungarian, African—all of us insignificant to them. Gradually we became nationless. I came to hate nations. We are deformed by nations."

When not simply testing cars or exploring for fun, serious work was also being carried out in the Sahara at this time, the most important tasks being to draw up national borders. The further one travelled from the coast and into the desert, the fewer clear borders would be found between the possessions recently claimed by European powers. In 1915 Frank Cana wrote in the *Geographical Journal*, "There remains the settlement of the boundaries of the Italian sphere, a settlement which affects French and British (Egyptian) interests. The exact frontiers of Libya (as the Italians style their North African possessions) is a matter of some importance, involving the control of the routes to the Central Sahara and then possession of the Kufra oases."

Once the Second World War started, control of desert paths and oases was crucial. As head of the Survey of Egypt, George Murray saw the problem in a professional capacity when he wrote, "Very little interest was taken in the Egyptian deserts before 1905, and by 1925 only 20 percent of the country had been mapped to the professional standards of the day." The British-run Egyptian Survey department was thus put in charge of surveying and mapping the whole of Egypt and, after the Italian invasion of Libya, settle the otherwise ill-defined border between these countries. Murray noted: "Hastily, it was agreed that the frontier should start from Bir Ramla on the coast and follow various devious camel tracks in turn until Siwa Oasis had been left in Egypt and Jaghbub in Cyrenaica. These objectives achieved, nobody cared where it went. So the twenty-fifth meridian was chosen for it to follow until it got tired or reached the

Sudan." The border was not accurately marked until the late 1930s, just in time for Italian and British troops to start marching back and forth across it.

In 1936, following a talk by a pioneer of motorized desert travel, Major W.B. Kennedy Shaw, later of the Long Range Desert Group and Special Air Service, Hassanein Bey was invited to offer his thoughts, which neatly sum up the evolution of desert exploration between the wars. "All my journeys in the Libyan Desert," Hassanein explained,

> were made by camel caravan, and I am pleased to hear that, modern methods of transport notwithstanding, the camel has still been of some use in dumping petrol for the expedition. I might add though that although there are bits of desert where the camel cannot go and the car can, there are a good many bits of desert where the camel can go and the car cannot show its face. There is also something to be said for the slow pace of the camel, three or four miles an hour, because it gives one leisure to look around and note the points of interest in one's surroundings. Please do not think that I am making propaganda against the car, for although I do not like inanimate transport, I recognize that the exploration of the last nine years in the Libyan Desert could not possibly have been covered by camel carrier.

Whether fans of the camel caravan, motor car or aeroplane, the men and women who spent their time exploring in the Sahara all did so because it held a special place in their heart. As Kennedy Shaw later noted in the preface to his history of the Long Range Desert Group, "There are no two ways about deserts—either you dislike intensely being in them or you find their attractions hard to resist." Yet even while Hassanein Bey was extolling the virtues of the camel, the shadow of war was growing on the horizon which, when it came, rudely ended the age of civilized, multinational expeditions by desert-loving ladies and gentleman.

French Chadian soldier, 1942

Chapter Nine

THE SECOND WORLD WAR

"The plain was littered with abandoned German equipment, destroyed vehicles, clothing, hats and shoes. I don't believe I ever saw such a bleak, desolate land except for the Sahara. Little white crosses marking German and Italian dead dotted the sand. 'God, what a place to have to die in,' Keith said. He was right."

Don Whitehead, diary, 14 November 1942

It is curious that wars, with all their destructive power, are so often the midwives of creativity, and in this regard, the Second World War was typical. Those who experienced the conflict in the Sahara produced a wealth of diverse material after their experiences, which tackled the futility, waste and boredom as well as the flashes of glory among otherwise ordinary men who lived through—and died in—extraordinary situations.

Combat was largely limited to the northern parts of the desert. After 1940 and the fall of France, the eight-state federation of French West Africa, which included Mauritania, French Sudan (now Mali) and Niger, remained with Vichy France, as did French North African Morocco and Algeria. The French protectorate of Tunisia was occupied by Vichy-allied German and Italian troops. In contrast, French Equatorial Africa, including Chad, sided with General de Gaulle's Free French government in exile. As a result, some 15,000 native Chadian troops fought during the course of the war, with other Free French units also fighting alongside British and Commonwealth units.

One feature of the war in the desert, missing from a number of other theatres of combat, was the sense of the Sahara itself as an implacable enemy, against both sides. All soldiers suffer in adverse weather, but in the desert the ubiquitous sand and dust, extreme temperatures and ever-present fear of being without water gave enemies a certain sympathy for one another.

The point is made in the closing lines of Christopher Landon's 1957 novel, *Ice Cold in Alex*. A semi-autobiographical account of Landon's war service, the story revolves around Captain Anson, a British officer and alcoholic, and Otto Lutz, a German spy posing as a South African officer.

Retreating across the desert in the face of a German advance, Anson is accompanied by his sergeant and a couple of nurses who are left behind when their unit withdraws one night. The journey across the desert is dramatic. Travelling via the tiny oasis of al-Qara and the salt-pans of the Qatarra Depression, they make it safely to Alexandria after much drama. Once there, they enjoy the beer Anson promised to buy them to celebrate their deliverance. As Anson remembers his favourite bar, he muses, "They served it ice cold in Alex."

At the story's close, when Military Police arrive to arrest Lutz, the German "walked to the door with the lieutenant, and then turned back to look at them once more. He said, 'It has been something. All against one—against the greater enemy. I have learned a lot.' Then he gave them that silly stiff bow again, the door flapped twice behind him and that was that."

Cecil Beaton recorded his thoughts on people confronting the desert in his wartime diaries, noting:

> Cairo demands too little of a man, and the desert too much. Existence in the desert is, in its way, as unnatural as that of Cairo, for a false reality prevails. The desert is an unnatural habitat for the average human being... Life here is primeval, and from this very simplicity seems to spring a new contentment. Often the men become so contented that they are said to be "sand happy".

Better known as a high-society photographer, Beaton was in the Western Desert to take photographs for the British Ministry of Information. He observed at first hand the truism that life in the military involves a high degree of "Hurry up and wait", with the lulls being longer and more numerous than any episodic action. He describes this inactivity in *Self Portrait with Friends*: "One of the worst aspects of desert life is the men's lack of reading matter. However conscientious they are about their duties, much of their time necessarily must be spent 'hanging about being bored'."

Beaton was also present at a time of movement, with both sides engaged in attacks, counter-attacks and retreats over hundreds of miles of flat desert. Remembering one such attack he writes, "Dudley Barker asked excitedly, 'Do you want to take some action pictures?' 'Then it has started in the desert?' 'Yes, this morning.' This was how I heard that Rommel had attacked. One of the Anglo-Egyptian secretaries squeaked up, 'Oh, I can't get a thrill out of the desert any longer. It's always a case of someone going backwards or forwards.'"

If the "going backwards or forwards" of the war had potential for farce, Spike Milligan articulated this and other more madcap aspects of the war. Milligan especially highlights the absurdity in the midst of what others would see rather as a time of historical import. Serving as a signaller with the Royal Artillery, Gunner Milligan took the most ridiculous elements of military life into his post-war comedic career, creating the *Goon Show*, the forebear to countless later absurdist comedians from Monty Python to Eddie Izzard.

In a series of memoirs about his wartime service including *"Rommel?" "Gunner Who?": A Confrontation in the Desert*, Milligan displays an artist's eye for detail as in the following passage:

> Twixt Tizi Ouzou and Beni Mansour we passed mountains each side of 8,000 feet, and numerous rock-hewn tunnels... "Attention! Rallientair!" signs appeared frequently. We saw camel trains all laden with goods. They followed ancient camel tracks two or three hundred feet above us, moving slowly with a dignity no civilization had managed to speed up. At sundown, the Arabs turned towards Mecca to carry out their devotions, a religious people, more than I could say for our lot, the only time they knelt was to pick up money.

Milligan displays sympathy towards the locals while further mocking his brothers-in-arms, observing: "Looking along the line, one caught sight of the odd Gunner piddling against the wheels. I don't understand it! They have to clean their own transport, and then, when they've got the whole of Africa, they piss on their own lorries!" His observations about cultural misunderstandings on the part of the British soldiers are also put to comic effect: "Marches took us through timeless Arab villages, Rouiba, Ain-Taya, Fondouk, when we halted I'd try the Arab coffee; piping hot, sweet, delicious. I watched Gunner White sip the coffee then top it up with water! I explained the water was for clearing the palate. 'I thought it was coolin' it down,' said the descendant of the Crusaders."

In a more traditional mode, the war also produced a number of exceptional poems rather than desert-poets, with the notable exception of Keith Douglas (1920-44). Killed three days after taking part in the D-Day landings, Douglas' desert-inspired poetry is his best, most poignant work. In "Vergissmeinnicht (Forget Me Not)", an Allied combatant returns to the scene of a battle three weeks after it took place and comes across a German corpse. Like others who wrote from the desert, Douglas displays no hatred towards his declared enemies but instead recognizes the random nature of survival and mortality, sparing a thought for those left behind. In the case of the dead German, "the soldier sprawling in the sun", his sweetheart is the focus:

> the dishonoured picture of his girl
> who has put: Steffi. Vergissmeinnicht.
> in a copybook gothic script.

Another verse by Douglas, "Cairo Jag", has a soldier on leave wondering, "Shall I get drunk or cut myself a piece of cake"? In spite of the available distractions, the soldier's mind returns to a recently fought battle, and he imagines the dead as neglected tourists:

> But by a day's travelling you reach a new world
> the vegetation is of iron
> dead tanks, gun barrels split like celery
> the metal brambles have no flowers or berries
> and there are all sorts of manure, you can imagine
> the dead themselves, their boots, clothes and possessions
> clinging to the ground, a man with no head
> has a packet of chocolate and a souvenir of Tripoli.

Hamish Henderson (1919-2002), once referred to as the most important Scottish poet since Robert Burns, saw active service as an Intelligence Officer in North Africa and Italy. Henderson's time in the desert inspired his *Elegies for the Dead in Cyrenaica*. First published in 1948, he described them as "poems of passive suffering… of stoicism". Like others who served in the desert, Henderson highlights the unity of soldiery. He never sees Germans as the enemy, preferring to single out individuals who have been forced by circumstances to confront each other, with the Sahara as the common enemy. In the first elegy, he writes:

There are many dead in the brutish desert,
who lie uneasy
among the scrub in this landscape of the half-wit
stunted ill-will. For the dead land is insatiate
and necrophilious. The sand is blowing about still.
Many who for various reasons, or because
of mere unanswerable compulsion, came here...
And sleep now. Sleep here the sleep of the dust.

In April 1945 Henderson was personally responsible for accepting the surrender of Italy from Marshal Graziani. He kept the signed order in his pocket until the day he died in 2002, 57 years after the war's end.

While the desert inspired many poets, journalists who wrote about the war did so with more immediacy, reflecting deadlines imposed on them by distant editors. Some of the more famous American names who reported from North Africa included Walter Cronkite, the *New Yorker's* A. J. Leibling, Don Whitehead and Ernie Pyle, who wrote for Scripps-Howard Newspapers. One of the most popular American reporters of his day, Pyle's column was syndicated in more than 300 newspapers in the US. His personal, even folksy, writing style and his tendency to see the war through the eyes of the ordinary soldier made his readers feel personally involved in the war in North Africa. Pyle's reports, often filled with informal observations and filed from the front line, provided details that Americans at home came to rely on for a sense of what was happening. A great supporter of the common soldier, Pyle's reputation among the troops was enhanced when his calls for "fight pay" led to Congress passing a bill that increased each American combat troop's salary by $10 a month.

In January 1943, while with American forces at Biskra, Algeria—but specifically not mentioning this in line with wartime censorship rules—Pyle offered a typically chatty description of the Saharan scenery:

The only way I can picture it for you is to suggest that you try to visualise some flat endless space in the desert of our own Southwest, with purple mountains in the distance and sand everywhere. Put an oasis of date palms down upon it, so big it would take an hour to walk from one end to the other... it does rain here, but very seldom. Soldiers who have lived knee-deep in the perpetual winter mud of the coastal belt call this the best place in Africa to be.

Ernie Pyle was awarded the Pulitzer Prize in 1944 for distinguished war correspondence. He was killed the next April, covering the war in the Pacific.

DESERT WARFARE

Of the many British journalists who covered the war, Alan Moorehead, with the *Daily Express*, and Alexander Clifford, with the *Daily Mail*, were among the best known. In *The Conquest of North Africa: 1940-1943*, Clifford writes about the hit and run tactics of the "Jock Columns", so-called after their originator, Brigadier Jock Campbell. Understanding the desert was all, as Clifford says: "The British commanders dug right down to the fundamental principle of the desert, to the rule that everyone up there sooner or later comes to recognize: use the desert, make the desert help you, play the desert's game."

The Jock Columns were small, self-sufficient vehicle patrols that would spring up seemingly from nowhere to harass German forces when they were least expecting it. Clifford goes on to say, "This was true desert warfare—something that could never be done in a country like France or England or the jungles of Malaya. It was making a friend of the desert, this taking advantage of every opportunity this peculiar battle-field offered... There was a German report found near Tobruk, written by a senior officer, which said that the British had forgotten more about patrolling than the Germans had ever learned."

These lessons were learnt in the decade before the start of the war by that assortment of desert-lovers who explored the Sahara, Ralph Bagnold foremost among them. While Bagnold was on his way to East Africa his ship was forced to stop in Egypt for repairs, so he went to Cairo to visit old friends. While there he was asked as the best-known exponent of desert driving whether he could form a specialist desert reconnaissance unit. The time he spent "messing about" in the desert was suddenly an asset. In double-time Bagnold created what was the Long Range Desert Group, or LRDG: its unofficial motto was *Non Vi Sed Arte*, Not by Strength but by Guile.

A combination of disparate factors, including Bagnold's knowledge of sand and cars and his love of adventure, went to make the LRDG the

Men of the LRDG on patrol

valuable force it became. Sending small units hundreds of miles behind enemy lines, it carried out invaluable intelligence operations, typically engaging the enemy only when forced to, if spotted or attacked. Writing in his *African Trilogy*, Moorehead describes them as "a collection of young men of the commando type. They were volunteers and trained men. They had their headquarters in the caves of Siwa Oasis and from there they used to set out on incredible journeys many hundreds of miles inside enemy territory. Their safety was the vastness of the desert. They struck unexpectedly by night and got away."

Winston Churchill, writing in his own history of the Second World War, spoke admiringly of the LRDG, noting in particular a detour British forces took around the Mareth Line, French-built fortifications in southern Tunisia that were supposed to keep the Italians out, but which they and the Germans actually used against the British. As Churchill explains, "The route had formerly been pronounced by the French as impossible for vehicles, but it had been reconnoitred in January by the Long Range Desert Group and declared feasible if difficult. Here was not the least valuable of the many services rendered throughout the African campaign by this hardy and highly mobile reconnaissance unit."

Inspired by the LRDG, David Stirling of the Scots Guards formed and commanded the Special Air Service, or SAS, which was the attacking counterpart to the LRDG's intelligence gathering. The importance of SAS activity in the Sahara was twofold: first, raids carried out behind enemy lines had an enormous impact on morale among the Allies; and second, the attacks were a tremendous nuisance to Axis forces. In the course of one raid, in January 1943, Stirling was captured by the Germans and after four escape attempts was sent to the infamous Colditz Castle.

An entry in General Rommel's diary clearly shows his delight at Stirling's capture, as he wrote: "Insufficiently guarded, he managed to escape and made his way to some Arabs, to whom he offered a reward if they would get him back to the British lines. But his bid must have been too small, for the Arabs, with their usual eye for business, offered him to us for eleven pounds of tea—a bargain which we soon clinched. Thus the British lost the very able and adaptable commander of the desert group which had caused us more damage than any other British unit of equal strength."

Another early member of the SAS was the some-time diplomat, Fitzroy Maclean. A close friend of Stirling, he was once rendered unconscious after a car-crash caused by Stirling's reckless driving. After recovering he joked that "Stirling's driving was the most dangerous thing in World War Two!" The many dramas in Maclean's early life, as recounted in his memoir *Eastern Approaches*, may give the impression that one is reading fiction, but while his adventures were real enough, there has been speculation that he was the inspiration for James Bond. Such a connection is not wholly unlikely as Ian Fleming and Maclean were friends, and after his exploits in North Africa, Maclean was sent to Persia and Yugoslavia on a number of secret missions.

If short on philosophical depth, Maclean's account is big on excitement. He recalls, for instance, a raid on an Italian fort in the desert behind enemy lines, after which German aircraft were harrying his force. Maclean explains the situation coolly: "We were separated from our base by eight hundred miles of waterless desert, dotted with enemy outposts and patrols, now all on the look out for us. We had lost several of our trucks, some of our food and a good deal of our ammunition. The enemy knew, within a few hundred yards, where we were… It was a nasty drive."

The war in the desert also inspired a slew of fictional accounts, including the Boys' Own adventures in *Biggles Sweeps the Desert*. Captain John's hero, who featured in nearly a hundred titles from 1932 until the author's death, began his career during the First World War but is apparently young enough to return to "do his bit" in the Second.

Written in a breathless style suited to its largely adolescent readership, Biggles sets the scene:

> "All right, you fellows," he said at last. "Let's get down to business. No doubt you are all wondering why the dickens we have come to a sunbaked, out-of-the-way spot like this, and I congratulate you on your restraint for not asking questions while we were on our way. My orders were definite. I was not allowed to tell anyone our destination until we were installed at Salima Oasis, which, for your information, is the name of this particular clump of long-necked cabbages that in this part of the world pass for trees. Even now all I can tell you about our position is that it is somewhere near the junction of the Sudan, Libya, and French Equatorial Africa." Biggles broke off to sip his coffee.

In slightly more measured tones, Ondaatje's fictional account of pre-war "desert Europeans" tells much of its story in flashbacks recalled by Almásy, the English patient of the title, as he is being nursed after a plane crash in the desert. Of Bagnold the fictional Almásy says, "We forgave Bagnold everything for the way he wrote about dunes. 'The grooves and the corrugated sand resemble the hollow of the roof of a dog's mouth.' That was Bagnold, a man who would put his inquiring hand into the jaws of a dog."

Like Bagnold, in real life Almásy's intimate knowledge of the desert led him to work for the war effort. As a Hungarian this meant working for Germans, although not apparently unwillingly. At the start of the war Germany had limited intelligence about the Sahara, but as the conflict progressed, and their forces pushed east, German high command needed more intelligence about British intentions. Almásy was given the task of taking German spies across the Sahara to the Nile, from where they travelled to Cairo, relaying information back to Rommel in the desert. Codenamed Operation Salaam, the story is retold in Ken Follett's novel *The Key to Rebecca*. For successfully carrying out his mission, Almásy was awarded the Iron Cross and promoted to the rank of a Luftwaffe major. On his death in 1951, Almásy's obituary in the *Geographical Journal*, written by George Murray, concludes, "On his desert record and on his war record, the judgement can be safely passed: 'A Nazi but a sportsman'."

After the Axis retreat across the Mediterranean, combat actions in the Sahara ceased. Although the war resulted in untold loss of life on all sides, including local civilians caught up in the terrible drama, once hostilities concluded life in the Sahara returned more or less to the pre-war status quo, with France and Britain still the region's major powers. Only Italian Libya moved quickly towards independence, which it attained in 1951 at the behest of the recently founded United Nations. For the other Saharan nations, foreign rule remained, for now, the norm.

Chapter Ten

HEAVEN AND HELL

INDEPENDENCE AND SINCE

As one of the world's best-known franchises, it should come as no surprise that there is a branch of al-Qaeda active in the Sahara. The actual size of al-Qaeda in the Maghreb, or AQIM, is unknown but it is clear that certain criminal groups with no connection to al-Qaeda happily claim to operate in their name; the region's governments are likewise delighted to proclaim that local disturbances are actually the work of an international terror network, especially when this is untrue. Al-Qaeda is not the first terrorist organization to find the isolation of the Sahara ideal for setting up and running training camps—Colonel Gaddafi once welcomed the Irish Republican Army and other such groups to Libya.

Against the backdrop of what is customarily known as the War on Terror, al-Qaeda also operates in the Saharan political environment about which the West is broadly ignorant. Certain Saharan regimes are able to capitalize on this disconnect to secure funding that allows them to crack down not only on al-Qaeda but also on innocent domestic groups that have genuine grievances about abundant levels of corruption, or the lack of representation and absence of investment in desert communities. The seeds for such problems were sowed when independence came to the Sahara.

Despite the fact that the strongest, or at least longest, resistance to the European invasions in the nineteenth and twentieth centuries came from the desert inhabitants, nationalist movements only really flourished in the region's cities. The drive towards independence was hence not so acute in the desert, where people always lived somewhat independent of the outside world. When, in the decades after the Second World War, those European nations that in one form or another controlled Saharan territory decided to leave, they tended to do so without any consultation with their Saharan subjects. Since independence the political experience of the region has been a mixed lot, with border disputes, coups and wars marking long periods of turmoil. At the same time, although certain regional tensions persist hostilities forecast by the jeremiads have usually failed to break out.

As mentioned in the last chapter, the last Saharan nation to be colonized, Libya, was the first to gain independence. This was followed by independence for Morocco, Sudan, Tunisia, and self-government for Egypt, in 1956; Chad, Mali, Mauritania and Niger in 1960; Algeria in 1962; and almost for Western Sahara in 1975 when Spain unilaterally declared it was giving up all claims to the region and leaving with almost immediate effect.

Libya's destiny was made clear through a 1949 declaration by the nascent United Nations, which stated that the country must be fully independent within three years. Just 25 months later—in spite of an attempt on the part of the Soviet Union to secure a mandate over the country—on 24 December 1951 Libya declared its independence as a constitutional and hereditary monarchy with Idris as king, becoming in the process the first country to gain independence through the United Nations. Maintaining the ancient administrative division of the country into the provinces of Cyrenaica, Tripolitania and Fezzan allowed for greater provincial autonomy, which suited the Saharan Fezzanis perfectly.

Under King Idris, amicable relations between Libya and the West were the norm, with first Britain and then the United States signing agreements allowing them to have military bases there, as well as using certain demarcated zones in the Sahara as firing ranges. In return, Libya received economic and military aid from the UK and the USA. Later, after the discovery of significant oil deposits in the Libyan Sahara, the balance of power changed somewhat, with Libya now viewing itself as less of a third-world nation and more on a par with the economically developed western powers. Yet in spite of its becoming rich, alienation among the people was widespread, especially for those living in the desert where the oil—and later gas—was being extracted, while the locals saw even fewer benefits than most people living in the towns and cities of the Mediterranean littoral.

Since the 1969 military coup by a group including a young Captain Muammar al-Gaddafi, the lot of Saharan Libyans has not seen great improvement. This lack of progress contrasts with Gaddafi's somewhat theatrical insistence on hosting meetings in a tent, which is meant to remind his guests—as if they would ever be allowed to forget—that he was born of humble Arab-Berber stock in a tent in the desert outside Sirte.

One of the threats to his power that Gaddafi most feared was that from the desert-rooted Sanussi, of which King Idris was once the head, and which had previously fought against both Italian and British rule in the Libyan and Egyptian Sahara until after the First World War. Seeing the Sanussi as a potential unifying force against his authority, especially in their Fezzan heartland, Gaddafi not only tried to write out of history the vital role they played in the struggle for independence but also destroyed the shrine and tomb of the movement's founder in the otherwise unimportant Berber oasis of Jaghbub, near the border with Egypt.

Although Egypt became an independent kingdom in 1922 in a declaration made by British rather than Egyptian authorities, it was really only after the "Free Officers" movement overthrew King Farouk in 1952 and declared a republic the next year that it became, more or less, the master of its domain, with Britain holding onto the Canal Zone until after the Suez Crisis of 1956. Throughout this period the Egyptian Sahara was spared the convulsions that affected the cities, and the urban elites responsible for pushing independence had little or no interest in the country's desert dwellers: from the other side, the feeling was mutual. For both Egypt and the Sudan the Nile will always be the main artery of power and influence, and the further one travels west, away from its banks, the easier it is for politicians in the capitals to ignore the Saharans, as long as they remain nominally obedient.

Independence was granted to Sudan on 1 January 1956 under the terms of a joint British Egyptian treaty. The year before, a civil war broke out between the Arab-orientated Muslim north and the African-looking, Animist and Christian south of the country, a fault line which has remained absolute since independence. Recognizing this division, a bold attempt to bring a halt to the seemingly never-ending civil war meant holding a referendum, in January 2011, which, depending on the results, allows the country to be divided in two. While a majority of southerners are certain to vote for secession, a peaceful division of the country is a far less likely outcome. Saharan portions of the Sudan have not been spared in this conflict.

The Islamist government in Sudan's capital has long attempted to enforce a vision of national unity across the country. However, Sudan, at the time of writing Africa's largest country, is also one of the continent's least homogeneous nations. Often employing proxy militias to carry out its mission, the government has presided over unrestricted violence, most infamously by the Janjaweed in Darfur, which has resulted in the mass rape, murder and dislocation of its own generally unarmed and innocent citizenry. Since 2003, when the then American Secretary of State Colin Powell referred to the Darfur conflict as a genocide, an estimated 400,000 have been killed in the region, with another two and a half million displaced. Many of these have fled into neighbouring Chad, which has resulted in increased tension between its capital N'Djamena and Khartoum. Those Saharan regions of Chad into which the Sudanese have flooded were barely able to support the existing population, let alone the influx of foreign refugees.

Two months after Sudanese independence, following negotiations between French authorities and Sultan Mohammed V, Morocco too became fully sovereign, with the vast majority of Spanish-controlled territory likewise being handed back in April of the same year. Morocco had become a French protectorate in 1912, after the Treaty of Fez, which also granted Spain control over the country's northern Rif and southern Saharan regions. The French and Spanish were most interested in the Atlantic and Mediterranean coastal regions, however, the remoter corners of the Sahara remaining a largely autonomous Berber-controlled zone. Since independence Moroccan troops have pushed into the Sahara beyond their borders—as the international community recognizes them—on two important occasions. The first of these wars lasted a matter of months; the second conflict rumbles on more than 35 years later.

In 1963, after a number of border skirmishes, Moroccan forces invaded Algeria, focusing on the oasis towns and areas around Tindouf and Figuig, thus marking the start of what became known as the Sand War. Pressing a spurious claim to an imagined Greater Morocco—an argument which has also been employed in the ongoing dispute over Western Sahara—Moroccan troops hoped to secure their land claims swiftly and without much opposition. They had not, however, reckoned on spirited resistance from the militarily capable Algerian army. After initially being forced into a stalemate, the Moroccans were soon forced back across the border, at which time they renounced all further claims to the area. Even so, the border between Morocco and Algeria remains closed to all traffic, and tensions, sometimes fierce, clearly still exist between the neighbours.

Although Morocco has dropped claims to Tindouf, the town and surrounding area remains important in Morocco's ongoing territorial dispute because Tindouf is a major centre of operations for the Popular Front for the Liberation of Saguia el-Hamra and Rio de Oro, better known by its Spanish acronym, Polisario, the most prominent organization that continues to press for independence for the Western Sahara.

In 1975, when Spain announced it was going to relinquish control of what was Spanish Sahara, and furthermore was going to do so in something of a hurry, Spanish authorities promised a referendum on the colony's future before reneging on this decision and signing a tri-partite agreement with Morocco and Mauritania. In this agreement Spain ignored the wishes of the local population by handing the territory—which by the fact of their withdrawal would appear not to be in their gift in the first place—to Morocco and Mauritania, both countries claiming certain historical ties to the region.

Simultaneously, the Hague-based International Court of Justice sent a mission to Western Sahara to investigate the situation. Though they accepted that Morocco and Mauritania had enjoyed historical links to the area, these were not sufficiently strong to overrule the wishes of the local people. Not only did the indigenous Sahrawis have the right to self-determination, but they had also made it absolutely clear that they wanted nothing less than independence. The Moroccan response was to send troops into Western Sahara, followed a few days later by some 350,000 civilians in what they called the Green March. This marked the start of a lengthy, wholly unlawful colonization of Western Sahara with the long-term goal of skewing the local population figures so that in any future referendum the "local" population would overwhelmingly vote in favour of Morocco.

Mauritania abandoned its claims to a portion of the Western Sahara in 1979, after a successful military campaign by the Polisario. Those areas from which Mauritanian forces withdrew were soon filled by Moroccan troops. Today most aid workers and archaeologists who wish to gain access to the unoccupied portion of the Western Sahara tend to do so via Tindouf.

Since the start of the conflict, Algeria has sided with the Sahrawis against the Kingdom of Morocco. One aspect of this support, and in spite of Moroccan protests, comes in the form of granting the Polisario the right to operate freely from Tindouf. Nervous as the Algerians are of their neighbour becoming too powerful in the region, they view the continuing nuisance caused to Morocco by the Polisario as a useful counterbalance.

Evidence of post-independence wars littering the desert

An uneasy cease-fire has been in place between Polisario and Morocco since 1991, which in part has held because of the presence of a 2000 mile-long earthwork *berm*, or earthen-work wall, illegally built and mined by the Moroccans. Morocco had learnt the efficacy of such defences when they employed the same tactics against Algeria in the Sand War. Although this Moroccan Wall, which is said to be patrolled by a greater number of troops than there are Sahrawi people, is maintained at great cost to Morocco's economy, it also encompasses everything of worth in Western Sahara, not least the mines that have made Morocco the world's number one exporter of phosphates. The area to the east of the wall covers only one third of the country's full territorial mass. This area, unoccupied Western Sahara, is a very thinly populated, flat and largely featureless, resource-free desert. Had there been anything of worth there, one can be sure that someone else would have laid claim to it by now.

THE FRENCH LEGACY

The antithesis of the relatively peaceful withdrawal of European nations from their Saharan colonies, dependencies and protectorates was the

French departure from Algeria and the story of this long and bloody war continues to haunt its politics today. When Algeria gained its independence from France in 1962, it did so only after an eight-year internecine war that was remarkable for its vicious and fratricidal nature. If the worst excesses of violence occurred primarily in the cities in the country's north, in the Sahara itself there was more violence after independence during a power struggle in the mid-1960s that saw old allies turn on one another, with the Front of Socialist Forces trying, unsuccessfully, to overthrow the regime of President Ben Bella.

Mass unemployment and a decline in energy prices in the mid-1980s saw a significant rise in support for Algerian Islamist parties, including the founding of the Islamic Salvation Front (FIS) in 1989. Nationwide elections held in December 1991 gave the FIS clear majorities in virtually half of the country's electoral districts. In January the panicked government declared the elections null and void and dissolved parliament. The Algerian civil war that lasted for the rest of the decade displayed gruesome echoes of the war of independence, with shocking massacres being committed by both pro-government and Islamist factions throughout the country. Approximately 100,000 Algerians were killed before the decade's end, when Abdelaziz Bouteflika was elected president. The official returns showed him receiving seventy per cent of votes cast, in spite of all other candidates pulling out in advance of the election because of claims of widespread fraud.

Tunisia was also forced to fight the French for independence, and although a nationalist movement had been active for decades, the final rush to independence, complete with civil disturbance, was a relatively short two-year affair, which was never stricken with the levels of violence that characterized Algeria's struggle. The result was warmer post-independence relations with France, as well as enhanced economic growth in Tunisia. Both before and after independence, the limited population that call the Tunisian Sahara home had little or no influence on national politics. In recent years the growth in adventure-style tourism has seen a somewhat larger degree of economic independence for those living in the Saharan south.

The new government in Chad found itself in a situation similar to that of Sudan in 1956, with the country exhibiting a *de facto* division between a largely Muslim Saharan north and a Christian-Animist Sahelian south. Chad's first president, François Tombalbaye, a southerner, soon betrayed his own prejudice against the north with a series of laws that led directly to the outbreak of a civil war in 1965, billed as pitting the loyalist south against a fractious Saharan north.

The government first called upon French troops to help them fight against the well-organized forces of the National Liberation Front of Chad (FROLINAT), which sought to end the southern dominance of the country. Meeting with limited success against FROLINAT, Tombalbaye next allied himself with the Libyan regime of Colonel Gaddafi. Although this initially meant greater success against the rebels, in 1975 Tombalbaye was ousted in a coup, not that his removal from power by any means marked an end to the war.

By the decade's end, any central authority in Chad had completely disappeared between a dozen independent factions. A 1981 declaration that Chad and Libya would work towards full unification spread anger and despondency in equal measure, even if it also meant a temporary reconciliation between certain rival factions who were able to push Libyan forces back through Bornu and Ennedi, into the far north of the country, where they halted their retreat in the Aouzou Strip, a desolate but mineral-rich band of land that runs through the Tibesti Mountains along the length of the Chadian-Libyan border. In early 1987 the last phase of the war took place. It became known as the Toyota War after the French-supplied hundreds of pick-up trucks to the Chadians, which they used to great effect both for swift mobility of military personnel and as carriers for anti-tank missiles. In spite of a ceasefire agreed later in the year, Libyan forces continued to occupy the Aouzou Strip until 1994.

Since then, relations between Chad and Libya have steadily improved. However, since 2005 Chad has instead found itself at war with its eastern neighbour. Chad declared that a state of war existed with Sudan because of that country's raids into its territory. The root of this conflict is closely linked to the situation in Darfur, which has driven hundreds of thousands of Sudanese refugees into Chad since 2003.

As part of French West Africa, Niger was controlled during the colonial period from Dakar, more than 1000 miles away. In the fifty years since independence the country has endured a depressingly predictable cycle of corruption and economic mismanagement and one coup after another. At the time of writing, the last coup, in February 2010, saw the establishment of yet another military junta, which like military dictatorships the world over has chosen to adopt a most populist-sounding moniker: Supreme Council for the Restoration of Democracy. Whether it lives up to this title remains to be seen.

The discovery of oil in the Ténéré desert should have brought some fringe benefits to the country's large Saharan north: it did not. In response to the almost total lack of development in the north and inequitable treatment of the country's significant Tuareg population, an armed anti-government insurgency has developed. Fighting a guerrilla war, including the planting of large numbers of land mines, the Mouvement des Nigeriens pour la Justice (MNJ) has been effective in terms of retarding foreign oil and gas investment and almost completely halting Saharan tourism in the country.

Mali declared its independence of the Mali Federation in August 1960. Since then, in common with the model seen in Niger, the country has been unable to demonstrate any meaningful development through a combination of economic woes, military coups and periodic debilitating droughts that have driven people out of both the desert and the Sahel.

When Mauritania gained independence, it is estimated that ninety per cent of the population was nomadic, which made impossible the sort of centralized, one-party control sought by the authoritarian President Moktar Ould Daddah. Daddah's attempts to impose his will on the country, moving it away from traditional lifestyles, created social tensions that continued even after he was ousted from power in a bloodless coup in 1978. The greater tension, however, was that of colour and culture that seems to afflict the whole of the Sahara, here dividing southern-black and northern-Moorish Mauritanians, with African-Arab prejudices exploited by both sides.

Across the Saharan south, Chad, Niger, Mali and Mauritania all became independent of France in 1960. During their respective periods of colonial rule, none of these countries was encouraged to look to a future of self-rule, with the result that none of them was ready for the challenges to come. The almost indecent haste with which France retreated meant that the odds were very much against any of these newly independent states becoming viable democracies, at least in the short term. For the Saharan parts of these countries, the challenges were even greater, one might argue insurmountable. As if it were not bad enough that local populations have to live in such a climate without basic amenities like a reliable source of water, the fact that central government only sheds its indifference to their plight when such resources as oil and gas are discovered adds insult to injury. Regrettably, those benefits that one might expect from a country discovering large energy supplies have too often proved to be a curse. Yet this is not to say that the situation is static.

With widespread concerns about future oil and gas supplies, the Sahara is already receiving significant attention from interested parties keen to find suitable sites for the generation of alternative energy. Plans for harnessing solar energy are well advanced, with an estimate by one European consortium, Desertec, suggesting that an area of 6000 square miles of solar panels—roughly the size of Connecticut—would be sufficient to supply the energy needs of both North Africa and Europe. Desertec also reckons that 35,000 square miles of solar panels, roughly one per cent of the Sahara's surface, could produce the same energy as all power plants operating around the world today, not that plans are in place for such an scheme. Although in the relatively early stages of development, even the most optimistic proponents of such grand schemes recognize that the biggest obstacle to their success is the necessity of cross-border cooperation, especially between nations that are hardly on the best of terms, Morocco and Algeria being the most obvious example. While the power of the sun is the Sahara's most obvious and readily accessed asset, plans have also been drawn up for the development of large-scale wind farms, primarily in western parts of the desert but also off the coast of Morocco and Western Sahara.

Overall, since independence regional experiments in democracy have not been successful. A dreary succession of civil and regional wars has taken the place of dialogue, corruption has supplanted accountability and dictators, whether suited or uniformed, use their nations' wealth, police forces, security apparatus and bribery to ensure re-election with nothing less than 95 per cent of the popular vote, which they do without any apparent shame or embarrassment.

It is hardly surprising that groups such as al-Qaeda in the Maghreb have managed to obtain a foothold in parts of the region, namely southern Algeria, Mali and Niger. Even less surprising is the willingness of regional governments to seize upon the presence of al-Qaeda to brand any of their own understandably fractious citizens as potential terrorists. It is,

Solar potential

after all, far easier to secure foreign financial assistance in the War on Terror than work to improve the lot of those who are not going to vote for a corrupt regime.

Part Four

IMAGINATION

Leopold Carl Müller, *The Caravan*, 1876

Chapter Eleven

CLASSICAL INSPIRATION

"I am getting confused in my mind between these various goddesses.
Are they all the same person?
Originally. She is older than all the gods. Perhaps her most archaic form
is the Goddess Libya."

"A Conversation at Paphos", imagined by Robert Graves in *The White Goddess*

However in thrall the western cultural landscape is to the mythological and literary imprint of ancient Greece and Rome, their myths did not spring into existence fully formed. Both civilizations relied on earlier, often non-European sources of inspiration. They frequently borrowed from foreign mythologies, adapting them to fit their worldview, and Egypt was the non-native source from which they borrowed most extensively. The Greeks in particular knew something of Egypt before they established close ties with the country, their earliest impression being that it was the archetype of a distant and mysterious place: the land of the Pharaohs and half-known things, where myth and reality lived side-by-side and indistinguishable from one another.

Evidence that Greece had an interest in lands outside its borders can be found in the story of how Africans came to have black skin. Greek mythology has it that the god Apollo, who is also the sun god Helios, drove his fiery chariot and four horses through the sky from the east to the west each day. One evening, either to impress his sisters or because friends had teasingly doubted his paternity, his son Phaeton pleaded to be allowed to ride the chariot. Apollo reluctantly acceded to his son's request but the horses sensed an inexperienced driver and bolted. As they veered from their usual course, the sun-chariot came too close to the earth as it passed Africa, burning everything in its path, which is why its inhabitants have black skin.

This story retained its appeal and the ancient Roman poet Ovid used it in his *Metamorphoses*. "The Aethiopes then turned black, so men believe, as heat summoned their blood too near the skin. Then was Libya's dusty desert formed, all water scorched away." The scorching was so severe that the Sahara remained evermore a barren desert, and the Africans black.

Egypt was important enough for the Greeks that Herodotus devoted the whole of Book Two of his *Histories* to it. By the time the *Histories* were written, between the 450s and the 420s, Herodotus' readers believed Egypt to be a land filled with sacred mysteries, ancient traditions and knowledge that was as close as possible to primordial. In contrast to the eighth century BCE of Homer, when myths were understood to be straightforward narratives without consideration for their accuracy, in Herodotus' time they came to be seen as something almost legendary, rather than the literal truth. To convey a sense of this ancient knowledge, it was still important for Herodotus, Cicero's "father of history", to write about meeting Egyptian priests when he was there, to show that he was learning about the world before recorded Greek history.

Although a proud Greek, Herodotus was happy to note the importance of these Egyptian guardians of tradition, seeing them as having access to an unbroken succession of ancient texts, which he frankly admits his countrymen did not. Despite Plutarch calling him the "father of lies", Herodotus is clearly telling the truth when he acknowledges the Egyptian origin of many Greek gods, saying, "As for the stories told by the Egyptians, let whoever finds them credible use them." The characteristics of deities are often altered but their Egyptian roots are clear, as with Osiris, who became Dionysus, and Apollo who replaced Horus.

After the full-scale invasion and absorption of Egypt into the Greek Empire under Alexander the Great and his successors more than a century after Herodotus' visit, the country was substantially, although never absolutely, Hellenized. Early in his career Alexander realized that he could not ignore Persian-ruled Egypt before pursuing conquests in the east. He also understood that to leave a secure Egypt he would have to be accepted by the local priests. Although it was billed as a fight to expel the Persians, Alexander's motives in invading Egypt were entirely self-interested. An important part of his strategy was his consultation with the Oracle of Zeus-Ammon. If he gained approval for his conquest of Egypt from the Oracle he would have the priestly class on side.

Alexander's boyhood education—Aristotle was one of his tutors—convinced him that when his empire grew he would pursue a system of syncretism, the unification and reconciliation of different religious beliefs into one new system. For this reason Alexander had to be recognized as an incarnation of Ammon. Upon his arrival at Siwa he was duly greeted as "son of Zeus", thus receiving confirmation of his divine antecedents and a blessing for his future conquests.

Although it grew up along the Nile, as previously noted, Egyptian civilization relied on the Sahara for much of its religious symbolism. Egyptians located the land of the dead in the desert, the land of shadows, which was central to Egyptian theology. The father of Egyptology, Professor Flinders Petrie, wrote about the "sacred league", a priestly union between Libya and the Greek mainland that dated back as far as the third millennium BCE, with the sacred Ammon oak cared for by the Garamantes. Robert Graves in his *White Goddess*, drawing on Petrie, describes Zeus-Ammon as "a sort of Heracles with a ram's head akin to ram-headed Osiris, and to Amen-Ra the ram-headed sun-god of Egyptian Thebes from where Herodotus says that the black doves flew to Ammon and Dodona."

Religious syncretism, by combining or altering existing features, also allowed for the re-creation of Egyptian gods as new Hellenic deities, for instance combining Ammon-Ra, with his/her (Ammon was thought to be a hermaphrodite at this time) oracle at Siwa to create the most senior deity, god of the universe, heaven, earth and most importantly empire. Any perceived foreignness around this new god was regarded favourably as an indication of its ancient roots, only enhancing the god's authenticity and reputation.

In his account of the abortive attempt of Cambyses to conquer Ammon, Herodotus refers to the Islands of the Blessed, a name which occurs elsewhere as the resting place of heroes and notable mortals, or paradise. Also known as the Fortunate Isles, the Islands of the Blessed are in Plato's *Gorgias* a place where "every man who has passed a just and holy life departs after his decease to the Isles of the Blest, and dwells in all happiness apart (safe) from ill."

Plutarch, in his life of the Roman statesman Quintus Sertorius, describes the climate there as one where, "the air was never extreme, which for rain had a little silver dew, which of itself and without labour, bore all pleasant fruits to their happy dwellers, till it seemed to him that these could be no other than the Fortunate Islands, the Elysian Fields." Commonly located by later writers in the furthest western ocean, possibly meaning the Canary Isles, Herodotus unequivocally places them in the Sahara, identifying the isles as oases. Complementing the Egyptian view of the desert as the Land of the Dead, it makes sense to imagine the oases as idyllic places of rest and reward.

Of all the gods in the Egyptian pantheon, those who became best known in a largely unchanged form were Osiris and his sister-wife, Isis. Even though the story of Osiris' murder and dismemberment at the hands of his brother Set, and his reincarnation, is one of the most important of all Egyptian religious stories, Egyptian texts are fragmentary and we rely on Greek texts to tell the story in full. Set's actions were often destructive, driven by his tempestuous mood and malevolent power, which is why early Egyptians felt most comfortable when they thought he was confined to his realm of desert wilderness. In an allusion to the desert, one of the *Pyramid Texts* states that Set killed his brother in "a quiet place".

Later retellings, however, such as Diodorus Siculus in the first century BCE and Plutarch in the first century CE, change important details of the story. For instance, Diodorus has Osiris murdered in a public place before witnesses by "his brother Typhon (the Greek name for Set)". In a more elaborate scheme, Plutarch, again referring to Typhon, claims that Osiris was first locked in a made-to-measure wooden chest, essentially a coffin, which was then filled with molten lead and thrown into the Nile, which carried Osiris to the Mediterranean, where he drowned. Certain later Greek texts place the murder of Osiris during "the night of the great storm". This may explain why since Herodotus, Set was identified as Typhon, son of Gaea and, according to Hesiod, the god of storm winds.

Set, as Lord of the Oases and protector of their vines, remained prominent through the entirety of the Greco-Roman period of Saharan history. Apart from deadly heat, Set was also associated with such aspects of the desert as flash floods and sandstorms. By the Greco-Roman period he was more likely to be reviled than worshipped, hated for rebelling against the gods and trying to kill Zeus. The name Set-Typhon was invoked by both Greeks and Romans to destroy enemies, as Set had destroyed his brother, or else to separate lovers as Set did with Isis and Osiris.

Although the myth of Osiris was well established among the Greeks, it was only after the Roman Empire settled in Egypt that it gained an even wider audience. *The Metamorphoses of Apuleius*, or *The Golden Ass*, by the Roman writer Lucius Apuleius, is the only full-length Latin novel to have survived intact and is known as the world's first novel. It tells the story of a sorcerer's apprentice, Lucius of Madaurus, who is turned into a donkey by a witch before being subjected to a number of humiliating misadventures. Isis eventually restores Lucius to his human form and, to offer thanks, Lucius becomes a priest of Osiris. As the ruler of the underworld, Osiris is indelibly linked to the Sahara but Osiris' story spread beyond the desert and even classical Europe. Beginning with the theological necessity of the death of Osiris, which allowed for his resurrection and subsequent rule over the dead, one does not have to think too hard to imagine this myth in a Christian setting.

As Osiris' sister and consort, Isis also enjoyed a cult following in Rome, sometimes accompanied by other Egyptian figures such as young Harpocrates, reinvented with wings as Eros, or Anubis, the dog-headed god who helped Isis to search for Osiris' body parts. It is the Roman cult of Isis that Mozart colourfully portrays in *The Magic Flute*, including the following prayer offered to the gods in Act Two:

> O Isis and Osiris, give
> The spirit of wisdom to the new couple!
> May that which guides the wanderer's steps,
> Strengthen them with patience in danger.

Egyptian mythology happily allowed for therianthropic gods, combining human and animal body parts. This included portrayals of souls as human-headed birds, living as ghosts, able to fly and enjoy such offerings that relations would leave at their tombs. For the Greeks, such beings were exclusively female. Retaining their wings and claws, they renamed them harpies and portrayed them as malevolent spirits responsible for punishing evil-doers, what Robert Graves in *The Greek Myths* refers to as "fair-haired and swift-winged daughters of Thaumas by the Ocean nymph Electra, who snatch up criminals for punishment."

According to the tradition cited by Graves, the Libyan Desert was also home to another fearful creature, the Gorgon Medusa and her sisters, Stheno and Euryale. Indeed, the Hellenes tended to view the whole of ancient Libya, that is the Sahara, as a world of demons and evil, lying as it did beyond the civilizing effect of mainland Greece. The goddess Libya herself, representing the whole of alien North Africa, was said to be a daughter of King Epaphus of Egypt, a son of Zeus, who appeared to Jason of the Argo fame, dressed in goatskins.

RIDDLE OF THE SPHINX

The most famous mythical Egyptian creature adopted and recast by the Greeks is the Sphinx. It is worth mentioning that the Greeks subverted the Egyptian idea of theiranthropes: whereas the Egyptians had animal heads on human bodies, the Greeks, with the exception of the minotaur, had human heads on animal bodies. This animal, whose name is from the Greek meaning "the strangler", was for the Egyptians the result of the union of Gaia, the earth, and Pontus, a sea-god and son of Gaea, whom she produced herself. In the Egyptian tradition the Sphinx represented the divine power of the (male) Pharaoh in the form of a human-headed lion, watching over Egypt in life and death. For the Greeks, the Sphinx was a winged female whose role was to torment the city of Thebes.

In this guise the Sphinx was famous for the riddle she posed to travellers who crossed her path. The most famous version runs: "What being, with only one voice, has sometimes two feet, sometimes three, sometimes four, and is at its weakest when it has the most?" Giving an incorrect answer to the riddle resulted in the Sphinx throttling and eating the unfortunate victim. The story goes that the Sphinx's reign of terror ended when Oedipus arrived at Thebes and guessed the correct answer. In Graves' version of Oedipus' encounter with the Sphinx, he replies, "'Man... because he crawls on all fours as an infant, stands firmly on his two feet in youth, and leans on a staff in his old age.' The mortified Sphinx... dashed herself to pieces in the valley below."

From the neoclassical period in Europe, Sphinx statues became commonplace at the entrance of buildings, freemasons in particular adopting the creature as symbolic of a wise, silent guardian. Like the Greeks and Romans, freemasonry used the antique to claim ancient legitimacy. In the late nineteenth century the Sphinx became a favourite subject of writers and artists looking to portray the darker side of myths of the sexually proscribed and echoing the Biblical story of Adam and Eve, the tree of knowledge and forbidden fruit.

The Sphinx was also a favourite subject of nineteenth-century artists, whose portrayals of the creature changed greatly between the century's start and end, from the literal interpretation of the myth in Jean-Auguste-Dominique Ingres' 1808 *Oedipus and the Sphinx* to Gustave Moreau's sexually charged 1864 painting of the same name. By 1895, in Franz von Stuck's *The Kiss of the Sphinx* it is hard to see anything but the supposed

Ask me no questions…

licentious nature or intent of the Sphinx, the original questioning of wayward travellers being transformed into a nightmarish, lust-filled vampiric embrace.

In the presumably less sexually charged atmosphere of the US Army Military Intelligence Corps, the Sphinx is that unit's regimental insignia, and it was also the cap badge of the now disbanded Gloucestershire Regiment, which adopted the emblem after battling the French in Egypt in 1801. At one point, being attacked from front and rear, the Glorious Glosters were forced to fight back-to-back. They were consequently accorded the unique honour in the British Army of wearing a cap badge on the front and rear of their headgear. It is pleasing to see that, whether conceived in a pre-literate or post-Enlightenment era, the Sahara still manages to give birth to myths, ancient and modern.

Chapter Twelve

POETIC MUSE

"Lesbia, you ask how many kisses of yours
would be enough and more to satisfy me.
As many as the grains of Libyan sand
that lie between hot Jupiter's oracle,
at Ammon, in resin-producing Cyrene,
and old Battiades sacred tomb."

Catullus (c. 84-c. 54 BCE)

The Sahara has been a source of inspiration for poets for as long as they have been exposed to it. What ancient European poets such as Catullus and Lucan knew about the desert was derived from myths and conquests. One of the more memorable of the classical verses based on historical events is by Lucan. In book nine of his *Pharsalia*, he recalls the Saharan meanderings of Cato the Younger and his band of followers during the course of the civil war in Rome when Cato was in opposition to Caesar:

Now near approaching to the burning zone,
To warmer, calmer skies they journeyed on.
...
As forward on the weary way they went,
Panting with drought, and all with labour spent,
Amidst the desert, desolate and dry,
One chanced a little trickling spring to spy.

In *Cato: A Tragedy*, written in 1712 by the poet, playwright, and politician Joseph Addison, Cato remembers his time in the Sahara, asking,

Have you forgotten Libya's burning waste,
Its barren rocks, parch'd earth, and hills of sand,
Its tainted air, and all its broods of poison?

Making use of the famous Roman's life-long struggle against tyranny, Addison's play embraced the theme of opposition to monarchies and government oppression, in favour of republicanism and libertarianism. The play, with its Saharan imagery, proved inspirational to George Washington and other Founding Fathers. So enamoured was Washington of the play that in the midst of the War of Independence he had it performed to inspire the Continental Army, while they were camped at Valley Forge in the winter of 1777.

A similar vein of myth and conquest ran through the verses of later eighteenth- and nineteenth-century western poets, although these also turned for inspiration to the non-Saharan *Alf Layla wa Layla*, or *A Thousand and One Nights*. Largely set in Baghdad and other lands far from the Sahara, the *Arabian Nights*, as they also became known, quickly became the staple reference for anything considered Oriental, including the deserts of North Africa, by otherwise ignorant European poets and writers. First available to European readers in French, by 1713 at least four English editions had been published. In the absence of anything more scholarly, the *Arabian Nights* established itself as a primary source on the East in the western imagination. Peculiarly, it was concurrently read and understood both as a record of the people and places of the region and as a work of fantasy, complete with spirits and sorcery.

A large part of the Sahara's poetic appeal for the non-native writer has been its image of pristine isolation. Depicting it as undisturbed and removed from the pollution of civilization, poets have often imagined that they would find peace there, contemplation supposedly being easier in a wild emptiness than in a city. Lord Byron writes about this desire for solitude in *Childe Harold's Pilgrimage*, exclaiming,

> Oh that the desert were my dwelling place,
> With only one fair spirit for my minster.
> That I might forget the human race,
> And hating no one, love her only.

While the majority of eighteenth- and nineteenth-century poets inspired by the Sahara did not travel there, this did little to dampen their enthusiasm for drawing on typical wilderness tropes, as they understood these in the abstract. These mainly consisted of silence, danger and the almost complete absence of human interference. Given the appeal of deserts as solitary places, it is not surprising that the Romantic poets found the

Sahara a particularly evocative subject. It is worth noting that the "big six", those poets who have for nearly two hundred years been at the core of the Romantic Movement—Blake, Wordsworth, Coleridge, Byron, Shelley and Keats—all allude to the Sahara in their work. Defending his choice of foreign subject matter, Coleridge once said, "A sound promise of genius is the choice of subjects very remote from the private interests and circumstances of the writer himself."

One advantage of the unseen Sahara was that it provided these poets with an imaginative landscape radically different from more domestic settings such as London or the Lake District. Choosing to write about the desert they were also freer to experiment with different poetic forms, working in the alternative metaphorical space provided by the imagined. Shelley's "Ozymandias" remains as popular now as when it was published in 1818; its opening lines are some of the most easily recognized in English verse:

I met a traveller from an antique land
Who said: Two vast and trunkless legs of stone
Stand in the desert.

"Ozymandias" was written in friendly competition with Shelley's fellow poet Horace Smith, both men having to produce a verse with the same title. Smith's version opens with the lines:

In Egypt's sandy silence, all alone,
Stands a gigantic Leg, which far off throws
The only shadow that the Desert knows.

Shelley's version became so popular that Smith renamed his own poem, hoping it might flourish if not in the shadow of Shelley. Unfortunately for Smith, his choice lost something of the power of its original single-word title. "On A Stupendous Leg of Granite, Discovered Standing by Itself in the Deserts of Egypt, with the Inscription Inserted Below" does not exactly trip lightly off the tongue.

A similar composition competition took place in 1818. Taking part in it, Keats wrote to his brothers, "The Wednesday before last [February 4] Shelley, Hunt, and I, wrote each a sonnet on the river Nile." Apart from the common theme, the self-imposed challenge also stipulated that the verses had to be composed in fifteen minutes or less. The results were as impressive as one would expect from such poetic heavyweights. Leigh Hunt produced "A Thought of the Nile", and Shelley and Keats both entitled their poems "To the Nile". Keats included the following evocative reference to the desert beyond the Nile:

> We call thee fruitful, and that very while
> A desert fills our seeing's inward span:
> Nurse of swart nations since the world began,
> Art thou so fruitful?
> ...
> 'Tis ignorance that makes a barren waste
> Of all beyond itself. Thou dost bedew
> Green rushes like our rivers, and dost taste
> The pleasant sunrise.

It was not just English poets who sought to evoke the Sahara. Johann Wolfgang von Goethe published *West-östlicher Diwan*, or *West-East Divan*, in 1819 and an updated version in 1827. *Diwan* is a twelve-book collection of lyrical poetry and Goethe's last major poetic cycle. A lifelong admirer of Middle Eastern cultures, Goethe saw in the East the pre-classical roots of western civilization, including the origins of language and poetry, and his magnum opus as both an exchange of cultural ideas between Occident and Orient and a philosophical or spiritual journey. In *Hegira*, and the 195 poems that follow it, Goethe's intention was to

> Travel with the caravans,
> Trade in musk through burning sands;
> All the coffee trails I'll wander,
> Deserts here to cities yonder.

Described by the French poet Théophile Gautier as a "cool oasis where art rests", Diwan had an enormous impact in Europe and America, inspiring a new decades-long aesthetic of Orientalism.

Nineteenth-century American poets also included the Sahara in their topographical repertoire. In 1842 Longfellow published his collection

Frontispiece to Goethe's *West-East Diwan*

Poems on Slavery, which he described as "so mild that even a Slaveholder might read them without losing his appetite for breakfast." The collection included "The Slave's Dream", the tale of a man taken by slavers from near the River Niger. While sleeping, the slave dreams of his homeland:

> And the Blast of the Desert cried aloud,
> With a voice so wild and free.

While the slave dreams about his desert home, he is released from bondage by death.

> He did not feel the driver's whip,
> Nor the burning heat of day;
> For Death had illumined the Land of Sleep.

Longfellow's 1850 collection *The Seaside and the Fireside* contains his most famous desert-inspired verse, "Sand of the Desert in an Hour-Glass", which includes the lines:

How many weary centuries has it been
About those deserts blown!
How many strange vicissitudes has seen,
How many histories known!...
Before my dreamy eye
Stretches the desert with its shifting sand,
Its unimpeded sky.

From 1874 Longfellow published an enormous 31-volume anthology called *Poems of Places*, with each volume focusing on poetry from or about a different locale. Volume 24 concentrates on Africa, and includes nine poems devoted to the Sahara, including "Song of Slaves in the Desert" by his fellow Fireside Poet, John Greenleaf Whittier, and three poems by the German Ferdinand Freiligrath. Another friend of Longfellow, Freiligrath's Saharan verses—"Mirage", "The Lion's Ride" and the Edgar Allen Poe-esque "The Spectre Caravan"—were inspired, the writer was proud to acknowledge, by Victor Hugo's *Les Orientales*. The last of the three imagines those who have died in the desert coming back from the dead one night, not unreasonably terrifying the traveller-poet and his entourage:

When, behold!—a sudden sandquake,—and atween the earth and moon
Rose a mighty host of shadows, as from out some dim lagoon;
Then our coursers gasped with terror, and a thrill shook every man,
And the cry was "Allah Akbar! 'Tis the Spectre Caravan!"

Like Longfellow, Ralph Waldo Emerson was comfortable drawing on Egyptian mythology, the quizzing Sphinx being a favourite theme as it was for artists of the period. For Emerson, writing in 1841,

The Sphinx is drowsy,
Her wings are furled:

Her ear is heavy,
She broods on the world.

Oscar Wilde's poem "The Sphinx" portrays the creature as "so somnolent, so statuesque!.../Come forth my lovely languorous Sphinx! And put your head upon my knee!" With Ammon as the Sphinx's lover, who "strode across the desert sand," Wilde also imagines the creature of mystery for all who have gazed upon it across the centuries:

And many a wandering caravan of stately negroes silken-shawled,
Crossing the desert, halts appalled before the neck that none can span.
And many a bearded Bedouin draws back his yellow-striped burnous
To gaze upon the Titan thews of him that was your paladin

One final nineteenth-century poem worth mentioning is "The Simoon" by the Englishman Martin Farquhar Tupper. A lyrical poem typical of its time, it refers to the hot, sand-laden winds that regularly sweep the Sahara and Arabia. Evoking their destructive and potentially fatal force, the poem speaks of their victims: "The desert is their grave, the sand their shroud." With these words we are able to make a connection between the nineteenth-century versifiers who imagined the Sahara and those twentieth-century poets who lived and died there.

THE BRUTISH DESERT : WAR POETS
Diametrically opposed to the Romantic Movement, the majority of poets who wrote about the Sahara in the twentieth century experienced the desert directly, often in war and as far from the Romantic worldview as possible. As we have seen, large swathes of the Sahara saw a great deal of the Second World War, and the desert experienced by soldiers was no pure, idealized setting, but an environment sullied by war machines and the burnt and blasted bodies of fallen combatants.

One of the predominant images of the First World War is the mud and dirt of the trenches. In the Saharan poetry from the Second World War the mud may be missing but the dirt is no less real; nor were the desert's open spaces any less lethal than the trenches. As Keith Douglas records in "Landscape with Figures",

> On sand and scrub the dead men wriggle
> in their dowdy clothes. They are mimes
> who express silence and futile aims
> enacting this prone and motionless struggle
> at a queer angle to the scenery.

The most famous of this group, a poetic school of circumstances, Douglas was by temperament a man of action, as he makes clear in his unfinished memoir, *Alamein to Zem Zem*. A soldier who loved soldiering, despite or perhaps because of fighting first-hand, Douglas wrote in his memoir, "To say I thought of the battle of Alamein as an ordeal sounds pompous: but I did think of it as an important test, which I was interested in passing."

Speaking of the war's drama, Douglas remarks, "it is exciting and amazing to see thousands of men, very few of whom have much idea why they are fighting, all enduring hardships, living in an unnatural, dangerous, but not wholly terrible world, having to kill and be killed, and yet at intervals moved by a feeling of comradeship with the men who kill them and whom they kill, because they are enduring and experiencing the same things." The back and forth of the desert war also gave both sides plenty of opportunity to come into contact with, now dead, enemies. Seeing these inevitably forced men to wonder what was the point of the fighting and the dying.

In contrast to Douglas, Sidney Keyes hated the army and the war. By nature a pacifist, Keyes once wrote in a letter home, "I was never bored until I joined the Army; now I am crazy with the utter futility, destructiveness and emptiness of my life, to which I see no end." Sadly for Keyes, the end came swiftly, when he was killed in action in Tunisia in 1943. Dying aged 21, he had been at the front for just two weeks. While his frontline Saharan service was limited, Keyes arrived full of ideas about the desert, which he soon translated after his arrival into a number of moving poems that betray keen awareness of their geography. Echoing Byron, Keyes writes in "The Wilderness",

> The red rock wilderness
> Shall be my dwelling-place...
> The rock says "Endure".

The wind says "Pursue".
The sun says "I will suck your bones
And afterwards bury you."

Others were inspired to write by the disconnect that existed between their experience of the fighting and how this would be remembered by those who were not there. One of these was John Jarmain, who wrote in "El Alamein":

It will become a staid historic name,
That crazy sea of sand!
Like Troy or Agincourt its single fame
Will be the garland for our brow, our claim,…
But this is not the place we recall,
The crowded desert crossed with foaming tracks,
The one blotched building, lacking half a wall,
The grey-faced men, sand powdered over all…

In similar vein, "Eighth Army" by T. W. Ramsey speaks of

… bones there where we left our own
Bleached by the drifting detritus of stone…
We never liked them, and we hated sand
So loving warm, so thirsty for our blood;
But still they might have sent us into mud
A fathom deep—this was at least dry land.

Like Douglas and Keyes, Jarmain and Ramsey were killed during the war, thus sealing or limiting their reputations. Hamish Henderson, one poet who survived the conflict, highlights the contrast between the dead and the survivors. In *Elegies for the Dead of Cyrenaica*, he reflects that the "conflict seemed rather to be between 'the dead, the innocent'—that eternally wronged proletariat of levelling death in which all the fallen are comrades—and ourselves, the living." Henderson also sees the desert as an enemy, a theme to which he gives prominence in the foreword to *Elegies*, observing that he had heard a German officer making the same point. The officer mused, "In reality we are allies, and the desert is our common enemy." Henderson adopts the sentiment in "End of a Campaign", where he writes of the dead:

> There were our own, there were the others...
> I will bear witness for I knew the others.

In the seventh elegy, "Seven Good Germans", Henderson mourns his avowed enemies, coming across some unburied German corpses:

> Seven poor bastards
> dead in African deadland
> (tawny tousled hair under the issue blanket)
> wie einst Lili
> dead in African deadland
> einst Lili Marlene.

The Gaelic poet George Campbell Hay resisted his call-up for military service on the grounds of his Scottish nationalism. After his eventual capture and a spell in prison, he was sent to North Africa. According to many critics, the desert war was the making of Hay as a Scots makar. Certainly, in English renderings of "The Young Man Speaking from the Grave", "Bizerte" and "Meftah Babkum es-Sabar?" (the title borrowed from an Arabic poem meaning "the key to your door is patience"), one is aware of the importance of the desert in Hay's work. Writing largely in Gaelic with occasional phrases in colloquial Italian, French, German, Arabic and Greek, his work never garnered the same reputation as his English-language counterparts, although his verse is just as powerful as any of Douglas' work.

Hay's Scottish nationalism also invades his poetry and he appears more sympathetic to the North African locals than to many of the English soldiers with whom he served—or is simply more anti-English than pro-indigenous Saharan. As he wrote to his brother in 1942, "I cannot imagine a more cosmopolitan place than the seaboard of North Africa... though curiously enough the average English soldier in his ignorance seems to find nothing but crowds of 'dirty bastards', who are much inferior to him in every respect, wherever his masters order him to go."

Chapter Thirteen

A BRILLIANT PALETTE

"I will salute with a profound regret that menacing and desolate horizon which has so rightly been called—Land of Thirst."

Eugène Fromentin

If nineteenth-century poets did not journey to North Africa, painters of the period did. The fact that such a trip could be costly and involved an element of danger was offset by the visual delights the travellers expected to find. The motivations that brought them to the Sahara were many and diverse. Like the poets, more romantically inclined painters could forget in North Africa the banality of European industrial modernity, finding the Sahara pristine by comparison. From the French invasions of Egypt in 1798 and Algeria in 1830, the region's Ottoman territories were coming under varying degrees of European control, which made the decision easier for those bearing easels.

Because of uneven foreign occupation or control not all of the Sahara attracted painters. In those Saharan lands with a Mediterranean border, Libya received the fewest artist-travellers, not being colonized until the twentieth century. Morocco attracted more painters than Libya, although few travelled south of the Atlas Mountains. The number of visitors to Morocco was as nothing, however, compared with those who journeyed to Algeria and Egypt in the second half of the century. As for the southern Saharan nations, apart from those painters who followed the British Army to the Sudan, Chad, Niger, Mali and Mauritania were left virtually undisturbed by foreign artist-travellers.

Before the political map of the Sahara was altered in favour of the Europeans, anyone wishing to travel there found that diplomatic protection was usually necessary. Invasion and occupation changed this, and opened up the Sahara to European and other artists. For many the impetus to travel to North Africa came about as a result of Napoleon's invasion of Egypt.

The artists who accompanied Napoleon, notably Dominique Vivant, Baron de Denon, were, among other things, given the task of producing topographical images of the country. Denon, one of Napoleon's close associates, worked in Egypt between November 1798 and the following August, when he returned to France. Made the first director of the Louvre by Napoleon in 1801, Denon published his illustrated account of his time in Egypt the next year. *Voyage dans la basse et la haute Egypte*, or *Journey in Lower and Upper Egypt*, proved immensely popular and was a powerful draw for future traveller-artists, as was Luigi Mayer's *Views in Egypt*, which came out the year before Denon's book. Although less well known than Denon, Mayer had travelled in Egypt two decades before the French invasion as the official draughtsman to Sir Robert Ainslie, British Ambassador to the Ottoman Empire.

After these early diplomat-artists came the traveller-artists who, instead of producing a sanctioned body of work for official purposes, were free to paint subjects of their own choosing. At the vanguard of the not-quite independent artists inspired by the Sahara was Eugène Delacroix. Born in the same year as Napoleon's ultimately unsuccessful invasion of Egypt, Delacroix travelled to Morocco and Algeria in 1832 as the official artist accompanying a diplomatic mission to the Sultan of Morocco.

At the time he received the invitation to travel as official artist Delacroix was already keen to visit North Africa, having read the poetry of Byron and Victor Hugo. Although he made just one six-month trip to the region, Delacroix was besotted with what he saw, writing of his experiences: "I am truly sorry for the artists gifted with imagination who can never have any idea of this virgin, sublime nature...I can only look forward with sadness to the moment when I shall leave forever the land of beautiful orange trees covered with flowers and fruit, of the beautiful sun, of the beautiful eyes and of a thousand other beauties."

Delacroix's love of the spectacular in everything he saw during his travels led him to produce a dramatic body of North African-inspired work that tends towards the fantastic and allegorical, for example *The Death of Sardanapalus* (1827). He also filled his work with imaginary battle and hunting scenes, as seen in pieces such as *Moroccan Military Exercises* (1832), complete with terrified horses, or the animated *Combat between the Giaour and the Pasha* (1826), inspired by Byron's 1813 poem, *The Giaour, a Fragment of a Turkish Tale*. Delacroix represented something of the acme of sensationalist Orientalist work, with many artists who travelled to North Africa after him tending towards more realistic representations of their subjects. Delacroix filled numerous notebooks with sketches while travel-

David Roberts, *The Simoon in the Desert*, 1838

ling in Morocco and Algeria, allowing him to sketch rough drafts often with watercolour notes, but his larger works were all completed in his studio in France. At home he would often use models dressed in local costumes, which he bought on his travels.

By the time David Roberts (1796-1864) set off for the Holy Land and Egypt in 1838, he was confident that his efforts would meet with financial success, so well received was the work of earlier artists, such as Delacroix. In eleven months Roberts travelled extensively in Egypt, Syria, Palestine and Lebanon, drawing en route virtually every tomb and temple he came across. On his return to England, he published, to great acclaim, six volumes of lithographic reproductions of these drawings. Although an already known painter, these lithographs, images of a land that was largely unknown to the British public, secured Roberts' longer-term fame and financial success.

Visiting Egypt, William Thackeray echoed Roberts' view of the potential financial rewards to be made drawing in the region. Writing in 1844 during the course of his trip to the Middle East, the novelist appeared positively envious of the artist when he wrote, "There is a fortune to be made for painters in Cairo... I never saw such a variety of architecture, of life, of picturesques, of brilliant colour, of light and shade."

Algeria at around this time was proving a popular destination for artists, especially after the capture of Abd al-Qadir made the country feel safer from a European perspective. The scene of the capture of Abd al-Qadir was famously recreated by Joseph-Louis-Hippolyte Bellange in his imagined if not imaginatively entitled piece, *Capture of the Retinue of Abd el-Kader in 1843*.

FROMENTIN AND THE ORIENTALISTS: DANGEROUS NOVELTIES

Yet as early as the 1850s, artists were complaining that the cities of the north coast were not "authentic" enough for their purposes of exploring new lands, so many Europeans having already settled there. With this in mind, they started heading further south, deep into the Sahara. As Guy de Maupassant wrote: "The moment you step onto African soil, a strange need takes hold of you: to go further south... The south! That quick, burning word: south! Fire!"

It was this south that attracted the poet and painter Eugène Fromentin (1820-76), whose critical success greatly promoted the cause of Orientalist art. Having discovered the Sahara for himself, Fromentin challenged his fellow artists to leave their studios and travel in order to paint the "dangerous novelties" that he believed one could only grasp through first-hand knowledge of the desert. As he wrote in his journal:

> The East is extraordinary, it gets away from conventions, it upsets the age-old harmonies of the landscape. I am not speaking of a fictitious East, I am talking of that dusty, whitish country, rather crudely coloured when it does have colour, with rigid shapes, generally broad rather than lofty, unbelievably clear with nothing to soften it, almost without an atmosphere and without distance.

Fromentin made good use of desert landscapes as a result of his three journeys to Algeria between 1846 and 1853, and Egypt in 1869, where he went for the opening of the Suez Canal. As well as his artistic output, Fromentin made a literary reputation for himself with works such as *A*

Summer in the Sahara (1857) and *A Year in the Sahel* (1859). The first of these recalls Fromentin's journey south to the oasis of Laghouat, which featured in a number of his paintings.

Fromentin's advice to travel was seized upon by Gustave Guillaumet, with both artists bringing to life the harshness of the desert and its risks to their work. Fromentin and Guillaumet were both trained as landscape artists, a skill they used to great effect in their Saharan output, their brushes removing some of the more fantastic elements that had worked their way into pieces by earlier artists. Increasingly accurate scenes are evident in Fromentin's *Land of Thirst* from 1869, or Guillaumet's 1867 painting, *The Sahara*. Neither of these pictures offers an idealized image, presenting viewers instead with unrelentingly grim aspects of death and dying in the desert.

Fromentin painted at least two versions of the *Land of Thirst*, a title which echoes the closing words of one of his memoirs, *A Summer in the Sahara*: "I will salute with a profound regret that menacing and desolate horizon which has so rightly been called—Land of Thirst." The scene shows the ordinary tragedy of a man's death in the desert and is a long way from the romantic horsemen and colourful robes of Delacroix. While mirroring Théodore Géricault's *Wreck of the Medusa*, its setting is not an ocean but a barren landscape of rock and sand. The men, who have become separated from a caravan that had provided them with some security, lie abandoned on rocky ground, beyond despair, waiting for death. The raised arm of one of the men perhaps shows a last gesture of defiance in the face of death, with the sun overhead and raptors circling patiently.

In *The Sahara*, also known as *The Desert*, Guillaumet likewise produced a work that did not pander to the usual western preconceptions. Devoid of dunes, the geography consists of little beyond some mountain peaks, placed definitively beyond easy reach, and the merest hint of a caravan, too far away for comfort. Those elements aside, there is little for the eye to linger on; no trees for shade, no water burbling in a spring-fed oasis, but instead a vast, flat, featureless plain typical of much of the Sahara. The main focus is a camel's carcass that dominates the foreground, melding a traditional *memento mori* motif with a Saharan icon. The dramatic use of light and the minimization of colours, bleached by the sun like the camel's carcass, make the painting reminiscent of Turner's masterful use of light and colour.

Guillaumet's time in the remote southern reaches of Algeria led him to sympathize with the local environment to a greater extent than many of his fellow Europeans. He especially hated the development of the country, which he referred to as "Frenchification". As he wrote with a certain melancholy, "Life here no longer seems as before, held together by dreams and bringing life to the shadows." Ironically, had it not been for the French invasion, Guillaumet would probably not have had the opportunity to travel to the country he came to love and, to an extent, idealize because of what he saw as its alien otherness. During his initial visit to the Algerian interior he contracted malaria, from which he never fully recovered. His first bout of the sickness forced him to spend three months recovering in the military hospital at Biskra, an oasis he would subsequently return to frequently.

Because of Guillaumet's encouragement, Etienne Dinet made his own journey to the Sahara. While there he learnt Arabic and converted to Islam, taking the name Nasr'Eddine Dinet, before settling virtually full-time in the oasis of Bou Saada from 1903 until his death on Christmas Eve, 1929. Though his output is quite distinct from that of Fromentin and Delacroix, who worked very much with European audiences and markets in mind, Dinet is an artistic reactionary compared with Matisse and the Impressionists who travelled to North Africa after him. Dinet was, like Delacroix, devoted to reproducing accurately the garb and accoutrements of the people he encountered and showed a greater respect for his subjects than many of his fellow artists who hardly registered the differences in ethnicity and costume from one area of the desert to another.

Typical of this realism is *The Snake Charmer* (1889). Painted in Laghouat, it shows an elderly, bearded snake charmer at the centre of the picture with a benevolent smile on his face and a snake on top of his head, with another held between his right thumb and forefinger. In the expressions of the semi-circle of spectators the viewer sees an array of emotions, including awe, fear, concern and pleasure. The faces of the men and boys who have gathered for the show are so beautifully observed that although it is taking place in a public arena, Dinet creates a sense of the intimacy of a private encounter.

Like Dinet, Fromentin and Guillaumet also drew inspiration from daily life in Saharan oases. The slice of life in Fromentin's *A Street in El-Aghouat* (1859) is clearly based on first-hand experience. A common enough scene, the picture shows half a dozen men doing their best to rest while hiding from the heat, recumbent in the midday shade that barely covers a portion of the village street, dividing the public space into two distinct spheres of light and dark. Another ordinary scene captured by Guillaumet is that of a group of women drawing water in *The Seguia, Biskra* (1884), an image which has essentially remained unchanged since the oasis was settled in Roman times. Other scenes of daily life inspired Guillaumet to paint *Saharan Dwelling, Biskra District, Algeria* (1882) and *Laghouat, Algeria* (1879), studies of such mundane activity as the preparation of food. In *Evening Prayer in the Sahara* (1863) by Guillaumet, the figures of the group of worshippers in various stages of prostration during sunset prayers bring the divine into the Sahara, as behind them the smoke rises from the campfires.

The American artist Frederick Arthur Bridgman (1847-1928), sometime student of French painter and sculptor Jean-Léon Gérôme, spent a number of winters in Egypt and Algeria during the 1880s, both on the coast and in the Sahara. A native of Alabama, Bridgman had seen slave markets first-hand in his home state before the American Civil War. As a result, he became a committed anti-colonialist, sympathies he transfers to the downtrodden North African locals, for instance in the affectionately executed *Interior of a Biskra Café, Algiers* (1884). Although eventually settling in France, he continued to paint Algerian scenes which became, perhaps because of the distance and a faulty memory, increasingly saccharine, taking on the look of syrupy illustrations for a children's edition of the *Arabian Nights*.

In stark contrast to Bridgman's chocolate-box period, the dramatic almost featureless landscapes by Guillaumet and others proved inspirational to Léon Belly, who created one of the most famous desert scenes of the nineteenth century in *Pilgrims Going to Mecca*. Although almost as much a part of the landscape as the stones and sand itself, until this time camels were not the first choice of artists painting Saharan scenes. This changed, however, when Belly's painting was unveiled in 1861. It is not hard to see why this epic work, which measures almost eight feet by five, has become a classic of its genre.

Unlike romanticized images, Belly's painting offers an altogether more realistic, indeed sympathetic, portrayal of pilgrims as individuals, rather than a group of stereotypes. The elderly and the exhausted feature with

Léon Belly, *Pilgrims Going to Mecca*, 1861

the heat and blinding light—all elements given equal weight in the tableau. The believers are marching in the heat with the sun at their back forcing the picture's detail into the dark places. The placing of the pilgrims too, looming front and centre, lends grandeur to the group of otherwise ordinary people. The seemingly infinite column of pilgrims forms a pyramid that reaches the top of the picture and back away across the endless plain, again devoid of soft colours or shade.

Where Belly led, many followed. At a brush-stroke, the camel caravan became not only acceptable as a subject, but *de rigueur*; virtually every artist who portrayed camels after Belly was in his shadow. Ludwig Hans Fischer's (1848-1915) treatment of the subject is beautifully shown in a pair of paintings, *An Arab Caravan* and *An Arab Caravan at Dusk* (1903). The first of these in particular creates a sense of heat, but both works impart that extreme stillness that is only found in the desert, where even the camel's padded feet seem to have been designed to maintain this silence.

In contrast to these tranquil scenes, Fischer also produced an extremely animated work in *The Simoom* (1878), a study of a sandstorm.

The presence of an ancient statue, suggesting the possibility of nearby water, is the only thing that prevents this from being an image of pure terror. The picture of men battling through a storm, accompanied by their distressed sheep and a lone donkey, is uncomfortably realistic. Adverse weather is also the subject of Fromentin's *Windstorm on the Esparto Plains* (1864), which features, for Fromentin, an uncharacteristically dark sky, the greys adding to the storm's menace. Apart from the storm, the picture's focus is the discomfort of a group of horsemen, caught on the plains with no shelter in sight, as their burnouses billow about their heads.

After camels, the animal that features most prominently in Saharan art is the horse. In 1851 the French general Melchior Dumas published *Horses in the Sahara*, aided by the exiled Abd al-Qadir. The book is a study of animal husbandry and the uses and treatment of horses in the West versus North Africa. Fromentin and others seized upon the book as invaluable source material.

In *Moroccan Horsemen in Military Action* (1832) by Delacroix, the majesty of the horses is tempered by the fear in their eyes as they take their mounts into battle. Horses also feature prominently in the work of Gérôme (1824-1904). In setting the standard for documentary realism—commonplace by the second half of the nineteenth century—Gérôme was disparaged by many who came after him as cold and static, especially by the Impressionists, who favoured a freer, more interpretive approach in their work. In *Arabs Crossing the Desert* (c. 1870), Gérôme places a noble-looking group of horses and riders directly in front of the viewer, with camels relegated to the background as little more than set dressing. The view he offers is that while camels may be the more useful animals for a desert crossing, the horse is endowed with greater nobility. The all-male setting, devoid of any hint of domesticity, likewise promotes masculinity in the imagined nobility of his desert-dwelling Arabs. Adding to the romance of what might otherwise be considered a realistic scene is the riders' garb, the rich, dust-free clothes shining out in contrast to the dun-coloured landscape surrounding them.

The portrayal of women in the general field of Sahara-inspired Orientalist art usually involves the convention of shrouded or naked forms. In the paintings of the nineteenth century, women are rarely depicted in harems—more commonly associated with palaces found in the major urban centres such as Constantinople or Cairo, and thus absent from the

Sahara proper. The questionable taste of many fantasy images of bondage and eroticism in many of these scenes no doubt contributed to the wholesale devaluation of Orientalist art as a genre.

For examples of a more restrained, even respectful portrayal of women in the region, one could look to *Morning Walk* by the Italian Rubens Santoro, or *Women in Biskra Weaving a Burnoose* (1880) and *Portrait of a Kabylie Woman* (1875), by Bridgman. None of these shows the female subjects in a demeaning light; instead they are almost shying away from the more salacious harem portraits of other so-called Orientalists. *Portrait of a Kabylie Woman* in particular portrays a subject whose strength and single-mindedness are clear in her face, in contrast to the naked, pale-skinned women examined in a slave market or waiting in a harem.

In this regard, *The Almeh's Admirers* (1882) by Leopold Carl Müller and Gérôme's *The Dance of the Almeh* (1866) are far more sexually straightforward images, both pictures featuring the *almeh* dancing for an all-male audience. Literally a learned woman, in reality an *almeh* was a dancer who would often also work as a prostitute. In Müller's piece, the dancer, who is staring directly at the viewer, seems unaware of her audience who are focusing on one or another of the woman's curves, laughing or, in the case of the musicians, concentrating on their work.

If so-called Orientalist art was a nineteenth-century phenomenon, it is not always obvious what legacy the artists of the next century who travelled in the footsteps of Delacroix *et al* inherited. Most of these moved away from the studio-executed or studio-finished work of their predecessors, now seeking more immediacy and spontaneity in their work. This change of direction meant that Orientalist art was actually replaced by a looser informal brotherhood of painters, sometimes referred to as colonialist artists, who travelled and lived in the region both before the Second World War and after independence.

By and large, the Impressionists found little inspiration in the Sahara. Claude Monet (1840-1926), for example, did his military service in Algeria, and although he wrote favourably of his time there this did not translate into any major works inspired by the country. Although Renoir (1841-1919) is sometimes said to be the most Orientalist of the Impressionists, making several trips to Algeria in 1881 and 1882, he likewise did not obviously take any Saharan subject matter away with him, concentrating instead on the cities and gardens of the Mediterranean coast. In this region, Renoir, as Matisse after him, delighted in the textures and colours offered by the vegetation of North Africa.

Renoir and Matisse were both happy to acknowledge the debt they owed to Delacroix, although as Matisse once said of himself "I am much too anti-picturesque to get much out of travelling." Even so, he did travel to Algeria in 1906, going to the oasis of Biskra, and made two lengthier Moroccan visits in 1912 and 1913 although these were limited to Tangier. His interest was less specifically in landscapes than figures, and his *Odalisque* series of paintings are much more like the studio-based Ottoman fare of the nineteenth-century artists than any of his contemporaries.

The work of the German Symbolist Paul Klee (1879-1940) may not at first speak of the Sahara, but it was in Tunisia in 1914 that he enjoyed a breakthrough in his work. Klee claimed to have discovered colour and abstraction in Tunis and Hammamet, after which he travelled to Kairouan and the desert beyond, which he described as the high point of his Tunisian tour. As he wrote during his trip, "Here is the meaning of this most opportune moment: colour and I are one. I am a painter." In 1928, during his first trip to Egypt, he described the quality of light and colours there in similar terms. Whether or not one cares to describe Klee as an Orientalist artist, it is undeniable that his work was informed by what he found in North Africa. As his diaries make clear, it was there that he learnt about light in the desert and simplicity from local architectural forms that informed the rest of his life's work.

Anyone who attempts to lump together the traveller-artists of the eighteenth, nineteenth and twentieth centuries as cultural imperialists misses the point by a considerable margin. Wrong as it is to assume the homogeneity of those who live in the Sahara, so is it misguided to think of the artists who travelled there as consistent in intention and outlook. Often criticized as little more than ignorant, paint-carrying tourists, it is true that some came in search of the seamy. Yet for every traveller who hoped to confirm some prejudiced view of the region as a land of harem-dwelling sex slaves, implacable pederasts and unholy despots, one can point to any number of artists whose interests lay in more innocent pursuits.

What is true is that numerous artists, including Delacroix, Fromentin, Renoir, Matisse and Klee, found their work altered by the time they spent in the Sahara. Each artist found his work developed in practical ways, opening up new sights and new directions. This was often the result of exposure to the Saharan sun, and the effect this light had on the colours of the region. More than anything else, it was the light which these artists took away with them from the desert—a brilliance they could not hope to find under European skies.

Chapter Fourteen

ORIENTAL DELIGHTS, STRANGE
WORLDS AND SPY STORIES

"Nothing of interest enlivened our journey by rail and caravan till we
came to the cluster of date-palms about the ancient well upon the rim
of the Sahara."

Edgar Rice Burroughs, *Pellucidar* (1915)

In spite of increased European contact with the Sahara following colonization, for many writers the desert remained shorthand for the unknown
and the fantastic. Whether the setting for wholly imaginary tales of
mystery or a half-invented land inhabited by white slavers, the Sahara of
literature proved to be fertile for writers and readers alike.

Even before the Scramble for the Sahara, European writers had occa-
sionally shown interest in the region. In the eighteenth century Charles
Fieux de Mouhy, a friend of Voltaire and a popular author in his day, was
responsible for numerous fantastic stories, one of the most famous being
*Lamekis, or The Extraordinary Voyages of an Egyptian in the Inner Earth,
With the Discovery of the Isle of Silphide, Enriched with Curious Notes*. His
work has recently enjoyed something of a revival thanks to a reference in
The League of Extraordinary Gentlemen, a series of graphic novels by Alan
Moore and Kevin O'Neill.

Published in 1737, the novel has multiple, intertwined plots that
begin in ancient Egypt, where Lamekis' father is a high priest. From
ancient Egypt, the action moves to a utopian world beneath the surface of
the earth. Back on the planet's surface, de Mouhy also invented the imaginary North African kingdoms of Abdalles and Amphicleocles. In these
the author is happy to outline all sorts of customs and behaviour for his
readers that would be most out of place in eighteenth-century France.

Like de Mouhy, Edgar Rice Burroughs, creator of the Tarzan stories,
also invented an imagined land that exists in our hollow earth. Called Pellucidar, this subterranean world that could be reached through the Sahara
featured in seven novels and, in an interesting melding of fantasy tales,
Burroughs used Pellucidar as the setting for one of his Tarzan stories

Tarzan at The Earth's Core (1929). In the second story in the series, *Pellucidar* (1915), the hero returns to the Sahara to reach the underground kingdom.

As the narrator explains:

Our trip through the earth's crust was but a repetition of my two former journeys between the inner and the outer worlds. This time, however, I imagine that we must have maintained a more nearly perpendicular course, for we accomplished the journey in a few minutes' less time than upon the occasion of my first journey through the five-hundred-mile crust. Just a trifle less than seventy-two hours after our departure into the sands of the Sahara, we broke through the surface of Pellucidar.

The French novelist Pierre Benoît (1886-1962) was based in North Africa while serving in the French Army, and he drew on this experience of the Sahara for his second novel, *Atlantida*. Set in 1896, the story involves two French officers drugged and kidnapped by Tuareg and taken to the kingdom of Queen Antinea, a descendant of the rulers of Atlantis, the poetic Atlantida of the title. Queen Antinea lives in a cave with 120 niches carved around its walls; each niche represents one of her lovers, each of whom "dies for love" when the queen tires of him. When all the niches are full, Antinea is supposed to rest for eternity. When the Frenchmen, Captains Morhange and André de Saint-Avit arrive, just over fifty niches have been filled, meaning that the queen has some way to go before she can rest. While in a trance-like state, captivated by the queen's beauty, Saint-Avit kills Morhange. Eventually coming to his senses, Saint-Avit manages to escape, riding across the Sahara to a French army outpost where he relates his story. Not surprisingly, his tale of the Queen of Atlantis in the Sahara is not readily believed, in spite of his previously unblemished reputation. As his fate is being decided, colleagues rush to defend him: "'He went alone to Bilma, to the Aïr, quite alone to those places where no one had ever been. He is a brave man.' 'He is a brave man, undoubtedly,' I answered with great restraint. 'But he murdered his companion, Captain Morhange, did he not?' The old Sergeant trembled. 'He is a brave man,' he persisted."

After the novel's publication in 1919, Benoît was accused of plagiarism, one critic highlighting the similarities between this story and Rider

Haggard's *She*. Affronted, Benoît sued for libel but lost. *Atlantida* was said to have inspired the swashbuckling adventurer-cum-archaeologist Byron de Prorok to head into the Sahara in search of lost treasure. His cavalier approach to excavations did more damage than good to the objects he uncovered, for instance tearing apart mummies in his search for jewels. As a result, de Prorok today remains universally loathed by professional archaeologists, decades after his death.

A prolific author of short stories and children's books, the English writer Algernon Blackwood (1869-1951) is best known for his ghost and "weird" stories. Born in London, he became devoted to the teaching of Madame Blavatsky, founder of the Theosophical Society, and his writing often drew on occult and psychic motifs. Often using Egypt and the desert as settings, Blackwood was drawn to the possibilities of magic in ancient Egyptian religion and the idea of spirits coming out of the Sahara.

In *Sand*, one of his best-known stories, the Sahara sand itself is at the centre of the tale, introduced as an almost anthropomorphic entity that draws people to it. The central human character is Felix Henriot, who travels to Egypt because the sand called him there: "For Henriot drew near to its great shifting altars in an attitude of worship. The wilderness made him kneel in heart. Its shining reaches led to the oldest Temple in the world, and every journey that he made was like a sacrament. For him the Desert was a consecrated place. It was sacred." Without giving away the end of the story, suffice to say all does not end well.

One of the greatest exponents of tales of fantastic places was the pioneering author of science fiction, Jules Verne. Verne's first published book (54 novels came out in his lifetime) takes place over and in the Sahara at a time when large portions of the continent were still unknown to Europeans. *Five Weeks in a Balloon* (1863) tells the story of a balloon trip across the desert from Zanzibar to Senegal via Agadez, the capital of the Aïr, and, naturally, Timbuktu. In part because of the great public interest in African exploration at that time, and because it is a good read, the book sold well and secured Verne's reputation.

The last novel Verne completed, and which was with his publisher at the time of his death, also features a Saharan setting. In *The Invasion of the Sea* (1905) a team of Europeans is examining the possibility of flooding a low-lying region of the Sahara through a canal that would run through Tunisia into eastern Algeria. In planning the creation of a Saharan sea the

Europeans, and local Arab traders, hope to reap the benefits of a new trading region in North Africa. In spite of the careful planning, a large volcano erupts unexpectedly, creating just such a sea without the need for human interference.

Sax Rohmer was the exotic-sounding pseudonym of Arthur Henry Ward, also known as Michael Furey, the English author and master of the gothic thriller, most famous for his Chinese criminal mastermind Dr. Fu Manchu. First appearing in 1912, the tales of Fu Manchu would eventually feature in thirteen of Rohmer's more than fifty full-length novels. Head of the Si Fan, an international crime organization, Fu Manchu is described by his nemesis, the controller of the British Secret Service, Sir Denis Nayland Smith, thus: "Imagine a person, tall, lean and feline, high-shouldered, with a brow like Shakespeare and a face like Satan, a close-shaven skull, and long, magnetic eyes of the true cat-green. Invest him with all the cruel cunning of an entire Eastern race... and you have a mental picture of Dr Fu-Manchu, the yellow peril incarnate in one man."

Apart from the Si Fan network having its headquarters in the Sahara at one point, many other books by Rohmer, such as *Tales of Secret Egypt* and *Brood of the Witch Queen* (both 1918), involve spirits living in and coming out of the deserts of North Africa to terrify his characters and readers alike. Combining the theme of the Yellow Peril with visions of the Sahara, *Dope: A Story of Chinatown and the Drug Trade*—one of Rohmer's best-known novels—features an opium-fuelled dream of the desert. Mrs. Sin, the madame of a drug den in Limehouse, London, is feeding a young woman, Rita Dresden, pipes of opium. As a result Rita's hallucinations take her far away:

> She and the parakeets were alone in the heart of the Great Sahara...
> She was dressed in a manner which Rita dreamily thought would have
> been inadequate in England, or even in Cuba, but which was appro-
> priate in the Great Sahara. How exquisitely she carried herself, mused
> the dreamer; no doubt this fine carriage was due in part to her wearing
> golden shoes with heels like stilts, and in part to her having been trained
> to bear heavy burdens upon her head.

Like Algernon Blackwood, not to mention W. B. Yeats and the occultist Aleister Crowley, Rohmer was a member of the Hermetic Order of the Golden Dawn, a popular cabbalistic society of the late nineteenth and early twentieth centuries, from which he and Blackwood derived many of their mystically inspired plots. Ironically, considering the accusations of racism that bedevilled Rohmer because of his evil Chinese villain, the author died during a pandemic of the so-called Asian flu.

Dorothy Gilman, creator of the Mrs. Pollifax series of mysteries, makes use of a less fantastic but nonetheless exotic Saharan location, in the traditions of damsels in distress. Although *Caravan* (1992) deals with issues including murder and sex slavery, it is all rather sanitized and incomparably less sinister than the work of Rohmer and his occult peers. *Caravan* relates the misadventures of a sometime wife, widow, slave and sex object in the form of Caressa, Lady Teal, née Bowman, née Horvath. The plot is a common one: a young, innocent, attractive foreign woman alone in the big, bad world:

> I had no knowledge then of what was happening in other parts of Africa, I knew nothing of the intrigues, assassinations, treaties and betrayals, battles, rivalries and ultimatums among the French, Turks, Italians, British and Belgians as each of them raced to swallow up as much of the continent as possible... After all, I had been travelling for a very long time in the only part of Africa that nobody wanted—the desert.

Tuareg tribesmen, the Blue Men, murder our impressionable heroine's husband while he and she are on the way to Ghadames. Caressa is taken prisoner; concubinage and slavery follow. In a play on the usual idea of foreign men bad, white men good, the heroine suffers as much at the hands of western men as she does at those of locals, allowing all races to take part equally in Caressa's victimhood. Framing the tale in the run up to the First World War allows Gilman to introduce historical titbits, to conjure up the more alien nature of the Sahara of a century ago. "'There's news,' he said. 'Italy has invaded Tripoli—there's fighting there... The desert tribes—led by the Senussi—have rallied to support the Tripoli natives.'" After three years in the Sahara Gilman allows Caressa to get back to Cairo and civilization in June 1914, just in time for the start of the Great War.

TALES OF THE LEGION

As a balance to Saharan natives, the French Foreign Legion has long provided one of the most easily accessible motifs for western readers wishing to engage with the desert. Founded in 1831, the year after the invasion of "French Algeria", the regiment was created after foreigners were banned from serving in the French army. One reason for growth of the legendary Legion was the fiction it inspired. The fact that the regiment accepted so many foreign recruits, Americans and British among them, also fed this trend, allowing as it did non-French readers to enjoy the vicarious pleasure of reading about military engagements fought under another's flag. This theme is central to one of the first works to deal with a foreigner serving in a French regiment.

The best-known of all Legion novels is *Beau Geste* by P. C. Wren, who claimed to have served in the Legion himself, although evidence for this is vague. The film versions of the story ensured that the Legion and the Sahara remained popular cultural motifs long after the end of the colonial presence in North Africa. The continuing popularity of stories of legionnaires in the post-war period is clear from the fact that, in the 1950s, the British publisher John Spencer successfully brought out a series of 23 paperbacks about the Legion, written under a number of in-house pseudonyms.

Even cartoon strips have used the Legion as a suitable storyline. Charles Schulz, creator of the cartoon *Peanuts*, penned a long-running storyline in which Snoopy, Charlie Brown's beagle, was dressed as a sergeant in the French Foreign Legion, leading Woodstock, his small yellow bird friend of indeterminate species, and fellow birds across the wastes of the Sahara, en route for Fort Zinderneuf, the fort featured in *Beau Geste*. In reality, these sandy wastes turn out to be a sandpit belonging to one of the children in the cartoon, or else a bunker on the local golf course.

Still in the world of colonial occupation, Brian Moore's last novel *The Magician's Wife* (1997) is set in Algeria in 1856-57, and takes a clash of European and Arab cultures as its central theme. Moore served in North Africa during the Second World War, and obviously retained some memory of the desert from this time. The magician of the title, Henri Lambert, is persuaded by the French authorities to travel to Algeria in the service of his country. The French head of Arab affairs wants him to perform a series of tricks for an influential holy man, Bou-Aziz, who lives in the desert and is thought to have healing powers. The French hope is that by witnessing these illusions, the holy man will be convinced that God is actually on the side of the French and so persuaded not to declare a jihad against the invaders.

At the successful conclusion of a trial of his new tricks, Lambert addresses his audience saying, "I am a sorcerer. I am Christian. I am French. God, whom you call Allah, protects me—as He will protect my country from any enemy who dares to strike a blow against France." Travelling across the desert to meet Bou-Aziz, Emmeline, Lambert's wife, voices her fears of the desert: "I just want to reach wherever it is we sleep tonight. To be inside, away from the sun. How big is this desert? It frightens me."

Lambert's mission is ultimately successful, but not in the way one is led to expect. Displaying great humility—in noticeable contrast to the hubris of Lambert and the French authorities—Bou-Aziz resigns himself to his fate and the fate of his people in the face of the foreigners' greater scientific knowledge, not to mention military strength, remarking of the French: "To conquer our enemies, we must first increase our obedience to God and to the Prophet. If we do, one day our faith will be so strong that the Christian world will be powerless against it and the infidels will pass forever from this land... The passage of the French through our country is temporal: it will not last... Everything comes from God."

The Day of Creation (1987) by J. G. Ballard is typical of a number of the author's other works in dealing with the fantastic in a commonplace setting. Dr. Mallory is the protagonist, a man determined to make the Sahara a fertile region, fed by an underground river he believes can be tapped. As he says of his presence in the imaginary zone in which the book is set, "Chance alone, I guessed, had not brought me to this war-locked nation, that lay between the borders of Chad, the Sudan and the Central African Republic in the dead heart of the African continent, a land as close to nowhere as the planet could provide." His plans for irrigating the desert include "a new game reserve in the Sahara, populated by every living species—except one." Men would be excluded.

When a mechanical digger working on the construction of a runway uproots an ancient oak tree, it also breaks the earth and a trickle of water appears. The spring grows into a river, which Mallory sees as his creation in the desert, the fruition of his dream for greening the Sahara, although Mallory's sanity by this stage is questionable: "I felt as if I had conjured up not just this miniature river that would irrigate the southern edge of the Sahara, but the entire consumer goods economy that would one day smother the landscape in high rises, hypermarkets and massage parlours." A degree of sanity only returns once the water stops flowing, and the desert reclaims the temporarily wet land. The book concludes quietly with Mallory musing matter-of-factly on the failure of the plans of men with the words, "The desert is closer today."

DESERT ESPIONAGE

> "Percy said, 'People only go south if they have a purpose. You don't go into the Sahara to hide. Are they looking for something?'"
> Len Deighton, *Twinkle, Twinkle, Little Spy* (1976)

Espionage fiction was conceived as early as the 1820s; Sherlock Holmes was engaged in military-espionage plots in, for example, *The Adventure of the Bruce-Partington Plans* and *The Naval Treaty*, but the genre really came of age around the end of the nineteenth century. The fin-de-siècle paranoia that accompanied the period nurtured such amateurs-in-the-service-of-the-Crown, defence-of-Empire tales as Rudyard Kipling's *Kim* (1901), *The Riddle of the Sands* (1903) by Erskine Childers and *Greenmantle* (1916) by John Buchan.

In the last of these, Buchan has First World War German villains fomenting a *jihad* in the Sahara and the wider Islamic world as far as British India—a plot once again in vogue and worth reading in light of contemporary events. It is not giving away too much to say that, against all odds, our heroes manage to prevent the German menace, saving the lives of countless British subjects in the process. For the British and French during the nineteenth century, if the enemy was not one of the European rival claimants for foreign lands, it was religiously inspired uprisings. In these, the Mahdi was first among equals, a prophetic figure in Islamic theology whose arrival signifies the advent of the end of times.

At the start of the twentieth century, with the almost complete subjugation of the native populations achieved, the enemy in British tales of espionage was almost exclusively a Prussian agent who lurked behind any number of planned acts of mayhem, which readers would expect to be thwarted by some loyal servant of the British Empire. In the 1930s the villains were jack-booted Nazi thugs, and after the Second World War writers on both sides of the Atlantic turned their attention to Soviet agents and Cold War concerns, foremost of these worries being the prospect of a nuclear war. Since the end of the Cold War, and particularly since 2001, Islamic-inspired terrorists are again at the top of the list of bogeymen.

Enormously successful in his lifetime, Dennis Wheatley wrote more than seventy novels and was one of the best-selling authors of the twentieth century, best known for his multi-million-selling occult novels, notably *The Devil Rides Out* and *To the Devil a Daughter*. The Julian Day series of books are more straightforward thrillers, the eponymous hero himself a victim of a plot by an international gang of master-criminals, which shockingly counts a member of the British upper class among its number.

Christened Julian Fernhurst, our hero is forced to quit a promising career in the Diplomatic Service and to change his name to Day, allowing him some degree of anonymity from social and professional disgrace. Fortunately, having a large inheritance, money is not a problem for Mr. Day, who is thus able to devote his life to wreaking his revenge on those responsible for his downfall, with the unofficial backing of a branch of the British secret service. Deriving great pleasure from his subject, Wheatley spatters his text with mini-lessons in Saharan history, folklore and exploration, covering everything from the required tyre pressure for driving over sand dunes to correct forms of hospitality when encountering a Bedouin caravan.

In *The Quest of Julian Day* (1939), Wheatley includes the whole gamut of criminal concerns of the period. The plot involves a conglomerate of foreign agents who are not only involved in espionage against Britain, but also in more straightforward criminality, including drug trafficking and the euphemistically entitled white slave trade. Aside from sex trafficking and every racial stereotype one might expect in a 1930s thriller, the Saharan link is crucial to the story, which starts and finishes with the search for the remains of the army of Cambyses by an eminent British archaeologist who is murdered, and his daughter. She, with grim inevitability, becomes a hostage of the international criminal gang who are also, naturally, searching for the Persian army.

At the beginning of the second book in the series, *The Sword of Fate* (1941), Day is again in Egypt. The Second World War has broken out, and Italy is about to join the German side. Day secures work in uniform as an army interpreter, having an acute ear for languages, and is sent to obtain information from Italian prisoners in the Western Desert. Unfortunately he is taken prisoner while on patrol south of Marsa Matruh. From there, the action moves to Fort Capuzzo just over the Egyptian border in Libya, which oscillated between Allied and Axis control several times during the North African campaign because of its strategic location. Day is not long a prisoner, allowing the plot and our hero to travel further afield, away from the Sahara to Europe.

Most early spy novels and thrillers set in the Sahara were by British authors. But since the Second World War and the Middle East's increasing importance as a source of American energy, this has changed. Although Americans entered the Sahara in the wake of the Europeans, they were quick to make up for lost time, with businessmen, energy prospectors and diplomats fanning out across the desert. American considerations in Saharan spy stories and thrillers can be divided into books concerned with energy resources, tales concerned with terrorism and stories that deal with both.

In the Cold War thriller, *Twinkle, Twinkle, Little Spy*, British author Len Deighton offers readers two heroes for the price of one in a joint Anglo-American mission that takes place in the Sahara. The story has many of the elements one might expect from a Deighton thriller. Although the action allows the two heroes to travel, Bond-like, back and forth across the globe, the action opens and ends in the heart of the Algerian Sahara. The opening is a typically sardonic exchange between the British and American spies and colleagues:

> "Smell that air," said Major Mann. I sniffed. "I can't smell anything," I said. "That's what I mean," said Mann. He scratched himself and grinned. "Great, isn't it?" There's not much to smell when you are one thousand miles into the Algerian Sahara; not much to smell, not much to do, not much to eat.

This portrait of the Sahara, revelling in an appreciation of emptiness, is later developed by the British agent-narrator as he muses, "Men become mesmerised by the desert, just as others become obsessed with the sea; not because of any fondness for sand or water, but because oceans and deserts are the best places to observe the magical effect of ever-changing daylight.

Small ridges, flattened by the high sun, become jagged mountains when the sunlight falls across them, and their shadows, pale gold at noontime, become black bottomless pools."

Technological advances in the real world did not take long to appear on the pages of spy fiction, but although agents in the Sahara may be issued with much gadgetry to help them in their work, fast cars rarely make an appearance, Saharan roads not generally being fit for fast driving. The 1973 Arab oil boycott sharpened more febrile imaginations, leading to a flurry of energy-related terrorism thrillers, which in various guises continue to the present day. The Arabian Peninsula is the main focus for these novels but they have also enveloped the Sahara.

The Sahara is not only there to host spies, master criminals and terrorists. On the contrary, many thrillers take as their central premise the naïve traveller, unwittingly caught up in an unwelcome adventure. One such story is *Rommel's Gold* (1971) by Maggie Davis, which involves an innocent young American woman. Sharon Hoyt is one of a group of young people doing some voluntary work in different parts of Tunisia for The Foundation, an organization similar to, but explicitly not, the Peace Corps. At the same time, rumours surround a former German soldier, the General, and his friends who spend time each year in the Tunisian Sahara. Allegedly searching for a fabled cache of gold that Rommel buried before Hitler summoned him to Berlin, many have their suspicions that this is not the real story.

Among the more unusual Saharan inspired thrillers is *Kicked to Death by a Camel* (1973), by the pseudonymous Clarence J.L. Jackson. The narrator, Roger Allenby, explains that he is in the Sahara researching a history of camels: "Camels. That was the reason. I was writing a book on the history of camels, and Tamanrasset was in the very heart of Tuareg country, where the finest riding camels in the world are reputed to come from. On the other hand, I could have sat at home and looked at coffee-table books of the colourful Sahara and probably found out as much as I was liable to find out in four days in Tamanrasset."

When a man is found dead, kicked by a camel, Allenby becomes a suspect and must try to solve the mystery himself. Complications and the apparent lack of motive befuddle and irritate him: "None of it fits together. It's like having several unrelated crimes squeezed into a short space of time on an absurd little spot in the desert. And besides that, everyone here just happens to have a ridiculous amount of Saharan expertise. It can't all be coincidence." Nor is it. Apart from the several plot twists that follow in this delightful, old-fashioned crime thriller, the story also evokes the loneliness of Tamanrasset, the destination for an incongruous group of foreigners.

Chapter Fifteen

SILVER SCREEN SAHARA

"Where would you go if you want to disappear completely and still have some excitement?"

Beau Geste (1939)

The Sahara has appealed to filmmakers since the earliest days of cinema. Its appeal lies in its foreignness, limitless space, unending horizons and seas of dunes—all of which are supported by a degree of ignorance. The combination of these factors has led to many spectacular films in which the Sahara has played a leading role, even if never credited as such. Indeed, there are two types of film where the Sahara plays a starring role: first are those about lands far-removed from North Africa but set in the Sahara; and the second are films about the Sahara shot in far-removed lands. One of the most famous examples of the former is *Star Wars* (1977), where the dramatic troglodyte dwellings of Matmata in the Tunisian Sahara stand in for Luke Skywalker's childhood home on the planet Tatooine, "a long time ago, in a galaxy far, far away." This is not to be confused with the genuine Tunisian town of Tatouine, even though the director George Lucas did use the name for his imaginary planet. The place's isolation is one important reason young Skywalker is keen to leave home and seek adventure.

In contrast, many great films with supposedly Saharan settings never see a member of the cast or crew going further than the American West or West London. Usually the high cost involved in shooting in foreign countries, the often stultifying bureaucracy of many Saharan nations and the frequent lack of suitable infrastructure make many directors reluctant to work on location.

The first major picture set in the Sahara was a silent film named *Sahara* and directed by C. Gardner Sullivan. One of the most prolific and accomplished early filmmakers, Sullivan was also responsible for the classic 1930 version of *All Quiet on the Western Front. Sahara* is a tragedy about love and betrayal in which a Parisian beauty marries an American engineer who goes to work in the desert with his wife and child. Unhappy with her life in the desert, his wife abandons the family and runs away to Cairo to live with a wealthy playboy. Years later, and still dissatisfied, the wife comes across her now blind, drug-addicted husband begging in the streets of Cairo with their child. The family are reunited and return to the desert and, surprisingly under the circumstances, live happily ever after. On its release in 1919, the New York Times described *Sahara* as "Desert sand and wind storms, picturesque Arabs, dashing horses, camels, beggars, turbans, flowing robes, bloomers and streets with the atmosphere of the Arabian Nights"—without mentioning the fact that it was filmed entirely in America.

Likewise, when directing *The Desert Song* (1929) Roy Del Ruth decided a journey to North Africa was unnecessary to capture the desert on film. As the promotional material says, "From out of the desert wastes of Morocco appeared a sinister figure. Men whispered his name—'Red Shadow!'" (And whispered it with an exclamation mark, no less!) The title song talks of "a desert breeze whispering a lullaby," as it happens a Californian rather than a Saharan breeze, the film's exteriors being shot on the Buttercup Dunes, a location which sounds as contrived as the film looks. Based on an earlier Broadway operetta, the film was promoted as containing "Romance, Adventure, Spectacle, Comedy, [which] Have been woven into one magnificent production—that will cause you to gasp—and agree that you've never seen anything like it." Starring John Boles as the Red Shadow, and Carlotta King as the love interest, Boles plays a handsome bandit leader whose domain is beyond the control of the authorities in French-occupied Morocco. The Red Shadow is, we are told, "Beloved by the Riffs whom he commanded—feared by the French—a mystery as deep as the desert silence."

Although it was the first colour film released by Warner Brothers, only a black and white print survives. Dated, it nonetheless remains important as Warner Brothers' first all-talking, all-singing operetta that was, according to their publicity, "the greatest achievement of the modern motion picture". However grand this claim, the subject matter demonstrates the early allure of the Sahara for filmmakers.

Romance in the Sahara was also central to the plot of *The Garden of Allah*. So popular was the story that three film versions were made between 1916 and 1936. Based on a 1904 novel by Robert Smythe Hichens, the first, silent adaptation of this tale of star-crossed love was filmed in America's Mojave Desert. The second, also silent, version, filmed in 1927, starred Alice Terry and Ivan Petrovich, and was at least partly shot in

Algeria, in Touggourt and Biskra. Clearly understanding what the audience expects from a Saharan film, the trailer promises "A thousand thrilling moments, fiery steeds, burning sands, flaming love, and a desert sandstorm that forms one of the most spectacular climaxes."

The best-loved version of the film stars Marlene Dietrich as Domini Enfilden and Charles Boyer as Boris Androvsky, the renegade Trappist monk turned lover. This version, like *The Desert Song*, was partly filmed in Buttercup Valley, California. Mirroring the pitfalls inherent in the love affair of the romantic leads, the film portrays the desert as a dangerous environment where divine protection is required from the perils of nature, both environmental and of human passions. As Count Ferdinand Anteoni, played by Basil Rathbone in a pre-Sherlock Holmes guise, muses philosophically, "A man who refuses to acknowledge his god is unwise to set foot in the desert."

An unconventional love affair is the subject of *Passion in the Desert*, a 1997 film based on a story by Honoré de Balzac set in the Egyptian Sahara in the wake of the Napoleonic invasion. In the heat of a battle against a force of Mamelukes, Augustin Robert, a French officer played by Ben Daniels, becomes detached from his company: "The silence was awful in its wild and terrible majesty. Infinity, immensity, closed in upon the soul from every side. Not a cloud in the sky, not a breath in the air, not a flaw on the bosom of the sand, ever moving in diminutive waves; the horizon ended as at sea on a clear day, with one line of light, definite as the cut of a sword." Balzac likewise had never visited the Sahara but his description is real enough:

> … the dark sand of the desert spread farther than sight could reach in every direction, and glittered like steel struck with a bright light. It might have been a sea of looking glass, or lakes melted together in a mirror. A fiery vapour carried up in streaks made a perpetual whirlwind over the quivering land. The sky was lit with an Oriental splendour of insupportable purity, leaving naught for the imagination to desire. Heaven and earth were on fire.

Although less contemplative than *Passion in the Desert*, *The Four Feathers* also takes place in the wake of the occupation of the eastern Sahara. Based on the 1902 story by A. E. W. Mason, late nineteenth-century Sudan is the main location, both in the novel and the seven film versions, from 1915 to the most recent, in 2002. The adaptation that perhaps best captures the feel of the late Victorian period, when the sun never set on the British Empire, is that directed by Hungarian-born Zoltan Korda, known for his love of African settings. Korda's 1939 film, filmed partly on location in Sudan, is outstandingly dramatic and made firmly in the empire stamp.

On the eve of his regiment's embarkation for the Sudan to battle the Mad Mahdi for control of the country, Harry Faversham, a young officer, resigns his commission. Stung by accusations of cowardice by his three closest friends and his fiancée, Faversham follows his erstwhile regiment to the Sudan determined to prove himself, and force his friends to take back the white feathers they gave him as a mark of cowardice. The parched Sudanese desert is captured in TechniColor and the film was considered one of the most advanced cinematic creations of its time. Two of its cast would later be knighted, Sir Ralph Richardson and Sir John Clements, who played Faversham.

On the other side of the Sahara, and a couple of decades after the events portrayed in *The Four Feathers*, *Fort Saganne* also has European oc-cupiers and locals clashing in the desert. A 1984 French film set in French Algeria, it features Gérard Depardieu as the hero, Charles Saganne, who is battling not just the Algerians but his own lowly background, and the political games of those responsible for promoting and condemning French colonialism.

BEAU GESTE

Considering their lengthier and broader colonial experience there, it is perhaps appropriate that the French should take the laurels for the most famous Saharan story and its numerous film versions. The very title *Beau Geste* is enough to conjure up images of weary legionnaires in kepis, pitched battles against defiant Tuareg and a seemingly deserted Saharan fort. This classic high adventure desert movie, based on the 1924 book by P. C. Wren, satisfied all the stereotypes of its day, including the heroic, upright British, a sadistic French sergeant-major and savage tribesmen.

Michael "Beau" Geste leaves home and joins the French Foreign Legion after the apparent theft of Blue Water, a precious stone belonging to his aunt who has raised Beau and his orphan brothers. By taking the blame for the alleged theft, Beau is satisfied that although these measures are drastic, he has done the right thing and saved something of the family's honour. When they learn what he has done, Beau's brothers, Digby and John, likewise run away from home and join the Legion, being as keen as Beau to make a conspicuous display of their chivalry.

The classic 1939 film version, starring Gary Cooper, Ray Milland and Robert Preston as the Geste brothers, was filmed in the deserts of Arizona. The importance of the desert is established before the first scene as the film's title is revealed written in sand, only to be concealed by more sand carried on a desert wind. The story's premise is summed up by an on-screen Arabian proverb that reads "The love of a man for a woman waxes and wanes like the moon... but the love of brother for brother is steadfast as the stars, and endures like the word of the prophet."

A slow opening shot of an empty desert establishes the Sahara's on-screen presence. Then, having crossed a sea of dunes, a relief column of the French Foreign Legion arrives at the embattled Fort Zinderneuf, only to find it silent but with its defenders still upright at their posts. With no

signs of the enemy, we discover that the fort is mysteriously manned by the dead. As the story says, "Everybody does his duty at Zinderneuf, dead or alive!"

The book was an instant success upon publication, as was the first film version, which came out just two years later with the tagline, "Hard lives, quick deaths, undying love!" A silent film, it featured some of the biggest stars of the day, including Ronald Coleman as Beau.

The 1966 film version is the least true to the story, losing not only one of the Geste brothers but dispensing with the missing gem and family dishonour to have Beau appear instead as an American businessman determined to take the blame for embezzlement by a dishonest partner. Starring Guy Stockwell as Beau, Leslie Nielsen in a rare non-comedic role as Lieutenant De Ruse and Telly Savalas as the tyrannical Sergeant-Major Dagineau, the film is less gripping than either of the earlier versions, perhaps because of the unnecessary meddling with the plot. One of the few links to earlier versions of the film is that it too was filmed in Arizona, rather than the Sahara.

Beau Geste is such an enduring favourite that it has sparked more film parodies than straight adaptations, including comic offerings from Abbot and Costello (*Abbott and Costello in the Foreign Legion*) and the British Carry On team (*Carry on... Follow That Camel*), whose interpretation of the story was filmed on Camber Sands on the south coast of England. The first of these spoofs is the 1931 silent film *Beau Hunks*, the first of two versions by the iconic comedy double act of Stan Laurel and Oliver Hardy. In both *Beau Hunks*, released in the UK as *Beau Chumps*, and the 1939 "talkie" *Flying Deuces*, the plot revolves around the cliché of a man joining the Legion in order to forget a lover. In both films a heartbroken Ollie decides to join the Legion, taking the perpetually compliant Stan away with him. In *Beau Hunks* Ollie's love interest is Jeanie-Weanie, or Jean Harlow, who only appears in the film as a photograph. When the pair reach their post, a fort in the Algerian desert, they discover that all their comrades have likewise signed up to forget Jeanie-Weanie, who is also the love interest of the rebel leader. To complete the Saharan motifs, Stan and Ollie become separated from their unit during a sandstorm, arriving at Fort Arid ahead of everyone else before single-handedly defeating the rebels and saving the day.

Profitable as the French Foreign Legion has proved for filmmakers, it is with Second World War films that the studios have really hit the jackpot. Replacing unfashionable empire-inspired story lines, directors were for decades able to draw on events that audiences understood as recent news rather than unremembered history. First among these was *Sahara*. Released in 1943, the action takes place in Egypt's western desert, beginning with an Allied retreat and concluding with news of victory at the first Battle of al-Alamein. Although an unashamed piece of Allied propaganda, *Sahara* remains an enjoyable film. Directed by Zoltan Korda, of *The Four Feathers* fame, it came out almost a year to the day after the end of the Second Battle of al-Alamein.

The film's leading actor is Humphrey Bogart, whose star was in the ascendant after the previous year's release of *Casablanca*, and he assured *Sahara*'s success. Billed as "A mighty story of adventure, courage and glory in the desert", the film follows a mixed-nationality group of Allied soldiers, consisting of Americans, British, Irish, French, South African and Sudanese who are, more or less, lost. Also in their company is an Italian prisoner, sympathetically portrayed railing against the idiocy of Mussolini and the evil of Hitler. The group come to a small, virtually waterless well only to be joined shortly thereafter by a similar-sized group of Germans. The crux of the film is a battle of wits between the two groups who face off and subsequently fight, while the desert threatens to kill them before they manage to kill each another. Bogart plays Sergeant Joe Gunn, a tank commander who brings the Allied stragglers to the well on his tank, Lulu Belle, and tries to negotiate food for water. Like other Saharan-based films, Korda's desert is as important as the soldiers, and one senses how terrified they are of the desert, the emotionless entity against both sides.

Sahara was Columbia Pictures top grossing film of the year, and with the film closing with an Allied victory it was an effective propaganda vehicle at a time when news of victories was scarce. Although Korda enjoyed working on location in Africa for other productions, it was impossible to shoot Sahara in situ, the war still being fought there, so it was filmed instead in Imperial Valley, California.

Released more than a decade after the war's end, *Ice Cold in Alex* (1958) perfectly captures the mayhem of any conflict but also aims to show heroism against the odds. The action centres on Captain Anson, played by John Mills, and his loyal but not-uncritical sergeant (Harry Andrews). While retreating from a German advance, the men are given the job of delivering two nurses, who have become separated from their unit, to Alexandria. An Axis attack forces the quartet to negotiate a path across the desert in an ambulance called Katy, while trying to avoid enemy troops. The group grow suspicious of Captain van der Poel, played by Anthony Quayle, a South African officer who claims to be lost. Added to this is the fact that battle-fatigued Anson is on the verge of becoming an alcoholic, and his forward progress depends on his vision of a bar in Alexandria where the beer is served ice cold, providing the film's evocative title.

During the course of their journey the British characters discover that Quayle is a German spy, although they do not tell him this until they are free of the Sahara, and in the comforting embrace of Alexandria and Captain Anson's favourite bar, the exterior shots of which were actually filmed in Tripoli's Cathedral Square, nearly 1000 miles west of Alexandria. The bond that has grown between them during the course of their struggle against the desert means that Anson reports Quayle to the authorities as a German prisoner of war who surrendered to them rather than as a spy, which would lead to his death by firing squad.

As the four sit at the bar with an ice cold beer in front of each of them, Anson does not wait for the usual niceties of raised glasses and "cheers", but empties his glass in a single, steady gulp as the others look on. Replacing his empty glass on the bar, Anson utters the immortal line, "Worth waiting for." Quayle's arrest allows the German officer to close the story by reminding viewers of the centrality of the desert in the production, to acknowledge that it was a case of, "All against the desert, the greater enemy."

One of the more intriguing Sahara-themed Second World War films is *The Hill* (1965), set in a British military prison camp in the Libyan Desert. While the war in the desert continues, the soldiers in the camp, who are mainly guilty of minor offences, are brutally mistreated by many of the prison's military police guards, who delight in handing out frequent and severe punishments for minor and imaginary infractions. Although he later wavers in his abuse of the men, one of the strictest disciplinarians is Regimental Sergeant-Major Wilson, played by Harry Andrews, who also played the sergeant in *Ice Cold in Alex*.

The unrelenting villain of the film is a new member of the prison staff, Staff Sergeant Williams, who takes sadistic pleasure from disciplining the prisoners, his favourite punishment being to force the men, in full kit and in the heat of the day, to repeatedly climb an artificial sand hill that stands in the middle of the prison yard, from which the film takes its title. The death of one of the prisoners, who fails to receive adequate medical attention from the camp's doctor (Michael Redgrave), precipitates a number of power struggles among the guards, with their different views on prisoner treatment, and the prisoners, who live in fear of being the hill's next victim.

The hero among the prisoners is Joe Roberts (played by Sean Connery, already established as James Bond in the previous year's *Goldfinger*). A former sergeant-major demoted for striking an officer, Roberts encapsulates the inherent predicament of prisoners and guards alike when he says, "Everyone is doing time here, even the screws." Although largely filmed in Spain, the director Sidney Lumet recalled in his autobiography that the weather was hot enough to recreate the feeling of a Saharan summer. Worried that the heat might lead to debilitating dehydration among his cast and crew, Lumet asked Connery if he was still urinating, to which Connery replied, "Only in the morning."

DESERT EPICS

More recently, the 1996 film adaptation of Michael Ondaatje's *The English Patient* achieved great critical success, winning nine Oscars and numerous other awards. Directed by Anthony Minghella, the film faithfully follows the novel, where the Sahara is the setting for romance and danger before and during the Second World War. An involved story, it tells a number of interconnected tales in non-linear fashion, revolving around themes such as crises of identity, betrayal and doomed love, all against the backdrop of pre-war desert exploration and the war itself.

The explorers of the story are based on the members of the Zerzura Club, the pioneering pre-war fraternity of Saharaphiles in the vanguard of motorized desert travel, including Ralph Bagnold, Patrick Clayton and the English patient himself, Laszló Almásy, played by Ralph Fiennes.

Although the Libyan Desert in Egypt, also known as the Western Desert, is central to the story, the all-star cast of Kristin Scott Thomas, Willem Dafoe and Colin Firth never set foot in Egypt, Tunisian authorities making it easier to shoot a film there. Because of budget constraints many purported shots of the Sahara, including some of the aerial views of the desert, were filmed in a soundstage, which is one of the film's few disappointing aspects.

With a post-war setting, another adaptation of a book to focus on the Sahara is *The Sheltering Sky* (1990). Based on Paul Bowles' 1949 novel, the director Bernardo Bertolucci's motion picture is considered by many to be one of the most beautiful works of cinema of the decade. Bowles hated it. In *Let It Come Down*, a film about his life, he says, "it should never have been filmed. The ending is idiotic and the rest is pretty bad,"—this despite having played the part of the film's narrator.

Starring Debra Winger and John Malkovich as Kit and Port Moresby, the film tells the story of an American couple in North Africa who are continually travelling south to ever-remoter desert locations. In part hoping to discover themselves, they are also ostensibly trying to salvage their moribund marriage although their friend from home, George Tunner, accompanies them on their travels. Tunner is the most excited by the prospect of the journey, exclaiming, "We're probably the first tourists they've had since the war." Kit replies disdainfully, "Tunner, we're not tourists. We're travellers." Unlike many of the films already discussed, Bertolucci was determined to film in the Sahara itself, which required the

Aït Benhaddou, Morocco, one location for *The Sheltering Sky*

crew to travel to locations in Morocco, Algeria and Niger. The extra effort of location shoots comes through on screen, with the enervating heat going a long way towards making civil, everyday relationships between the characters almost impossible.

Part Five

ENCOUNTERS

INDIGENES AND VISITORS

Chapter Sixteen

MEN WITH A MISSION

"We soon arrived among them, and were struck by terror at the sight: - huge mountains of loose sand piled up like drifted snow, towered two hundred feet above our heads on every side, and seemed to threaten destruction to our whole party."

Capt. James Riley, *Sufferings in Africa* (1817)

From the first meeting between a native Saharan and an outsider, goods and knowledge have been traded across the desert. These exchanges were not always carried out willingly; the interaction has often been marked by violence, but it has continued without interruption. When steps were taken to formalize relations between states, the presence of diplomats was required. When knowledge was sought, scientists from innumerable specialist fields were dispatched to obtain it. Apart from the Sahara itself, there was often little or nothing that bound together the otherwise disparate collection of individuals who were drawn into the desert's orbit.

Diplomats today benefit from the protection afforded by the recognition of other countries but for many years those sent out by their political masters could not always rely on such niceties. The arrival of a foreign diplomat was often met with unease by local authorities. Some were seen as an economic threat, wishing to pursue direct trade in territories where local rulers would rather maintain economic control. In other cases insularity made rulers wary of outsiders, who could be a threat to their power; in many cases, local chiefs lived to see these fears realized.

By the mid-seventeenth century European powers were sending representatives to Tripoli, in recognition of the state's *de facto* independence from Constantinople. Courting the *deys*, or rulers, of Tripoli was not always an easy task. For one thing, the city's most important commercial activity the rulers oversaw was state-sponsored piracy. Although foreign representation was largely restricted to the coastal ports, as termini of trans-Saharan trade, a base in one of those cities allowed diplomats to gather more information about the interior than their hosts would like.

One legendary British diplomat to the "Sublime Porte" in North Africa was Colonel Hanmer Warrington. Born two months after the

American Declaration of Independence, Warrington was an army officer for twenty years before being appointed British consul-general to Tripoli in 1814. At that time the city's ruler, Yusuf Pasha Karamanli, had seen corsair activity curtailed by the Royal Navy.

One result of this development, Warrington understood, was that the *dey* had turned his attention southward, developing ambitions to control the Saharan slave states of Bornu and Sokoto. Warrington believed that this was a great opportunity to garner information about the interior and possible new trading partners in that direction. As a result of the close relationship between the consul and the pasha, which Warrington once boasted meant he could "do anything and everything in Tripoli," there followed a remarkable period of British exploration, trade and anti-abolitionist agitation. If Warrington saw a conflict of interests between Britain's anti-slavery policy and the pasha's interest in the slaving empires of the south, he was apparently able to resolve this to his personal satisfaction.

Warrington's relationships with representatives of other foreign powers in Tripoli were often less friendly than those with the *dey*. In part because of his closeness to Karamanli, Warrington had an inflated sense of self-importance that his western counterparts considered haughty and arrogant. Recounting the details of one diplomatic battle with a foreign colleague, he closed his report to London with the words, "I am an Englishman (thank God). He is not."

While his own travels did not take him deep into the Sahara, he delighted in spending time with those explorers who came to see him during his 32-year tenure in Tripoli. He later became father-in-law to one of the more famous of these explorers when, in July 1825, his daughter Emma married Alexander Gordon Laing. Laing and Miss Warrington were married in a civil ceremony because there was no vicar available and Warrington insisted that the marriage remain unconsummated until an ordained priest could bless the couple.

Two days later, Laing set off for Timbuktu. He was lucky to survive one Tuareg attack en route, during which a number of his party were killed and Laing was left with 24 sword wounds to his skull and arms, resulting in the loss of one hand and an ear lobe. Laing eventually reached the famed city after an arduous journey via Ghadames and In Saleh, becoming the first European in modern times to do so. Resting in Timbuktu for about five weeks, Laing was, according to native reports, killed a few days after setting off on his homeward journey.

In spite of the Ottomans retaking direct control of the city in 1835, Warrington survived the change in political circumstances with élan, continuing to press for greater British representation in the Sahara. By persistence and force of his enormous, if flawed, personality, he convinced the Ottomans and the Foreign Office to accede to his demands, and the British established vice-consulates in Murzuq and Ghadames. As a result, Britain enjoyed unparalleled influence on trade and communications along the central Sahara routes. The vice-consul appointed to Ghadames was Charles Hanmer Dickson, grandson of the now late Consul Warrington, who died in retirement in Greece.

Dickson's duties included observing and reporting on trans-Saharan trade, promoting British trade interests and thwarting French ones. With French influence growing in neighbouring Algeria, there was a real fear of armed clashes between the British and French, who were exploring the area with increasing frequency from their own desert outposts. Dickson's first letter to the British foreign secretary Lord Palmerston after his arrival at Ghadames suggests he had much to learn when he wrote: "Yesterday the British flag was hoisted on my residence amid repeated volleys of Musquetry (sic)… The establishment of the first Christian in this city, which may well be recorded as an interesting event in its annals, has given universal satisfaction."

After the European nineteenth-century division of the Sahara the new powers were able to impose as much diplomatic representation as they chose, in many cases for the first time. In some cases these were "advisers" to the ruling potentate, in others the façade of cooperation was wholly absent. Whether before or after the gelding of local authorities, the Europeans rarely viewed the North Africans as political equals, frequently resentful if they had to negotiate with local notables at all.

With thoughts of life in the Sahara furthest from his mind, the American sea captain James Riley had the misfortune of experiencing it and slavery first-hand after his ship ran aground off the west coast of the Sahara. In the best tradition of lengthy Victorian titles, Riley's book was published as *Sufferings in Africa: Captain Riley's Narrative. An authentic narrative of the loss of the American brig Commerce, Wrecked on the Western Coast of Africa, in the month of August, 1815. With an account of the sufferings of her surviving officers and crew, who were enslaved by the wandering*

Arabs on the great African Desart (sic)*, or Zahahrah* (sic)*: and observations historical, geographical, etc. made during the travels of the author while a slave to the Arab, and in the Empire of Morocco.*

Riley's tale had an enormous impact upon publication, because even though slavery would be familiar to an early nineteenth-century readership, his text turned this state of affairs upside down, with white men enslaved by black masters. The crew's ordeal at the hands of their Saharawi captors, and those to whom they were sold, was indeed awful. Even so, the mistreatment doled out to Riley and his crew was probably not much worse than that endured by any number of the nearly four million slaves resident in America at the same time.

The crew of the *Commerce* started their captivity with a forced march through the deserts of the western Sahara and Mauritania, undergoing such indignities as being forced to drink their own and camels' urine if they wanted to drink at all. As Riley relates, "We were placed on our camel soon after daylight, having nothing to eat, and drinking a little camel's water, which we preferred to our own: its taste... though bitter was not salt." While it was then commonplace for foreign captives to be ransomed off, such transactions tended to take place at Mogador (modern Essaouira) in Morocco, or on the coast at St. Louis, 1200 miles south, in Senegal. Unfortunately for the *Commerce*, it ran aground at Cape Boujadour, midway between these trading posts.

Riley's book is also notable as the first American bestseller. Encouraged to write his memoirs by President Monroe, the publisher of *Sufferings* and its sequel said it was "read by more than a million now living in these United States. Probably no book that was ever published, in either this or any other country, obtained so extensive a circulation in so short a period, as did that Narrative, and probably none ever published, made so striking and permanent an impression upon the minds of those that read it." The book also has an important place in American history because among its one million readers was Abraham Lincoln upon whom it had such an impression that, along with the Bible and *The Pilgrim's Progress*, it was the book he said that most influenced his life and thinking on slavery.

In many cases, Americans and Europeans who became the prisoners of local tribesmen were lucky to receive the services of British consul William Willshire. Willshire, a Londoner, lived and worked in Mogador with his wife and children from 1814 to 1844, during which time he saved hundreds of foreign seamen and others from slavery. So instrumental was he in securing Riley's release that the grateful captain, on returning to America, founded a town in Ohio and named it Willshire.

In spite of having amassed a personal fortune through his business interests in Mogador, Willshire lost everything during a French attack, during the course of which Arabs from the interior looted the city. After the attack Willshire left the city, dying seven years later in Adrianople (today Edirne, Turkey) in a state of penury. Having fought to secure an annual pension of £100 from the Foreign Office in London, for his thirty years of loyal service in Africa and five in Adrianople, he was eventually granted his pension by Palmerston's government on 18 August 1851. Sadly he had died on the fourth.

Sometimes diplomats were also soldiers. Such was the case with William Eaton, the US consul at Tunis under President John Adams, an army officer and adventurer, and the first American to cross Egypt's Western Desert. A graduate of Dartmouth College, Eaton was selected for the trans-Saharan mission because so few Americans had any knowledge of North Africa. The purpose of his mission was twofold: to make contact with and reinstate Hamet Karamanli as pasha of Tripolitania, and to free Captain William Bainbridge and the 300 crew of the USS *Philadelphia*, prisoners in Tripoli because the US had stopped paying tribute to the Barbary states. (Yusef Karamanli, Hamet's younger brother, had responded to this refusal by declaring war on the Americans.)

Eaton himself was partly responsible for the change in US government policy, writing to Secretary of State, James Madison, "The more you give, the more the Turks will ask for." Appointed Navy Agent to the Barbary states, Eaton sailed to Alexandria and found Karamanli. Having promoted himself to the rank of general, Eaton outlined his plans to Karamanli, who warmly welcomed the American plot to return him to his throne. Leading a mixed force of 300 Arab cavalry, 70 Christian mercenaries, two sailors, eight Marines and 1000 camels, Eaton marched nearly 600 miles across the desert. Having failed to secure adequate funds or supplies for the march, the party almost starved to death during the two-month journey to Derna. The ensuing Battle of Derna was the first engagement involving American forces on foreign soil, providing part of the opening line of the US Marines' Hymn, "From the halls of Montezuma to the shores of Tripoli."

The contingent of Marines were led into battle by Lieutenant Presley O'Bannon, whose bravery so inspired Hamet Karamanli that he presented O'Bannon with his personal sword, since when a Mameluke-style sword has been traditional for Marine Corps officers' ceremonial uniform. Unfortunately for Hamet, however, news arrived that a treaty had been made recognizing his brother the usurper. Signed by Tobias Lear V, newly created American consul-general in North African and former personal secretary to George Washington, the treaty forced Hamet, Eaton and the other non-Arabs to sail away, having fought and won a battle for no reason.

Ninety-three years after Eaton's trek, Major Amédée-François Lamy of the French Army was at the head of another military column crossing the Sahara. In 1898-99 he led a French force south through French Algeria to Lake Chad. En route his force occupied the principal oases, including Tuat, Tamanrasset, Aïr and Zinder, which they were keen to ensure remained in French hands.

The success of the mission not only allowed the French to travel at will in the desert, but in conquering Chad Lamy connected all of France's West Africa territories. Meeting with two other French missions—coming from Congo and Niger respectively—at Kousséri in modern Cameroon, Lamy led a force of 1200 infantry and cavalry in a long-anticipated clash against the Sudanese rebel leader Rabih as-Zubayr and his forces. Having formed his own empire in the Chad Basin, as-Zubayr was the main obstacle to French domination of the region.

During the course of the battle both Lamy and as-Zubayr were killed, but when as-Zubayr's forces were routed, the French victory meant the creation of a single French Saharan super-state, the capital of which was named Fort-Lamy in honour of the French man of the hour. In 1970 the Chadian government issued a 1000-franc gold coin to mark the tenth anniversary of independence, of which one side bore the legend "Commandant Lamy 1900" and an image of the French soldier. Three years later Fort Lamy was renamed N'Djamena, eliminating one more name from the Sahara's short-lived, European imperial past.

PROFESSIONALS

The work conducted by non-military professionals such as archaeologists is by its nature painstakingly slow, with few discoveries having any impact on the public consciousness. The single most impressive discovery in the

Howard Carter opens Tutankhamen's tomb

past century is without doubt the tomb of Tutankhamen. Discovered by Howard Carter in the Valley of the Kings in 1922, the unearthing of the virtually undisturbed tomb of a Pharaoh was of peerless importance, containing as it did an incredible array of royal property including a large quantity of gold-work and precious jewellery. Carter spent numerous digging seasons living in a small house on the Theban Necropolis on the edge of the Sahara, from where he directed the digging, convinced he was going to make a significant find. By 1922 Lord Carnarvon, Carter's financial backer, had lost faith in the project and declared that digging season would be the last he would fund.

The discovery of Tutankhamen's tomb more than repaid Carnarvon's investment and made Carter, with the help of the British journalist H. V. Morton (later author of the popular *In Search of* series of travel books), the most famous archaeologist of all time. The fact that the tomb contained so many riches was what captivated the public. For gasp-inducing wonder, a pottery shard, however important, can never hope to compete with a golden death mask.

Of all the accounts left behind by foreigners who worked in the Sahara, one of the most pleasing is *A Cure for Serpents* by the Count Alberto Denti di Pirajno (1886-1968). When he first arrived Dr. Pirajno was responsible for a small group of Italian troops under the command of the Duke of Aosta. Nearly twenty years later, and after time in Eritrea, Ethiopia, and Somaliland, Pirajno was a count and the last Italian governor of Tripoli. As such, he handed control of the city over to British forces when they arrived in 1943.

A more sympathetic colonial administrator than many of his peers, Pirajno's medical training also made him a careful observer of the people and places he visited, recognizing and appreciating the differences between the people he encountered. Writing about Ghadames, for example, Pirajno notes that it "is a strange country, and I learnt many things in the shade of its palm trees. The Ghadames speak Arabic with Arabs, Tamahak with the Tuaregs and Hausa with their servants, but among themselves they use a Berber dialect which no one speaks outside the walls of the city... Enclosed within their oasis and isolated in the vast desert, the Ghadames nevertheless maintain contacts all over the world; they combine the flabbiness of sedentary people with the broad vision of the nomads."

When not tending the human sick, Pirajno turned his attention to sick animals which he was just as happy to treat. Here he describes a sick lion:

> People who have never had a young lion with a fractured femur in the house will be unable to imagine how unsettling it can be. In the first place, someone had to take care of the beast... I sounded Jemberie and when, appealing to his religious sense, I mentioned that Neghesti was also one of God's creatures, he agreed, but observed gravely that God had placed lions in the forest and not in men's houses.

Another man who did not start his career as a government official was Hanns Vischer, who became a member of the British Colonial Administrative Service after starting out as a missionary. Originally Swiss, Vischer became a British citizen and gave up the missionary life to work among the Hausa of northern Nigeria. Although the majority of his career was spent working in the education sector in Nigeria, for which services he was knighted, he also produced an account of a 1906 journey, *Across the Sahara from Tripoli to Bornu*.

On a significant journey, crossing the desert along a former slave route, Vischer's caravan of forty men and women and forty camels suffered a frequently waterless journey through British, French and Ottoman territory, gathering much original knowledge along the way. Vischer had hoped to do the reverse journey the next year but was denied permission by his superior in Nigeria. Major Sir Hanns Vischer retired from colonial service in 1939, spending the war working for the British Underground Propaganda Committee until his death in 1945.

MISSIONARIES

The arrival in the Islamic Sahara of individuals preaching the Christian gospel was often seen as a threat not only to the quiet life of those living unremarkably in remote oases, but also to the authority, and possible stability, of the state. Where one foreign preacher was allowed to wander, others might follow, and men of the Good Book were sometimes the forerunners of men of the gun. Suspicion thus fell on Christian missionaries, who were viewed as theologically unsound and harbingers of conquest, perhaps reporting back on a town's defences or the disposition of its inhabitants.

Few nineteenth-century missionaries were in the direct employ of their national governments but the majority of them unquestionably arrived with a strong belief that European imperial rule was in the best temporal and spiritual interests of the natives. Yet Islam was, and is, so dominant that any success on the part of European missionaries in finding converts among the denizens of the Sahara probably enjoyed no more than single figures.

The most famous foreign missionary to live in the Sahara was Charles Eugène de Foucauld (1858-1916). As a young man, the Strasbourg-born, aristocratic Foucauld was fond of those things most young men appreciate, including women and wine. General Laperinne, known in French history as the conqueror of the Sahara, and military cadet with Foucauld at the École Spéciale Militaire de Saint-Cyr, used to say that when they trained together, "The only thing Foucauld liked about the mass was the wine." Laperinne's fame was such that during French rule Tamanrasset was called Fort Laperinne, becoming Tamanrasset only after Algerian independence. Although somewhat dissolute, Foucauld did well as an army officer, attracting some fame in France for his travels through southern Morocco, disguised as one Rabbi Joseph Aleman, gathering topographical and other intelligence for French military cartographers, for which exploits the Société Géographique of Paris awarded him their Gold Medal.

Whatever else in his background or upbringing might have influenced his development, it was Foucauld's travels in the Sahara that were the catalyst for his transformation in adulthood. Leaving the army, he toyed with the idea of converting to Islam before becoming a Trappist monk, to the surprise of everyone who knew him. Twelve years later, after living and studying in Palestine, whose deserts he found too heavily populated for his extreme ascetic tastes, he asked to be sent back to the Sahara. Foucauld moved to one of the Sahara's most remote spots, Assekrem, which means "the end of the world" in Tamasheq, the Tuareg language. In the Ahaggar Mountains, thirty miles from the famed if hardly accessible Tamanrasset, the site provided Foucauld with the solitude for which he yearned.

Like St. Anthony 1600 years earlier, the desert's loneliness was precisely what appealed to Foucauld. As one diary entry noted, "I find this desert life profoundly, deeply sweet. It is so pleasant and healthy to set oneself down in solitude, face to face with eternal things; one feels oneself penetrated by the truth." Yet in spite of choosing the life of a hermit, Fou-

De Foucauld, the hermit of Assekrem

cauld also frequently bemoaned his isolation and enjoyed the company of his compatriots on the rare occasions they visited.

Over time the Tuareg accepted Foucauld's presence, allowing him to live among them for the next fifteen years. In terms of his mission to convert them, Foucauld must be considered a failure. As he wrote in a letter, those he converted consisted of "an old black woman at Beni Abbès. I also baptised a small baby who was in danger of dying, who had the joy of leaving this earth almost immediately for heaven. Lastly, I baptised a 13-year-old boy, but it was not I who converted him. He was brought to me by a French sergeant who had taught him his catechism and prepared him to receive the sacraments. You see, my dear brother, I am really a useless servant."

Of more practical use, Foucauld produced the first dictionary of Tamasheq. One of the more intriguing discoveries he made while compiling this was that the language has no word for virgin.

The coming of the First World War increased political tensions in the Sahara, so that not even in the remoteness of the Ahaggar was Foucauld able to retreat from the world. The Sanussi fraternity, which had long been agitating for independence, started acting in force against French interests, including raids against remote military outposts.

In December 1916, Foucauld was staying in a French compound at Tamanrasset when it was attacked by a band of Sanussi, searching for weapons and information about French forces in the area. During the course of the robbery Foucauld was accidentally shot in the head by a nervous youth who was guarding him. He died almost immediately. Today Assekrem is a place of pilgrimage; the numbers who visit the hermitage would no doubt have forced Foucauld to move elsewhere in search of a quieter spot in which to pursue his life of contemplation.

Another example of the European religious presence in North Africa since the nineteenth century is that of the French Roman Catholic religious order, the Pères Blanc, or White Fathers. Founded in 1868 by the first Archbishop of Algiers, later Cardinal, Charles Martial Lavigerie, the order's stated mission was the conversion of Africa. With this aim in mind, it dispatched its first missionaries to the Sahara in 1876. As Lavigerie wrote at the time, "At this moment, three of our missionaries are with the Tuaregs en route for Timbuktu. They are resolved to establish themselves permanently in the capital of the Sudan or to give their lives in the cause of eternal truth." All three were killed, along with their Chaamba guide, within days of entering the Sahara, possibly even before Lavigerie had written his rather optimistic note. Five years later, the next group of White Fathers to venture into the Sahara met with the same fate. Much more recently, a number of White Fathers were murdered during the course of the Algerian Civil War.

Paul Bowles was also familiar with the work of the White Fathers, paying the following tribute to them in *Their Heads Are Green and Their Hands are Blue* (1963):

> More extraordinary were the Pères Blancs, intelligent and well-educated.
> There was no element of resignation in their eagerness to spend the re-

mainder of their lives in distant outposts, dressed as Moslems, speaking Arabic, living in the rigorous, comfortless manner of the desert inhabitants. They made no converts and they expected to make none. "We are only here to show the Moslem that the Christian can be worthy of respect," they explained.

To this day the order maintains houses in a number of Saharan nations, including Algeria and Tunisia, although they now concentrate their energies on education rather than proselytizing.

The Sahara has attracted the religiously inspired since time immemorial. Its appeal for anyone seeking solitude is obvious. Life in the desert can be demanding, and perhaps there is an underlying association between the intrinsic discomfort of living in such a physically challenging environment and the challenge of a life of contemplation. In the desert though, life is simpler. With physical needs reduced to a minimum, it is expected that the purity and simplicity of desert life will help those who are searching for God, by whatever name they refer to him. As Merton once wrote, quoting St. Anthony, "The basic principle of desert life: that God is the authority and that apart from His manifest will there are few or no principles."

ASCENT OF THE GREAT PYRAMID.

Chapter Seventeen

LITERARY TRAVELLERS AND TOURISTS

"Caravan tours across the Sahara may well be organized by the tourist agencies in a not distant future."

Frank Cana, article in *Geographical Journal* (1915)

The Sahara has been a destination for foreign travellers for millennia. In centuries past many of these were soldiers; today they are more likely holidaymakers. Tourist souvenirs have replaced the spoils of war. Soldiers and settlers aside, there have always existed those who have journeyed to see what they might see, following different impulses; these usually forgotten journeymen and women passed through the desert, some intending to return home, others not. For centuries after the Arab invasion, the largest annual migration was by those performing the *hajj* to Mecca, and back.

The idea of tourism proper only came about with the rise in leisure time enjoyed by an ever-growing number of Europeans, one result of the Industrial Revolution. Not coincidentally, the opportunity and ability to travel for pleasure was at first monopolized by wealthier citizens from those European nations responsible for the large-scale invasion of the region. By the late 1880s, when the Berlin Conference had established the rules by which European nations would play out the Scramble for Africa, France had claimed Algeria and Tunisia, and was making significant inroads into Chad, Mali and Mauritania. Britain, meanwhile, had occupied both Egypt and the Sudan, and Thomas Cook and Sons were selling Nile tours.

These first modern tourists, who were treated to excursions into the Sahara, paid a single price to cover the cost of the journey, accommodation and food. Thus the package holiday was born. Founded in 1841, Thomas Cook and Sons became massively successful, and not entirely through its package holidays. Business also boomed because the company won a contract to run a postal service between Britain and Egypt, the opportunity arising from Egypt's unexpected declaration of bankruptcy and subsequent occupation by Britain. Visitors flooded the land in ever-greater numbers for the rest of that and the next century, sailing the Nile and stopping at the Pyramids in droves.

Instead of enjoying the desert, Anthony Trollope was wholly focused on government business—he was there to set up the Egyptian postal system—and meeting his daily word count. As he notes matter-of-factly in *An Autobiography*, "While I was in Egypt I finished *Doctor Thorne* and on the following day began *The Bertrams*." Mark Twain was likewise there to write, casting his sardonic eye over his surroundings and the proceedings of the natives before writing in *The Innocents Abroad*: "[I] landed where the sands of the Great Sahara left their embankment… A laborious walk in the flaming sun brought us to the foot of the great Pyramid of Cheops. It was a fairy vision no longer. It was a corrugated, unsightly mountain of stone."

More sympathetic, if no less disgruntled, William Golding wrote in *An Egyptian Journal* about his holiday there after winning the 1983 Nobel Prize for Literature: "There was nothing about the scene to distinguish it from any river scene in any city. The pyramids, of course, were hidden by buildings." To go beyond the pyramids and into the Sahara proper required, as it still does, a degree of planning that excluded all but those who were set on seeing more of the desert.

EARLY OBSERVERS

Before the First World War those parts of North Africa administered by Britain and France were seen as safe. In a sense, countries like Egypt and Algeria had ceased to be foreign, becoming instead part of European North Africa. As a result, increasing numbers of tourists, many of them writers, were travelling there.

André Gide (1869-1951) first travelled to these countries in 1893. In *Amyntas: North African Journals*, Gide writes:

> I love the desert more than anything else. The first year I was a little afraid of it because of the wind, because of the sand… But last year I began taking immense walks, with no other purpose than to lose sight of the oasis. I would walk—I walked until I felt myself immensely alone in that vast expanse. Then I began to look. The sands had velvety touches of shadow under each hillock; there were wonderful rustlings in every breath of wind; because of the great silence, the least sound could be heard.

These notebooks, published in 1906, cover the five-year period Gide spent travelling in the region, and are rightly considered an important work in his development as a writer. Indeed, Gide once declared, "Few realize I have never written anything more perfect than *Amyntas.*"

Gide travelled widely in Algeria and Tunisia, and enjoyed the relaxation afforded by escaping the moral and sexual strictures of contemporary France. In the course of his travels he met Oscar Wilde in Blida, northern Algeria, in January 1895, just three months before Wilde's libel trial against the Marquess of Queensberry. Although the two had met once before in Paris, both men were more at ease in North Africa because they were far removed from, their own societies. As Gide records in his diaries, it was during his initial trip to French North Africa that he enjoyed his first homosexual and heterosexual encounters.

Of all Gide's writings, *L'Immoraliste* draws most inspiration from the Sahara. A contemporary parable set in the desert, Gide described the book as "a fruit filled with bitter ashes. It is like those colocynths of the desert which grow in barren, burning places; you come to them parched with thirst and are left with a burning all the more fierce. Yet on the golden sands they are not without beauty." The book, which was considered scandalous when it was published in 1902, deals with the rejection of societal norms by a newly married, upper-middle-class French couple travelling in North Africa, with results that are not positive for either party. As they move further from the French environment they are used to, the couple are able, or perhaps forced, to shed more and more layers of their Europeanism. The further into the Sahara he travels, the more the agnostic protagonist, Michel, finds himself enamoured with the beautiful young boys of the oases, feelings he keeps from his religious wife.

Having returned to France for a period, Michel and his wife then travel again to North Africa where Michel is disappointed by his former infatuations, who have either married or lost the beauty of youth. Although his wife is ill, his disillusionment forces them to travel further south where, in the sad oasis of Touggourt, his wife dies and Michel decides to take her body to el-Kantara for burial because, as he says, "the French cemetery at Touggourt is a hideous place, half devoured by the sand."

Another writer who spent time exploring North Africa was Norman Douglas. Like Gide's, Douglas' journeys were made in part to leave something of Europe behind. Although his first visit to the Sahara was ten years earlier, it was a three-month period Douglas spent in the south of Tunisia

Touggourt, Algeria

during the winter of 1909-10 that forms the basis of his book about the region, *Fountains in the Sand: Rambles among the Oases of Tunisia*. Douglas' only book with a North African theme, *Fountains* was published in 1912, five years before *South Wind*, the novel that established his literary fame. Despite being full of the casual racism which was the norm at the time— for example, he scathingly dismisses the locals saying, "In a land where no one reads or writes or thinks or reasons, where dirt and insanity are regarded as marks of divine favour, how easy it is to acquire a reputation for holiness"—*Fountains* remains a text that offers useful insights about the country as it was then.

Douglas also makes himself the target of certain unflattering observations, although one cannot be entirely sure if these are genuine or literary artifice. Giving his thoughts regarding the Arab work ethic, Douglas tries to convince us that he is the same as those he is slandering, remarking: "The chief mental exercise of the Arab, they say, consists in thinking how to reduce his work to a minimum. Now this being precisely my own ideal of life, and a most rational one, I would prefer to put it thus: that of many kinds of simplification they practise only one—omission, which does not always pay." His views on local women are no less damning: "The

Arab woman is the repository of all the accumulated nonsense of the race, and her influence upon the young brood is retrogressive and malign." It should be said that Douglas shows no less disdain for the Europeans he meets, and for what he sees as their ill-informed view of the local population.

Yet when Douglas turns his attention to the desert landscape, his descriptions are often moving. Writing about the silence of the desert, he offers a poetic meditation:

> Face to face with infinities, man disencumbers himself. Those abysmal desert-silences, those spaces of scintillating rock and sand-dune over which the eye roams and vainly seeks a point of repose, quicken his animal perception; he stands alone and must think for himself—and so far good. But while discarding much that seems inconsiderable before such wide and splendid horizons, this nomad loads himself with the incubus of dream-states.

When Agatha Christie, or Agatha Miller as she then was, first journeyed to Egypt with her mother in 1910, the trip remained lengthy but it was a destination which the moderately well off could afford, leaving northern Europe in search of winter sunshine. Indeed, one of the reasons Agatha Miller's mother decided to spend a winter in Egypt was that her daughter's coming-out as a debutante would be more affordable than in England.

During her first visit to the Middle East Agatha showed little interest in either the Sahara or the monuments of Ancient Egypt. Writing in her autobiography about her mother's attempts to take her to Luxor, she confessed, "I protested passionately with tears in my eyes. The wonders of antiquity were the last thing I cared to see." Yet her first sight of the Sahara obviously had some impact on her because, on her return to England, she wrote her first, unpublished, novel, which she set in Egypt and called *Snow on the Desert*.

She returned to Egypt twice in the 1930s, with her husband, the archaeologist Max Mallowan. By now her interest in the desert had grown, and she used it to good effect when writing *Death Comes as an End*, published in 1945, and a play, *Akhnaton*, which was not published until 1973. Christie's only murder mystery with an ancient setting, she described

Death Comes as an End as "my 11th-Dynasty Egyptian Detective Story". During the war Agatha and Max were separated on account of his wartime service, which took him, via Cairo, to the Sahara in Tripolitania and the Fezzan.

Edith Wharton also ventured into the Sahara in the early days of tourism first travelling to Algeria and Tunisia in 1914, having already moved permanently from America to settle in France. When Wharton went to Morocco three years later, she was working for people whom the war had made refugees; she was also the doyenne of American literary society. The opportunity for her Moroccan journey followed an invitation from General Hubert Lyautey, then serving as Resident-General of the French Protectorate in North Africa, and to whom Wharton dedicated *In Morocco*, her 1920 book about her travels there. Lyautey was a leading figure in France's expansion into Algeria, a political position which matched Wharton's view of herself as a "rabid imperialist". Parts of *In Morocco* read uncomfortably like a panegyric to the general ("It is not too much to say that General Lyautey has twice saved Morocco from destruction"), and displaying extreme prejudice against the local population, Jews and Muslims alike, Wharton saw the region's only hope to lie in the French "civilizing mission".

If one can ignore her far-from-neutral assessment of the colonial experiment, Wharton's views on travelling at that time are interesting, coming, as she notes, at a unique moment in the history of tourism and the Sahara:

> The next best thing to a Djinn's carpet, a military motor, was at my disposal every morning; but war conditions imposed restrictions, and the wish to use the minimum of petrol often stood in the way of the second visit which alone makes it possible to carry away a definite and detailed impression… These drawbacks were more than offset by the advantage of making my quick trip at a moment unique in the history of the country; the brief moment of transition between its virtually complete subjection to European authority, and the fast-approaching hour when it is thrown open to all the banalities and promiscuities of modern travel.

Travelling to the Tunisian Sahara in 1921, Carl Gustav Jung wanted to believe he was travelling to a place that existed somehow outside of time, not a realm transformed by European occupation. As he wrote in *Memories, Dreams, Reflections*, "In travelling to Africa to find a psychic observation post outside the sphere of the European I unconsciously wanted to find that part of my personality which had become invisible under the influence and the pressure of being European." The Sahara, for Jung, represented something unchanging, literally time-less. He remarked: "While I was still caught up in this dream of a static, age-old existence, I suddenly thought of my pocket watch, the symbol of the European's accelerated tempo. This, no doubt was the dark cloud that hung threatening over the heads of these unsuspecting souls. They suddenly seemed to me like the game who do not see the hunter but, vaguely uneasy, scent him—'him' being the god of time who will inevitably chop into the bits and pieces of days, hours, minutes, and seconds that duration which is still the closest thing to eternity." Warming to his theme of time and the desert, Jung went further:

> The deeper we penetrated into the Sahara, the more time slowed down for me; it even threatened to move backwards. The shimmering heat waxes rising up contributed a good deal to my dreamy state, and when we reached the first palms and dwelling of the oasis, it seemed to me that everything here was exactly the way it should be and the way it had always been.

Among those in the modern world who pursue adventurous travels so that others do not have to, the former member of the Monty Python team and television personality Michael Palin is perhaps the most famous. Through a combination of engaging encounters, an almost saint-like patience and a gift for not taking himself too seriously when confronted by any manner of bizarre situations, Palin's television series and book *Sahara* are fine examples of why the genre of adventure travel with a film crew is so popular today. Viewers are allowed to live vicariously through the (mis-) adventures of a frequently tireless, always genial host and guide.

The journey undertaken by Palin and his crew covered 10,000 miles through nine countries in 99 days. Although *Sahara* was undoubtedly very entertaining, what made it special was the way it exposed its audience to some of the remotest corners of the planet, and revealed otherwise ignored or unknown lives of those who call the desert home, including the fate of refugees in the ongoing dispute between Morocco and the independence-starved people of Western Sahara. From their favourite armchairs, millions who would otherwise never get close to the North African desert were able to do so.

WILFRED THESIGER

Writing in 1930, Evelyn Waugh said, "Every Englishman abroad, until it is proved to the contrary, likes to consider himself a traveller and not a tourist." This sentiment would undoubtedly have resonated with, indeed might have been written for, Wilfred Thesiger. In many ways the archetype of an old-school British explorer, Thesiger shunned motorized transport in favour of the hardship and concomitant pleasure of travelling with animals and men. Although he became a household name—at least in those houses where books about deserts are read—with *Arabian Sands*, which is about crossing the Empty Quarter in Arabia, his first expedition was in the Sahara.

In 1938, while working as an assistant district commissioner in the Sudan, Thesiger crossed the Ennedi Plateau from Darfur to the Tibesti Mountains. About his chosen, car-free means of travel Thesiger wrote, "I

The inhospitable Tibesti Mountains

had hired camels to take me as far as Borkou, after which it would be necessary to use Tibbu camels used to travelling among the mountains… We travelled light, the distance before us being great and the time at our disposal short… We had no kit other than our rifles, sheepskins, blankets, and a small tent."

It was in the Ennedi that the last lion in the Sahara was spotted two years after Thesiger's visit. (Another Saharan-based species that managed to avoid extinction by living in the Ennedi is the Nile crocodile, which is noted for its dwarfism, because of the harshness of the environment and the limited availability of prey.) Although not guilty of eliminating the last lion in the Ennedi, Thesiger was a keen hunter in his early years, usually for food on the trail for his guides and himself. In his account of the Tibesti journey Thesiger's party does not encounter any animal more threatening than a gazelle. He did, however, come across and record a number of items of rock art, as pointed out to him by his guide. These pictures included hunting scenes and petroglyphs of numerous animal species long since vanished both from the Ennedi and the Sahara as a whole.

During the course of the journey, Thesiger and his guide, Idris Daud, climbed to the top of the volcano Emi Koussi, which at 11,302 feet, is the highest point in the Sahara. Downplaying the importance of his journey in a region then almost unknown to outsiders, Thesiger modestly remarks, "I had covered a considerable distance during these three months, some 200 miles in all, but only at the cost of continuous travelling. Many of my observations were in consequence superficial."

Even in Thesiger's day cars were virtually ubiquitous in those places they could travel. Yet this does not mean that for desert travel the camel has been consigned to the past. Since Thesiger there have been a number of individuals whose pleasure it has been to walk in the Sahara, renouncing cars in favour of camels (myself among them). Michael Asher is one such traveller who has wandered many miles on foot in the Sahara, and who fully appreciates the importance of local knowledge when doing so. In 1986 Asher embarked on a camel-borne journey to demonstrate that the age of non-mechanical travel is far from a thing of the past. Having lived and worked for a number of years in Sudan's Darfur region, Asher and his wife, Mariantonietta Peru, walked the breadth of the Sahara. Heading east from Mauritania, their epic 4500-mile foot journey with camels ended at the Nile at Abu Simbel. It took them nine months and was the first crossing of the Sahara at its widest point. The title of his account of the trek, *Impossible Journey*, is only just short of the truth.

Eschewing camels, Bruce Chatwin's own Saharan outings were more touristic in nature than those made by Thesiger and Asher. In deciding to travel to the talismanic oasis of Timbuktu, Chatwin understood that he was perhaps not making an entirely rational choice. And indeed, the legend did not survive his initial encounter. As he writes, "There are two Timbuctoos. One is the administrative centre of the Sixth Region of the Republic of Mali … And then there is the Timbuctoo of the mind—a mythical city in a Never-Never Land, an antipodean mirage, a symbol for the back of beyond or a flat joke. 'He has gone to Timbuctoo,' they say, meaning 'He is out of his mind.'… 'Was it lovely?' asked a friend on my return. No. It is far from lovely; unless you find mud walls crumbling to dust lovely—walls of a spectral grey, as if all the colour has been sucked out by the sun."

ADVENTURE TOURISM
If the basic business arrangements involved in package holidays have not changed much since Thomas Cook started taking travellers to Egypt, the type of experience customers now want means they bear little resemblance to those holidays enjoyed by our Victorian forebears. The rise of adventure travel is one of the more obvious departures from the more traditional Nile cruises, which brush against one of the Sahara's sandy fringes.

Those inclined to take adventure holidays do not sleep on beaches with unread paperbacks beside them. If it is possible to draw up a league table of adventurousness, one likely element to feature would be the effort or endurance required to complete, or survive, the so-called adventure holiday. The Sahara is able to provide the setting for such individuals in the form of the Marathon des Sables. An annual foot race that takes place in the Moroccan Sahara, contestants cover 150 miles in five days. They also have to carry everything they will need for the duration of the race, except water and tents.

In spite of two recorded competitor deaths, this ultra-marathon annually attracts an international field of runners, professionals and very fit amateurs alike, and with a limited number of available places, there is generally a waiting list of those hoping to join in the fun. First run in 1986, the event has been dominated in recent years by local athletes, the Moroccan Ahansal brothers, Lahcen and Mohammed, winning an impressive thirteen times since 1997. Described by the event's organizers as the word's hardest foot race, a self-effacing friend of mine who successfully completed the race in 2008 described it as "the hardest race anyone could do." I have yet to test the veracity of this claim.

Although the Marathon des Sables is unquestionably an extreme race, there is an exclusive group of three athletes who might consider that challenge little more than a training run. Starting in November 2006, Ray Zahab from Canada, Kevin Lin from Taiwan and American Charlie Engle ran an incredible 4,300 miles across the Sahara, starting from the Atlantic coast at St. Louis, Senegal. Followed by their support team and a small film crew, on hand to record the unique event, the three ran approximately forty miles every day for the next 111 days, their journey ending when they ran into the waters of the Red Sea.

The documentary about their journey, *Running the Sahara*, highlights both how fraught with emotion the atmosphere can become when three athletes are undergoing such a challenge and also how small three people running across the Sahara are. Others have already walked, run and cycled around the globe, but in taking on the Sahara the three-man team were tacitly acknowledging the unique place this desert still has in the popular imagination. More than any other similar massive stretch of the planet, and none is truly comparable, the Sahara continues to excite and terrify, even at a safe distance.

For those who shun foot races, the Sahara until recently also hosted the world's most famous motor race. First held in 1978, the Paris-Dakar Rally is so famous that organizers and followers these days more usually refer to it as The Dakar. In spite of its name, the rally has not been held in the Sahara since 2007 because of fears about al-Qaeda terrorist activity in the Maghreb. As a result, subsequent races, while retaining the Dakar Rally name, have taken place in South America.

Competitors are divided into categories for cars, motorcycles, and lorries and, when it took place in the Sahara, the rally attracted criticism from various quarters, including environmental groups, who were concerned about the impact the race would have on delicate Saharan ecosystems and other campaigners who questioned what benefits the race would bring to those who live in the desert, the populations there being among the poorest in the world. The rally has also resulted in nearly sixty deaths since it was first held, mostly local bystanders. Perhaps note should be made of the Tuareg saying: "Patience comes from God, and haste from the devil."

The most famous incident to occur during the rally was in 1982, when Mark Thatcher, son of the then British Prime Minister Margaret Thatcher and proudly sponsored by the condom manufacturer Durex, got lost in the desert. The disappearance of Thatcher, his co-driver and their mechanic set off a full-scale land and air search of the area. They were found safe and un-injured after six days, having become lost after stopping to carry out es-sential repairs to their car.

As the decision to relocate made by the organizers of the Paris-Dakar Rally proves, a recent increase in kidnappings, particularly in Algeria, Mali and Niger, has had a negative impact on the numbers willing to visit remoter parts of the desert. However, with planning and careful manage-ment, there is every reason to be optimistic about the possibilities that travel and tourism will become future sources of income for the desert dwellers. On the other hand, without careful planning, any untrammelled expansion in this sector will inevitably damage a unique environment, one that is a great deal more delicate than most people realize.

❧

Thinking about foreign visitors to the Sahara brings to mind the closing words of Chatwin's article on Timbuktu, where he writes, "The inhabi-tants of Timbuctoo are Arabs, Berbers, Songhoi, Mossi, Toucouleur, Bambara, Bela, Malinke, Fulani, Moors and Touaregs. Later came the English, French, Germans, the Russians and then the Chinese. Many others will come and go, and Timbuctoo will remain the same." Although the catalogue of ethnic groups that have come to the Sahara is accurate, the romantic idea of the Sahara and its people as something unchanging is far from the truth.

As we have already seen, the Sahara's physical landscape, its outward appearance, has changed beyond all recognition over the centuries. But the desert is not just a landscape; it is also made up of people, who like-wise continue to change over time. Each of the nationalities and races mentioned has had some impact on the desert. Future migrations will doubtless do the same.

Chapter Eighteen

PEOPLE OF THE SAHARA

"No one lives in the Sahara if he is able to live anywhere else."
Saharan Arab saying, quoted in Paul Bowles, *Their Heads Are Green
and Their Hands Are Blue* (1963)

While tourists come and go, there are those for whom the Sahara is home. Whether indigenous North Africans, Arabs or Europeans, a few million natives and foreigners have managed to find a place in the desert in which to settle. The best known, whom most associate with the Sahara, are the Bedouin or Bedu, Berber, Toubou and Tuareg, but there are others, smaller, less well-know tribes, sub-tribes and confederations.

The Bedu themselves, having settled in the region more than a millennium ago can comfortably claim indigenous status, so much so that they are often seen as the least distinct of the region's racial groups. This is especially true for those who have abandoned the traditional, nomadic way of life.

The most numerous and widespread of all the indigenous people who live in the Sahara are the Berber, who can be found from the Isle of Djerba, in Tunisia to the north to as far south as the River Niger and whose settlements are spread from as far east as the oasis of Siwa to the Atlantic coast in the west. In spite of this extensive range, their heartland remains the north-west parts of the Sahara in Morocco, Algeria, Tunisia and Libya. Famous Berber names include such diverse characters as St. Augustine, Ibn Battuta and the French-born international footballer Zinedine Zidane.

Although known in the West as Berbers, it is very rare for the people to use this name, referring to themselves rather as Amazigh or Imazighen, which Leo Africanus claimed meant "free people" in their native language, Tamazight. The Tamazight language group demonstrates, as one would expect considering the distance over which it is spread, great variety from one side of the Sahara to the other. These dialects do, however, have a common Punic ancestry. Now extinct, Punic was derived from ancient Phoenician, which the Tamasheq script, Tifinagh, resembles.

Although it is not known where the Berbers came from, nor when they first entered the region, Ibn Khaldun says of them, "They belong to a powerful, formidable, brave, and numerous people; a true people like so many others the world has seen—like the Arabs, the Persians, the Greeks, and the Romans. The men who belong to this family of peoples have inhabited the Maghreb since the beginning." The Romans also used specific names for specific Berber communities, for instance the Numidians and Mauri, from which latter term we derive Mauritania.

THE TUAREG

The Tuareg are actually a branch of the Berber family, whose origins are likewise unknown. As Hanbury-Tenison observed in *Worlds Within*, "They are a Berber people, who consider themselves white, although their skin is burnt dark by the sky. Babies are born snow white." He adds: "The Touareg, an ancient offshoot of the Kabyle Berbers of Algeria, were unappreciative of the 'civilizing mission' of the Roman legions and decided to put a thousand miles or more of desert between themselves and their would-be educators." Many Tuareg still live according to their traditional nomadic pastoral lifestyle but they are increasingly found leading settled lives, albeit still largely confined to their traditional Saharan heartland in southern Algeria, northern Mali and Niger. Their familiarity with the desert means the Tuareg have an unparalleled understanding of what it means to be a Saharan, being unique in their ability to survive the unforgiving desert. This knowledge, or philosophy, is encapsulated in the Tuareg saying, "The desert rules you, you don't rule the desert."

As a culturally and historically nomadic people, the Tuareg suffered in the colonial and post-colonial divisions of the Sahara, with their traditional lands being divided among modern nation states, including Algeria, Libya, Mali, Mauritania and Niger. The Tuareg were known as great warriors before the arrival of Europeans bearing rifles, which immediately made swordsmanship redundant. Today Tuareg blacksmiths still produce traditional swords, but very much as decorative items. Tuareg silversmiths are renowned for their fine jewellery, which is now primarily made for tourists conducted across the desert to the craft vendors by Tuareg guides.

Like the main branch of the family, the name Tuareg is a foreign term of ancient standing, the Tuareg themselves using various other names including Imazaghan and Kel Tamasheq, or speakers of Tamasheq. According to Paul Bowles, Tuareg means "lost souls", and has only been in use since the sixteenth century. Some writers have consequently wondered if

A Tuareg craftsman, Algeria

perhaps these central Sahara people are not in fact the otherwise long-since vanished Garamantes.

Whatever name is used by or for them, the Tuareg's most famous moniker remains the Blue Men. The nickname comes from the brilliant blue turban or veil that the men wear, which they use to cover their heads and most of the face. Known locally as a *tagelmust*, the cloth traditionally gets its colour from being dyed with indigo, and can be up to forty feet in length. Over time the indigo will leech from the cloth, staining the wearers' skin a distinctive shade of blue, making them literally the Blue Men of the Sahara. Interestingly, in Tuareg society it is only the men who cover their faces, women going about with head and face completely exposed. Tuareg women also have a saying: "A good husband is the one who brings enough water." This is as practical a test of masculine mettle as any in their dry world.

Although not at present a significant economic sector, tourism once held out the promise of large income in the heart of traditional Tuareg

Tinariwen

lands. Today the industry is in tatters, with many would-be desert tourists put off by the threat of kidnapping and more general banditry by genuine or otherwise al-Qaeda-affiliated groups. By far the biggest Tuareg cultural event to draw foreign visitors is the music-oriented Desert Festival, which is held annually in Mali, terrorism permitting.

Among Tuareg musicians, Tinariwen—from the plural of *tenere*, or desert, in Tamasheq—have undoubtedly met with the greatest international success. Apart from the appeal of a gutsy, bluesy, guitar-driven sound, the band became the darlings of western promoters and the media alike with their background as desert warriors, literally veterans of fighting in Libya and Mali. Having hung up their weapons, Tinariwen have since graced the stages of western music festivals from Glastonbury to Womad, and have had their music lauded by, among many others, U2, Radiohead, Carlos Santana and Henry Rollins.

Many early European travellers believed the Tuareg made their living solely by robbing desert travellers. As a result, the *tagelmust* was thought to be primarily a device for concealing the wearer's identity, rather than an important means of keeping sand out of eyes, nose and mouth. By the late twentieth century they had largely managed to shake off this reputation for thievery, and now increasingly work as guides in the burgeoning market for Saharan tourism. Hanbury-Tenison, who spent forty days with a group of Tuareg, wrote of his experience:

> One of the best things about this whole time has been how happy my team has been, consistently. There has not been a cross face or a bad mood from any of them. They start and end each day in the same way, chatting, smiling and laughing as they crouch around the fire. I know "Africans" are supposed to be happy people, but the Tuareg dismiss all black people from the south as "les Africains" and would be horrified to be lumped in with them. This is a Tuareg thing.

TOUBOU AND SAHRAWI

The main ethnic group found in the Tibesti region of northern Chad and southern Libya is the Toubou (or Tibou or Tebu). For centuries the nomadic Toubou were as little known to outsiders as their homeland, the secluded massif in northern Chad that still receives fewer visitors than any other part of the desert. For this reason, many older references to Ethiopian or Sudanic races in all likelihood actually apply to the Toubou. As the great 1911 edition of the *Encyclopaedia Britannica* states, "The allusions by classical writers to Ethiopians as inhabitants of the Sahara prove little, in view of the very vague and general meaning attached to the word." The same entry on the Sahara goes on to observe: "The Tibbu (q.v.) or Tebu, once thought to be almost pure negroes, proved when examined by Gustav Nachtigal in Tibesti, where they are found in greatest purity, to be a superior race with well-formed features and figures, of a light or dark bronze rather than black... Physically, the Tibbu appear to resemble somewhat the Tuareg."

Long separated from the main Chadian Empires such as Kanem-Bornu, which grew up around Lake Chad, the Toubou were historically ignored by the country's centre. When the French ruled Chad, which was only one part of French Equatorial Africa, the situation was not radically altered. With limited resources to police the enormous northern expanses of the country, French authorities were forced to reach an unspoken, mutually beneficial understanding with the Toubou; the French would not interfere with the Toubou as long as the Toubou did not attack their camel caravans or outposts.

Saharawi women in a refugee camp

Sahrawi is an Arabic word that means "people of the Sahara" or "desert people". The term is most commonly used by and for the people of Western Sahara, and usually carries nationalist connotations for the people of that country which has yet to achieve independence. Sahrawi is not, however, transposable for a citizen of Western Sahara, a colonial-era border which would have been meaningless to the people—as is the case for all Saharan borders—before the arrival of European mapmakers. Inaccurately, Sahrawi has now become almost synonymous with the Western Sahara, what the UN calls one of the world's last major non-self governing territories. Sadly, this has become the rather negative defining characteristic of the region's inhabitants: a landless people, refugees waiting for a nation. Many self-identifying Sahrawis live in Morocco, Mauritania and Algeria, as well as migratory populations in Mali, Niger and beyond.

The people themselves are a mixture of indigenous, that is to say pre-Islamic Berbers, Moors, Arabs from the seventh and subsequent centuries and black African ethnic groups from the Sahel and West Africa, both willing migrants and slaves.

Like those Sahrawi who call an Algerian refugee camp home, many denizens of the Sahara today—Berber and Bedu alike—find themselves unemployed and without the prospect of work. The Sahara continues to support numbers of livestock farmers: shepherds tending their flocks of sheep and goats in close proximity to the oases and camels and their owners living further out, beyond the pale, in the desert's more remote and wilder corners. Some, with the largest flocks or herds, can grow very rich in this line of business but many never rise beyond a basic, subsistence level, with a single animal providing a family as much wool, milk, and meat as it possibly can.

Apart from the farmers and those working in tourism, employment options in the desert are limited. Where oil and gas is found so too are jobs. However, many of these are for skilled workers, engineers and the like, leaving those with limited formal education, into which category most habitués of the Sahara fall, overlooked or unemployable. Looking to the future, planned projects such as solar energy plants seem unlikely to offer anything like the numbers of jobs needed among the desert natives. Instead, the more likely course of action is for the continued migration of young men out of the desert into the towns and cities, where the persistent belief is that the streets are paved with gold. The majority of those seeking work will realise that if they do find what they think is gold on the streets of Cairo or Lagos it is probably sand that has followed them out of the Sahara.

One thing that all nomads—Saharan or otherwise—need to survive is a vital understanding of their landscape, whether it relates to where they are, where they have been or where they are going. As Chatwin wrote in *Songlines*:

> To survive at all, the desert dweller—Tuareg or Aboriginal—must develop a prodigious sense of orientation. He must forever be naming, sifting, comparing a thousand different "signs"—the tracks of a dung beetle or the ripple of a dune—to tell him where he is; where the others are; where rain has fallen; where the next meal is coming from; whether if plant X is in flower, plant Y will be in berry, and so forth.

Such skills are in decline today, as more people opt to turn their backs on a traditionally nomadic way of life, favouring instead the less arduous life of the settled.

The decision about whether to stop moving or retain the nomadic life is not always a straightforward one, but nor, as Chatwin was to discover, are the reasons for making such a choice necessarily complex. Meeting an Adrar chief in a village two days from the Mauritanian trading centre of Chinguetti, Chatwin asked him about his life in the desert: "The sheikh, Sidi Ahmed el Beshir Hammadi, spoke perfect French. After supper, as he poured the mint tea, I asked him, naively, why life in the tents, for all its hardship, was irresistible. 'Bah!' he shrugged. 'I'd like nothing better than to live in a house in town. Here in the desert you can't keep clean. You can't take a shower! It's the women who make us live in the desert. They say the desert brings health and happiness, to them and to the children.'"

TWO INCOMERS: ISABELLE EBERHARDT AND PAUL BOWLES

Others take the decision to adopt the nomadic lifestyle although such a life is not part of their cultural heritage. Born in Geneva in the last quarter of the nineteenth century, Isabelle Eberhardt fell in love with the Sahara and eventually settled there after years wandering its northern fringes. The illegitimate daughter of an Armenian anarchist, ex-priest and later convert to Islam, Eberhardt was brought up wearing boy's clothes, which unorthodox background and upbringing prepared her well for the unconventional life she led. She and her mother first went to North Africa in 1897, but her mother died suddenly in the Algerian coastal town of Annaba, historically Hippo. After her mother's death Eberhardt spent most of the rest of her life in Algeria, exploring and living in the desert, often maintaining a masculine disguise, which made it possible for her to travel alone in the region.

Of her life in the desert she wrote, "Everything is so clear here, too clear! No more obstacles to overcome, no more progress, no more action. You wouldn't know how to act anymore, or almost how to think: you'd die of eternity... I wanted to possess this country, and this country has instead possessed me. Sometimes I wonder if this land won't take over all her conquerors, with their new dreams of power and freedom, just as she has distorted all the old dreams... Is it not the earth that makes men?" As much as any native-born Saharan, once she settled in the desert, Eberhardt came to understand the necessity of living according to its terms.

She writes movingly about her adopted lifestyle. In the following extract from *In the Shadow of Islam*, she notes in particular the peace and simplicity of life in the desert, reduced to the basics needed for survival:

> So it is on the desert roads of the south; long hours without sadness, without worry; vague and restful, where one may live in silence. I have never regretted a single one of these "lost" hours… I live this life of the desert as simply as the camel drivers… I have always preferred simplicity, finding in it vibrant pleasures which I don't hope to explain… When I sleep under the starry skies of this region, religious in their vastness, I feel penetrated by the earth's energies; a sort of brutality makes me straddle my mare and push straight ahead unthinkingly. I don't want to imagine anything; the stages of the journey only count as insignificant details. In this country without green, in this country of rock, something exists: time. And the spectacle of morning and evening skies.

Eberhardt died at the tragically young age of 27, ironically drowning in the desert, the victim of a flash flood that swept through the town to which she had travelled for a reconciliation with her frequently absent Algerian soldier-husband. After the flood many of her papers were rescued and her diaries and stories later published, some translated by Paul Bowles. Although Eberhardt had written for numerous French newspapers, including working as a war correspondent near Oran, it was these stories that secured her reputation.

Although a non-Saharan resident of North Africa, the work of the American composer and writer Paul Bowles is so closely associated with the desert that it is virtually impossible to separate the two. A long-term resident of Tangier, his residency there encouraged a stream of foreign visitors including Truman Capote, Gore Vidal, Tennessee Williams and numerous prominent so-called Beat writers, including Jack Kerouac, Allen Ginsberg and William Burroughs. Apart from his writing, Bowles was a noted translator, not just of Eberhardt but also of numerous Moroccan authors such as Mohamed Mrabet and Mohamed Choukri.

Bowles' own writing has, with good reason, come to be more closely associated with the Sahara than that of any other writer in modern times. Unlike many expatriate writers, his fiction and travel diaries distinguish

Paul Bowles

themselves through consistently creating characters as individuals and recording genuine scenes of daily life, as opposed to falling back on stereotypes and unchallenged assumptions. His Saharan settings, too, set him apart, so convincingly capturing a sense of place that the words are a more than adequate substitute for the real thing, the literary as a substitute for the literal.

Here for example, is Bowles' evocation of the stillness encountered upon first entering the Sahara:

> An incredible, absolute silence prevails outside the towns; and within, even in busy places like the markets, there is a hushed quality in the air, as if the quiet were a conscious force which, resenting the intrusion of

sound, minimises and disperses sound straightway... You leave the gate of the fort or town behind, pass the camels lying outside, go up into the dunes, or out onto the hard, stony plain and stand awhile, alone. Presently, you will either shiver and hurry back inside the walls, or you will go on standing there and let something very peculiar happen to you, something that everyone who has lived there has undergone and which the French call le baptême de la solitude. It is a unique sensation, and it has nothing to do with loneliness, for loneliness presupposes memory... For no one who has stayed in the Sahara for a while is the same as when he came in.

This spirit of the desert that changes people, not necessarily for the better, is central to Bowles' debut novel and most famous book, *The Sheltering Sky*. Published in 1949, it tells the story of an alienated expatriate couple travelling deeper into the Sahara, the seemingly empty desert central to the novel's nihilistic credo, summed up in the line, "The difference between something and nothing is nothing." Bowles replicates this sense of emotional emptiness in the barrenness of the desert geography, brilliantly and disturbingly.

In *The Waste Land* by T. S. Eliot, a poem which Bowles said influenced him a great deal, there is a similar sense of desiccation, and it is easy to draw a line directly from Eliot to Bowles, as is evident in the following few lines from part five of Eliot's masterpiece:

Here is no water but only rock
Rock and no water and the sandy road
The road winding above among the mountains
Which are mountains of rock without water
If there were water we should stop and drink
Amongst the rock one cannot stop or think
Sweat is dry and feet are in the sand.

The appeal of emptiness, which can inspire and terrify, the space—literally awful in that it is full of awe—that provides equilibrium for an otherwise unquiet mind, also threatens to lead the way to madness. As Bowles wrote, "Here, in this wholly mineral landscape lighted by stars like flares... nothing is left but your own breathing and the sound of your heart beating… no other surroundings can provide the supremely satisfying sensation of existing in the midst of something that is absolute." This sense of place and nothingness such as Kit and Port Moresby experience while travelling through the Sahara in *The Sheltering Sky* is outlined in Bowles' foreword to *Their Heads are Green and Their Hands are Blue*, where he remarks, "With few exceptions, landscape alone is of insufficient interest to warrant the effort it takes to see it. Even the works of man, unless they are being used in his daily living, have a way of losing their meaning, and take on the qualities of decoration."

The desert ought to be at least as much about its people as its landscapes. Outsiders rarely see this, and for residents, natives and blow-ins alike, it is simply home. Bowles, the outsider who moved in, recognizes this, and is not alone among those who have enjoyed some intimacy with the great desert, able to see many Saharas at once, but the people first. As he put it, "North Africa without its tribes, inhabited by, let us say, the Swiss, would be merely a rather more barren California."

Further Reading

TRAVEL GUIDES

The *Lonely Planet* series of country-specific and regional guidebooks, i.e. North Africa, are a useful source of information for tourists, including very basic language guides and some background to the history, politics and culture of the country or countries concerned. For anyone interested in organizing their own journeys across the desert, *Sahara Overland* (2nd ed.) is indispensable, detailing as it does tried and tested routes, choice of vehicle, navigation and suchlike.

LANDSCAPES

For classical accounts of the region's natural history, no reader should be without both Pliny the Elder's *Natural History* and Strabo's *Geography*. E. F. Gautier's *Sahara: The Great Desert* (Cass, 1971) is a great read, even if the original text is approaching its centenary.

HISTORY

The *Encyclopaedia of African History* (ed. Kevin Shillington, 2004) is an excellent three-volume work that deals in some detail with much of the region's history. Two smaller volumes that cover Saharan history in a simpler and often more accessible form are the *Travellers' History of North Africa* (Cassell, 1998) and the *Travellers' History of Egypt* (Interlink Books, 1997).

The following limited list consists of first class, established works that cover one or more aspects of Saharan history: Dr J. Ball, *Egypt in the Classical Geographers* (Cairo, 1942); E. Bovill, *The Golden Trade of the Moors* (OUP, 1968); Michael Brett and Elizabeth Fentress, *The Berbers* (Blackwell, 1997); E. W. Bulliet, *The Camel and the Wheel* (Columbia University Press, 1990); Fergus Fleming, *The Sword and the Cross* (Granta, 2003); Anthony Sattin, *Sahara: The Gates of Africa* (Harper Collins, 2003).

IMAGINATION

Many creative works born in the Sahara, real or imagined, are mentioned in the text. Here I offer some personal choice for a week's reading holiday in the desert: *Metamorphosis* by Ovid; *The Greek Myths* by Robert Graves; *The Sheltering Sky* by Paul Bowles; *Desert Air: A Collection of the Poetry of*

Place (Eland, 2003); and *Wind, Sand and Stars* by Antoine de Saint-Exupéry.

ENCOUNTERS

Among the most important classic accounts of Saharan journeys and expeditions are W. G. Browne, *Travels in Africa, Egypt, and Syria, from the Year 1792 to 1798*; Heinrich Barth, *Travels and Discoveries in North and Central and Africa*; Friedrich Hornemann, *Missions to the Niger (1797-1798)*; Gustav Nachtigal, *Sahara and Sudan* (Hurst, 1975), an epic among epics. The journal of Hugh Clapperton, *Difficult and Dangerous Roads* (Sickle Moon Books, 2000), offer a new and welcome perspective on the Denham, Oudney, Clapperton expedition.

The Lost Oases by Hassanein Bey (American University in Cairo Press, 2006) is a joy to read, while *Libyan Sands* (Hippocrene Books, 1987) by Ralph Bagnold was the first book that made me love the desert.

Post-independence volumes would have to include Michael Asher's *Impossible Journey* (Viking, 1988), a gripping account of his nine-month walk with camels, and his wife, across the Sahara. Geoffrey Moorehouse's account of an earlier, unsuccessful attempt to do the same is equally readable: *The Fearful Void* (Hodder & Stoughton, 1974). Justin Marozzi's *South from Barbary: Along the Slave Routes of the Libyan Sahara* (Harper Collins, 2001) is a great modern take on the joys of non-motor-powered Saharan journeying.

Index of Literary & Historical Names

Abbot and Costello 203

Abd al-Qadir (also Abd el-Kader and Abdel Kader) 111-112, 117, 176, 181

Abu Ishaq as-Sahili 70

Adam 160

Adams, President John 215

Addison, Joseph 163

African Association 85-90, 92, 94, 95, 100, 101, 104

Ainslie, Sir Robert 174

Alexander the Great, of Macedon 22, 36-39, 58, 156

Allenby, Roger 195

Almásy, László 17, 127-128, 139-140, 206

Almoravid 73

Amen-Ra (see also Ammon and Ra) 157

Ammon, Oracle at Siwa 36-39

Ampère, Jean-Jacques 16

Andrews, Harry 204, 205

Androvsky, Boris 199

Anson, Captain 131-132, 204-205

Anteoni, Ferdinand 199

Anthony, Mark 40

Anthony, St. 52-55, 220, 223

Antinea, Queen 186

Anubis 159

Aosta, Duke of 218

Apollo 155, 156

Archaeoceti 4

Argo 159

Aristobulus of Cassandreia 36

Aristotle 156

Arrian 36, 38

Ascherson, Paul Friedrich August 122

Asher, Michael 233-234

Askia Ishaq II 80

Athanasius, St. 51, 52, 53

Atum 31

Augustine, St., of Hippo 51, 52, 55, 237

Bagnold, Ralph 121, 126-127, 136, 139, 206

Bainbridge, Captain William 215

Al-Bakri, Abu Ubayd Muhammad 61, 65, 66, 72, 73

Ballard, J. G. 191

Balzac, Honoré de 199-200

Banks, Joseph 88, 92, 94

Barker, Dudley 132

Barra, King of 91

Barth, Heinrich 11, 81, 90, 106-108

Bartholomew, St. 49

Battiades 163

Beaton, Cecil 132

Bellange Joseph-Louis-Hippolyte 176

Belly, Léon 179

Benjamin of Tudela, Rabbi 67

Benoît, Pierre 186-187

Berenice 38

Berlusconi, Silvio 119

Bertolucci, Bernardo 207

Bismark, Otto von 109

Blackwood, Algernon 187, 188-189

Blake, William 165

Blavatsky, Madame 187

Bogart, Humphrey 204

Boles, John 198

Bond, James 138, 194, 206

Boniface 55

Bonnet, Dr. 16

Book of the Dead, Egyptian 30-31

Bosch, Hieronymous 55

Bou-Aziz 190, 191

Boudica 60

Bouteflika, Abdelaziz 147

Bowles, Paul 48, 207, 222, 237, 238,

245-248
Boyer, Charles 199
Boyle, T. C. (Tom Coraghessan) 92
Bramley, Wilfred Jennings 121
Bridgman, Frederick Arthur 179, 182
Brown, Charlie 190
Browning, Robert 112
Buchan, John 192
Burns, Robert 134
Burroughs, Edgar Rice 185
Burroughs, William 245
Burton, Richard 67
Byron, Lord George Gordon 164, 165,
    170, 174

Caillié, René-Auguste 81, 104-106
Caligula, Emperor 99
Callisthenes 36
Cambon, Jules 114
Cambyses II 34-36, 157, 193
Campbell, Jock 136
Cana, Frank 225
Capote, Truman 245
Caressa, Lady Teal 189
Carnarvon, Lord 218
Carter, Howard 218
Catherine the Great 89
Cato the Younger 163
Catullus 163
Champollion, Jean-François 100
Chatwin, Bruce 73, 234, 236, 243, 244
Childers, Erskine 192
Choukri, Mohamed 245
Christie, Agatha (née Miller) 229-230
Churchill, Winston 137-138
Cicero 156
Clapperton, Hugh 102-104, 105
Clayton, Patrick 128, 206
Clayton, Sir Robert 128
Clements, Sir John 200
Cleopatra 38, 40
Clifford, Alexander 136
Clive, Everard 112

Coleman, Ronald 203
Coleridge, Samuel Taylor 165
Connery, Sean 206
Cook, Captain James 88, 89
Cooper, Gary 201
Cornelius Balbus Minor 43
Croesus 21
Cronkite, Walter 135
Crowley, Aleister 188
Cyrus the Great 34

Daddah Moktar Ould 149
Dafoe, Willem 206
Dagineau, Sergeant-Major 203
Daniels, Ben 199
Daniken, Erik von 14
Darwin, Charles 101
Daud, Idris 233
Davis, Maggie 195
Day, Julian 193
Defoe, Daniel 104
De Gaulle, General Charles 131
Deighton, Len 192, 194
Delacroix, Eugène 174, 175, 177, 178,
    181, 182, 183
Denham, Dixon 102-104, 105
Depardieu, Gérard 201
al-Dhahabi, Ahmed al-Mansur (or
    Golden Conqueror) 80
Dickson, Charles Hanmer 213
Dietrich, Marlene 199
Dinet, Etienne (later Nasr'Eddine
    Dinet) 178
Diocletian, Emperor 49
Diodorus Siculus 158
Douglas, Keith 133-134, 169-170, 171,
    172
Douglas, Norman 227-229
Dresden, Rita 188
Dumas, Melchior 181

Eaton, William 215-216
Eberhardt, Isabelle 244-245

Electra 159
Eliot, T. S. 247
Emerson, Ralph Waldo 168
Enfilden, Domini 199
Engels, Frederick 101
Engle, Charlie 235
Epaphus, King of Egypt 159
Eros 159
Euryale 159
Eve 160

Farouk, King 143
Faversham, Harry 200
Fiennes, Ralph 206
Firth, Colin 206
Fischer, Ludwig Hans 180
Fleming, Ian 138
Follett, Ken 140
Forbes, Rosita 47, 122-123
Foucauld, Charles Eugène de 220-222
Foureau-Lamy, Expedition 117
Freiligrath, Ferdinand 168
French Foreign Legion 108, 190-192
Freud, Sigmund 52
Freudenberg, Joseph 95
Fromentin, Eugène 173, 176-177, 178,
    181, 183
Fu Manchu, Dr. 188
Furey, Michael 188

Gaddafi, Colonel Muammar 45, 119,
    141, 142-143, 148
Gaea 158, 160
Galton, Francis 46
Gaudí, Antoni 22
Gavotti, Lieutenant Giulio 119
Geiseric, King 55, 56
Gelimer 56
George, St. 49
Géricault, Théodore 177
Gérôme, Jean-Léon 179, 181, 182
Geste, Digby 201
Geste, John 201

Geste, Michael "Beau" 201
Gibbon, Edward 57, 58, 61
Gide, André 226
Gildo 43
Gilman, Dorothy 189
Ginsberg, Allen 245
Goethe, Johann Wolfgang von 166
Golden Conqueror (see also al-
    Dhahabi, Ahmed al-Mansur) 80
Golding, William 226
Gorgon Medusa 159
Graves, Robert 121, 155, 157, 159, 160
Graziani, Marshal 135
Grünewald, Matthias 55
Guillaumet, Gustave 177-179
Gunn, Sergeant Joe 204

Haggard, Rider 187
Al-Hamawi, Yaqut 68
Hammadi, Sidi Ahmed el Beshir 244
Hanbury-Tenison, Robin 238, 241
Hardy, Oliver 203
Harlow, Jean 203
Harpocrates 159
Hassanein, Ahmed, Bey 122-123, 129
Hay, George Campbell 172
Helios 155
Henderson, Hamish 134, 171-172
Henriot, Felix 187
Heracles 157
Hercules 38
Hermes Trismegistus 29
Herodotus 21, 34, 35-36, 42, 47, 68,
    85, 156, 157, 158
Hesiod 158
Hichens, Robert Smythe 198
Hillman, William 102
Hitler, Adolf 195, 204
HMS *Egyptienne* 100
HMS *Resolution* 89
Holmes, Sherlock 192, 199
Homer 5, 156
Hornemann, Friedrich 94-96, 106

Horus 156
Houghton, Major Daniel 90-91
Hoyt, Sharon 195
Hugo, Victor 110, 168, 174
Hunt, Leigh 165
Hussein, Saddam 22

Ibn Battuta 68-70, 75, 76, 77, 237
Ibn Hawqal, Mohammed Abul-Kassem 64
Ibn Juzayy 68
Ibn Khaldun, Abu Zaid 'Abdul Rahman 60, 64, 65, 73, 77-78, 81, 237
Idris, King 142
Al-Idrisi, Muhammad 66-67
Ingres, Jean-Auguste-Dominique 160
Isis 158, 159
Izzard, Eddie 133

Al-Jabarti 96, 97
Jabberen 14
Jackson, Clarence J. L. 195
Jarmain, John 171
Jason, son of Aeson 159
Jefferson, Thomas 89
Johns, Captain W. E. 139
Jones, Owen 97
Jonson, Ben 80
Juba, King 47
Judar Pasha 80-81
Jugurtha 112
Julius Caesar 39, 40, 99, 163
Julius Maternus 40
Jung, Carl Gustav 230-231
Jupiter 163

Al-Kahina 60-61
Kankou Musa, Emperor (see also Mansa Musa) 75
Karamanli, Hamet 215, 216
Karamanli, Yusuf Pasha 212, 215, 216
Keats, John 165, 166

Kerouac, Jack 245
Keyes, Sidney 170, 171
Kimble, George 69
King, Carlotta 198
Kipling, Rudyard 48, 192
Kitchener, Herbert, later Lord 23, 113, 118
Klee, Paul 183
Korda, Zoltan 200, 204

Laing, Alexander Gordon 212
Lambert, Emmeline 191
Lambert, Henri 190-191
Lamy, Major Amédée-François 216
Landon, Christopher 131
Laperinne, General 220
Laurel, Stan 203
Lavigerie Cardinal Charles Martial 222
Lawrence T. E. 120, 121
Lear, Tobias, V 216
Ledyard, John 89, 90, 91
Leibling, A. J. 135
Leo X, Pope 79
Leo Africanus, Joannes 78-80, 88, 237
Lhote, Henri 14
Libya, Goddess 155, 159
Lin, Kevin 235
Lincoln, President Abraham 214
Longfellow, Henry Wadsworth 166, 168
Louis XIV, King of France 110
Louis-Philippe I, King of France 99
Lucan 163
Lucas, George 197
Lucas, Simon 88, 90, 91
Lucius Apuleius 158
Lucius of Madaurus 158, 159
Lulu Belle 204
Lumet, Sidney 206
Lutz, Otto 131-132
Lyautey, General Hubert 230

Maclean, Fitzroy 138

Madison, James 215
Mahdi, The (*see also* Muhammad ibn-Abdalla) 23, 117, 192, 200
Malkovich, John 207
Mallory, Dr. 191-192
Mallowan, Max 229
Mann, Major 194
Mansa Musa (*see also* Kankou Musa, Emperor) 75, 76
Mansa Suleiman 76
Mark, St. 49
Al-Marrakushi, Ibn Idhari 58
Mason, A. E. W. 200
Matisse, Henri 178, 183
Mattingly, David 42
Maupassant, Guy de 176
Mayer, Luigi 174
Merton, Thomas 53, 223
Michelangelo 55
Midas, King 75
Milland, Ray 201
Milligan, Spike 133
Mills, John 204
Mills, Robert 98
Minghella, Anthony 206
Mohammed V, King of Morocco 144
Monet, Claude 182
Monica, St. 51
Monroe, President James 214
Montezuma 215
Moore, Alan 185
Moore, Brian 190
Moorehead, Alan 136
Moreau, Gustave 160
Morhange, Captain 186
Morton, H. V. 218
Mouhy, Charles Fieux de 185
Mozart, Wolfgang Amadeus 159
Mrabet, Mohamed 245
Muhammad, Prophet 61
Muhammad III as-Sadiq, Bey of Tunis 109, 117
Muhammad IV, Sultan of Morocco 108

Muhammad ibn-Abdalla (*see also* The Mahdi) 23, 113, 117
Mukhtar, Omar 119, 120
Müller, Leopold Carl 182
Al-Muqaddasi 63, 64
Murray, George 128, 140
Mussolini, Benito 204

Nachtigal, Gustav 109-110, 241
Napoleon Bonaparte 85, 94, 95, 96, 97, 100, 102, 173, 174, 199
Nash, Ogden 45
Nebuchadnezzar 34
Newman, John Philip, Bishop 112
Nielson, Lesley 203
Nilus 5

O'Bannon, Lieutenant Presley 216
Oceanus 5
Octavian, Emperor Augustus 40
Oedipus 160
Olympias 36
Olympiodorus of Thebes 41
Ondaatje, Michael 128, 139, 206
O'Neill, Kevin 185
Osiris 31, 156, 157, 158, 159
Oudney, Walter 102-104, 105

Palin, Michael 231
Palmerston, Lord Henry John Temple 213, 215
Park, Mungo 85, 91-92, 102
Paul, St. 51
Pei, I. M. 100
Penderel, Commander 128
Pères Blanc (also White Fathers) 222-223
Perseus 38
Peru, Mariantonietta 233
Petrie, Flinders 32, 157
Petrovich, Ivan 198
Phaeton 155
Pirajno, Count Alberto Denti di 218

Plato 157
Pliny the Elder 42, 80, 85, 88, 117
Plutarch 156, 157, 158
Poe, Edgar Allan 98, 168
Polisario 25
Polo, Marco 69
Pollifax, Mrs. 189
Polyaenus 34
Polybius 34, 39
Pompey 39
Pontus 160
Pory, John 79, 80
Possidius 55
Powell, Colin 144
Preston, Robert 201
Prévot, André 124
Procopius 55, 56
Prorok, Byron de 187
Ptolemaeus, son of Lagos 38
Ptolemy 38, 40, 80, 85, 88
Ptolemy I Soter 38
Pyle, Ernie 135

El-Qadir, Abd 101
Quayle, Anthony 205
Queensberry, Marquess of 227
Quintus Sertorius 157

Ra, see Amen-Ra 157
Ramsey, T. W. 171
Rathbone, Basil 199
Redgrave, Michael 206
Red Shadow 198
Renoir, Auguste 182, 183
Richardson, Sir Ralph 200
Riley, Captain James 211, 213-215
Rise, Ned 94
Robert, Augustin 199
Roberts, David 175
Roberts, Joe 205
Roger II, King of Sicily 66
Rohlfs, Friedrich Gerhard 108, 122
Rohmer, Sax 188-189

Rollins, Henry 240
Rommel, Irwin, Field Marshal 132,
    133, 138, 140
Rosetta Stone 100
Royal Geographical Society, The 104,
    109, 123
Royal Society, The 88
Ruse, Lieutenant De 203
Ruth, Roy Del 198

Saganne, Charles 201
Saint-Avit, Captain André de 186
Saint-Exupéry, Antoine de 124-126
Salisbury, Lord 114
Santana, Carlos 240
Santoro, Rubens 182
Satan 188
Saturninus 51
Savalas, Telly 203
Schongauer, Martin 55
Schulz, Charles 190
Scipio 39
Seabrook, William 124
Septimus Flaccus 40
Sereno, Paul 5
Set, also Seth 31, 32, 158
Shakespeare, William 188
Shaw, Bill (W. B.) Kennedy 127, 129
Shelley, Percy Bysshe 165, 166
Siméon, Count 97
Sin, Mrs. 188
Sinhaja 78
Skywalker, Luke 197
Smith, Horace 165
Smith, Sir Denis Nayland 188
Société Géographique de Paris 81, 106,
    200
Sokoto, Sultan of 108
Solinus 80
Speke, John Hanning 67
Speratus 51
Sphinx 160-162, 169
Stheno 159

Stirling, David 138
Stockwell, Guy 203
Strabo 39, 42
Stuck, Franz von 160
Sullivan, C. Gardner 197
Sunni Ali 78
Sykes, Sir Mark 120

Tacitus 43
Tarzan 185
Ténérian 9
Tennyson, Lord Alfred 70
Terry, Alice 198
Tertullian 51
Tethys 5
Thackeray, William Makepeace 112, 175
Thatcher, Margaret 236
Thatcher, Mark 236
Thaumas 159
Thesiger, Wilfred 232-233, 234
Thomas Cook and Sons 225, 234
Thomas, Kristin Scott 206
Timothy, St. 51
Tombalbaye, François 148
Trollope, Anthony 225
Trust for African Rock Art 18
Tunner, George 207
Tupper, Martin Farquhar 169
Turner, J. M. W. 177
Tutankhamen 218
Twain, Mark 226
Typhon 158

Al-Umari, Chihab Addine Abul-Abbas Ahmad 75
Ummayad 58, 60, 63
Unesco 3, 4, 18, 22, 24, 65
United Nations (UN) 18, 140, 142, 242
Uqba bin Nafi 58

Van Der Pol, Captain 205

Verne, Jules 94, 187
Vidal, Gore 245
Vischer, Major Sir Hanns 219
Vivant, Dominique, Baron de Denon 97, 173, 174
Voltaire 185
Voulet-Chanoine Mission 117

El-Walati, Ammer 107
Wallace, Alfred 101
Ward, Arthur Henry 188
Warner Brothers 198
Warrington, Emma 212
Warrington, Colonel Hanmer 211-213
Washington, President George 98, 164, 216
Waugh, Evelyn 232
Wauthier, Captain René 123
Wharton, Edith 120, 230
Wheatley, Dennis 193
White Fathers (also Pères Blanc) 222-223
Whitehead, Don 131, 135
Whittier, John Greenleaf 168
Wilberforce, William 90
Wilde, Oscar 169, 227
Wilhelm I of Prussia, Emperor 109
William the Bad 67
Williams, Tennessee 245
Willshire, William 214-215
Wilson, Regimental Sergeant-Major 205
Winger, Debra 207
Wolfe, Tom 125
Wordsworth, William 165
Wren, P. C. 190, 201

Yeats, W. B. 188
Young, Thomas 100

Zaghawa 81
Zahab, Ray 235
Zeus 38, 157, 158, 159

Zeus-Ammon, and Oracle of 38, 156, 157
Zidane, Zinedine 237
As-Zubayr, Rabih 82, 216

Index of Places & Landmarks

Abbasids 63
Abdalles 185
Abu Ballas (also Pottery Hill) 122
Abu Simbel 233
Abyssinia 109
Adrar 22
Adrianople (also Edirne) 215
Africa, African(s) 22, 45, 55, 57, 79,
    89, 92, 96, 98, 102, 109, 113-115,
    128, 133, 136, 138, 149, 155, 168,
    172, 176, 189, 191, 204, 215, 222,
    225, 231, 243
Africa Nova 40
Africa Vetus 40
Agadez (also Agades) 124, 187
Aghlabids 63
Agisymba 40
Ahaggar 14, 25, 42, 220, 222
Ain-Taya 133
Aïr 7, 13, 186, 187, 216
Alabama 179
Al-Alamein 204
Alaouite 108
Alexandria 49, 53, 99, 132, 205, 215
Algeria, Algerian(s) 8, 14, 16, 22, 24,
    25, 51, 101, 109, 110-111, 112,
    114, 117, 131, 135, 142, 144, 146,
    147, 150, 173, 174, 175, 176, 178,
    179, 182, 183, 187, 190, 194, 199,
    201, 203, 208, 213, 216, 220, 222,

223, 225, 226, 227, 230, 236, 237,
    238, 242, 243, 244-245
Algiers 65, 111, 222
Amazigh (see also Berber and
    Imazighen) 237
Ammon, Ammonians (see also Siwa)
    35-36, 38, 157, 163, 169
Amphicleocles 185
Anatolia 5
Anglo-Egyptian Sudan 113, 117, 118
Annaba (also Hippo) 244
Aouzou Strip 148
Arabia, Arabian, Arab(s) 22, 45, 46, 56,
    57-61, 63, 64, 65, 80, 102, 120,
    125, 133, 138, 142, 143, 149, 169,
    172, 188, 190, 195, 201, 214, 215,
    218, 225, 228-229, 232, 238, 242
Arlit 22, 26
Asia 46
Assekrem 220, 222
Assyrians 47
Atar 25
Aterian industry 7, 8
Atlantis 186
Atlas 40, 58, 106, 173
Aujila 95

Babylonian 34
Baghdad 63, 164
Bahariya 35, 39, 49

Bambara 236
Banu Hilal 64, 65
Banu Sulaym 64, 65
Barbary 79, 80
Bardo, Treaty of 117
Bedouin (*see also* Bedu) 64, 65, 119,
    124, 125, 127, 128, 169, 193, 237,
    243
Beirut 49
Bela 236
Ben Bella, President 147
Beni Abbès 221
Beni Mansour 133
Berber(s) (*see also* Amazigh and
    Imazighen) 15, 23, 32, 33, 34, 41,
    47, 50, 51, 52, 56, 57, 58, 60-61,
    63, 78, 112, 142, 143, 218, 236,
    237, 238, 242, 243
Bilma 42, 82, 186
Bir Ramla 128
Biskra 135, 178, 179, 183, 199
Blida 226
Bokani 95
Bornu, Empire and region (*see also*
    Kanem, Empire) 81-82, 94, 95,
    103, 104, 109, 148, 212
Bou Saada 178
Britain, British and British Empire 17,
    88, 90, 100, 101, 104, 106, 112,
    113, 117, 118, 120, 122, 129, 131,
    133, 136, 137, 139, 140, 142, 143,
    162, 173, 175, 188, 189, 190, 192,
    193, 204, 212, 213, 218, 219, 225
Buttercup Valley, Dunes 198, 199
Byzantine(s) 56, 57, 58

Cadiz 43
Cairo, Cairene 3, 23, 59, 64, 65, 75,
    77, 89, 94, 120, 121, 132, 136,
    140, 176, 181, 189, 197, 198, 230
Cameroon 110, 216
Cape Boujadour 214
Cape Juby (also Tarfaya) 126

Capsian 8
Carthage, Carthaginians 13, 33, 34, 39,
    43, 51, 56, 58
Casablanca 120
Central African Republic 191
Ceuta 66
Chaamba 222
Chad, Chadian 25, 95, 109, 114, 117,
    131, 142, 144, 147-148, 149, 173,
    191, 216, 241
Chad, Lake 40, 46, 81, 82, 95, 104,
    108, 109, 124, 216, 225, 241
Chinguetti 26, 244
Conakry 104
Congo 117, 216
Constantinople 114, 181, 211
Cydamae 43
Cyrenaica 8, 118, 119, 128, 134, 142
Cyrene 163

Dakar 26, 90, 126, 148, 235
Dakhla 108, 122, 123
Damascus 75, 111, 112
Darfur 81, 109, 123, 143, 144, 148,
    232, 233
Delta, Nile 31, 32, 100
Derna 215
Djenné 81
Djerba 237
Djinguereber, Mosque of 74
Dodona 157
Dongola 23
Douala 110

East Africa 136
Edirne (also Adrianople) 215
Egypt, Egyptian(s) 15, 16, 17, 29, 32,
    34-36, 39, 40, 47, 49, 50, 52, 57,
    58, 64, 68, 69, 71, 75, 89, 94, 95,
    96-100, 105, 108, 118, 122-123,
    128, 136, 142, 143, 155, 156, 157,
    158, 159, 160-162, 168, 172, 174,
    175, 176, 179, 183, 185, 187, 194,

199, 204, 206, 215, 225, 226, 229, 234
El-Kantara 227
Emi Koussi 233
Empty Quarter 232
England, English 44, 49, 82, 85, 88, 103, 113, 119, 120, 121, 122, 128, 136, 164, 166, 171, 175, 188, 203, 236
Ennedi 7, 148, 232, 233
Eritrea 218
Essaouira (also Mogador) 214

Ethiopia, Ethiopian(s) 35, 42, 82, 218, 241
Europe, European(s) 22, 49, 55, 61, 68, 70, 80, 81, 82, 85, 88, 89, 92, 95, 96, 97, 99, 100, 101, 102, 103, 104, 106, 107, 108, 110, 113-115, 117, 118, 121, 122, 128, 141, 146, 150, 155, 159, 160, 163, 164, 173, 176, 178, 183, 185, 187-188, 190, 194, 201, 211, 213, 220, 222, 225, 226, 229, 231, 237, 242

Fatimids 64
Fez 79, 113
Fez, Treaty of 119, 144
Fezzan 13, 15, 40, 41, 42, 43, 45, 88, 118, 119, 142, 143, 230
Figuig 144
Fondouk 133
Fort Arid 203
Fort Capuzzo 194
Fort Lamy 216
Fort Laperrine (see also Tamanrasset) 25, 220
Fort Zinderneuf 190, 201
Fortunate Islands 157
France, French 25, 61, 81, 82, 89, 94, 95, 96, 100, 106, 111-112, 113, 114, 117, 118, 122, 128, 131, 136, 138, 140, 144, 147, 149, 162, 164,

172, 173, 178, 179, 185, 190-192, 198, 201, 204, 213, 215, 216, 219, 220-222, 227, 230, 236, 241, 244, 247
Freetown 104, 105
French Equatorial Africa 139, 241
French Sudan 131
French West Africa 131, 148, 216
Fulani 104, 236

Gades 43
Gadoufaoua, Valley 5
Gafsa 8
Gambia 88, 90, 91
Gana 68
Gao 78, 80, 81
Garama, Garamantes 41-45, 47, 64, 157, 239
Germa 42, 45
Germany, German(s) 94, 108, 109, 110119, 120, 122, 125, 128, 131, 132, 134, 136, 137, 138, 139, 140, 168, 171, 172, 192, 193, 195, 204, 205, 236
Ghadames 24, 43, 189, 212, 213, 218
Ghana 66
Ghana, Empire of 67, 71-73, 77
Gholaia 44
Gibraltar, and Strait of 55, 120
Gilf Kebir 17, 123, 128
Giza 30
Gobero 8, 9
Goree Island 90, 91
Grand-Bassem 110
Great Sand Sea 22, 26, 123, 127
Greece, Greek(s) 33, 34, 41, 51, 52, 71, 79, 85, 121, 155, 156, 157, 158, 159, 160, 172, 213, 238
Guinea 104

Hammamet 183
Hausa 90
Heliopolis 99, 121

Helwan 68
Hippo (also Annaba) 52, 56, 244
Hungary, Hungarian 17, 128, 139, 200

Iberia 80
Ifriqiya 57, 58, 60, 63, 65
Imazighen (*see also* Amazigh and
    Berber) 33, 237
Imperial Valley 204
India 5
In-Guezzam 124
In Salah 22, 26, 212
Iran 5
Iraq 5, 22
Ireland, Irish 141, 204
Irkutsk 89
Iroquols 89
Islands of the Blessed 157
Italy, Italian(s) 53, 100, 114, 118, 119,
    120, 122, 128, 129, 131, 134, 135,
    140, 143, 172, 189, 193, 194, 204,
    218
Italian North Africa 115, 128
Ivory Coast 110

Jaghbub 122, 143
Jebel Arkenu 123
Jebel Uweinat 123
Jerusalem 64

Kabara 105
Kabyle 111, 112, 238
Kairouan 58, 183
Kanem, Empire (*see also* Bornu,
    Empire) 81-82, 241
Kano 104
Kashna 95
Kharga 35
Khartoum 109, 144
Kiffian 9
Kordofan 109
Kouar 42
Kousséri 216

Kufra, also Kufara 108, 122, 18
Kukawa 109
Kush 35

Laghouat 178
Lagos 243
Lebanon 175
Leptis Magna 39
Levant 5
Libya, Libyan(s) 8, 13, 17, 24, 25, 34,
    38, 41, 44, 45, 52, 68, 80, 109,
    114, 118, 119, 120, 122-123, 128,
    139, 140, 141, 142, 143, 148, 155,
    157, 163, 240, 241
Libyan Desert 108, 129, 159, 173, 194,
    205, 206, 237, 238
Limes Britannicus 44, 79
Limes Tripolitanus 44
Lower Egypt 31, 32
Lower Saxony 94
Luxor 99, 100, 229

Macedon, Macedonians 34, 36
Madrid   , Conference of 118
Maghreb, Maghrebi(s) 58, 61, 63, 64,
    65, 77, 78, 141, 150, 235, 238
Malaya 136
Mali 9, 22, 25, 33, 69, 91, 114, 117,
    131, 142, 149, 150, 173, 225, 234,
    236, 238, 240, 242
Mali, Empire of 72-78, 89
Malinke 236
Malta 49
Mameluke 75, 200, 216
Mareth Line 137
Marsa Matruh 38, 194
Mascara 111
Matmata 197
Mauri 57
Mauritania, Mauritanian(s) 23, 25, 33,
    40, 43, 57, 69, 114, 117, 131, 142,
    145, 149, 173, 214, 225, 233, 244
Mecca 75, 96, 133, 225, 238, 242

Mediterranean 5, 33, 34, 41, 46, 50, 56, 61, 65, 140, 142, 144, 158, 182
Memphis 35, 39
Middle East 45, 194, 229
Mogador (also Essaouira) 214
Moor(s) 79, 91, 94, 149, 236, 242
Morocco, Moroccan(s) 7, 24, 25, 40, 50, 77, 80-8188, 90, 108, 112, 113, 114, 118, 119, 131, 142, 144-146, 150, 173, 174, 175, 183, 198, 208, 214, 220, 230, 232, 234, 237, 242
Mossi 236
Murzuq 95, 213

N'Djamena 144, 216
Niger 5, 8, 13, 22, 25, 33, 82, 105, 114, 117, 131, 142, 148, 149, 150, 173, 208, 216, 236, 238, 242
Niger, River 67, 70, 77, 78, 81, 88, 89, 91, 92, 95, 102, 105, 167, 237
Nigeria 95, 104, 219
Nile, Nile Valley 7, 9, 17, 23, 29, 30, 31, 32, 35, 38, 47, 57, 67, 77, 81, 88, 89, 109, 140, 143, 157, 158, 166, 225, 233, 234
Nitra 53
Nouakchott 23
Nubia, Nubian(s) 16, 42, 81
Numidia, Numidian(s) 34, 39, 40, 42, 43, 47, 51, 52, 56, 112, 238

Oasis 35-36
Al-Obeid 123
Oea 39
Olympus, Olympians 5
Oran 111, 245
Ottoman Empire, Ottomans 102, 110, 114, 117, 118, 119, 173, 174, 213, 219
Ouadane 26

Palestine 121, 175, 220
Papua, Mount 56
Paraetonium 38
Paris 26, 94, 99, 100, 106, 124, 125, 197, 220, 235
Paris Natural History Museum in Algeria 16
Pellucidar 185
Pelusim, Battle of 34
Persia, Persian(s) 34-36, 80, 138, 156, 192, 238
Phazzania 43
Philae 16
Phoenicia, Phoenician(s) 32-34, 41, 57, 237
Poland 89
Port Said 34
Pyramids, at Giza 225, 226

Al-Qara 132
Qatarra Depression 132

Red Sea 235
Regenfeld 108
Rif 144
Rio de Oro 145
Rome, Roman(s) 39-41, 42-44, 47, 49, 50-51, 52, 57, 58, 60, 61, 71, 79, 95, 85, 112, 118, 155, 158, 159, 160, 163, 238
Rouiba 133
Russia 89, 236

Sabha 68
Sabratha 39
Saguia el-Hamra 145
Sahel, Sahelian 15, 117, 147, 149, 177, 243
Sahrawi 25, 145-146, 214, 241-244
St. Louis 214, 235
Sakkara 30, 32
Salima 139
Sanussi 120, 122, 142, 189, 222

Sankore, Mosque of 74
Scilium 51
Scotland, Scottish 44, 91, 92, 134, 138, 172
Senegal 88, 90, 105, 117, 187, 214, 235
Senegal River 104, 105
Sicily 66
Sidi Yahya, Mosque of 74
Simbing 91
Sinai 34
Sirte 142
Siwa (see also Ammon) 22, 23, 35, 36, 39, 95, 108, 122, 128, 137, 157, 237
Smara 25
Sokoto 104, 212
Somaliland 218
Songhai, Empire 78, 80-81
Songhoi 236
Sosso 71
Souk Ahras 51
South Africa, South African 204, 205
South America 235
Soviet Union 142, 193
Spain 55, 79, 102, 113, 114, 118, 142, 144, 145, 206
Spanish Sahara 25, 114, 144-145
Sudan, Sudanese 17, 23, 35, 38, 40, 46, 65, 82, 95, 113, 117, 118, 123, 129, 139, 142, 143, 144, 147, 148, 173, 191, 200, 204, 222, 225, 232, 233
Suez Canal 34, 143, 176
Suluq 119
Syria 47, 49, 175

Taghaza 69
Taiwan   235
Takrur 77
Tamanrasset (see also Fort Laperrine) 25, 124, 195, 196, 216, 220, 222
Tangier 69, 106, 183, 245

Tarfaya (also Cape Juby) 126
Tassili n'Ajjer 14
Tatouine 197
Tebu (see also Tibbu and Toubou) 81
Tehenu 32
Temehu 32
Ténéré 81, 149
Tessalit 22
Tethys, Ocean   and Sea 3, 5
Thagaste 51
Thebes 35, 157, 160, 218
Tibesti 7, 25, 40, 42, 81, 148, 232, 241
Tibbu (see also Tebu and Toubou) 233
Tieme 104
Timbuktu 21, 22, 67, 69, 70, 73-76, 78, 79, 80, 81, 82, 88, 89, 90, 92, 95, 104-106, 124, 212
Tindouf 24, 144, 145, 187, 222, 234
Tizi Ouzou 133
Tobruk 119, 136
Togoland 110
Tondibi 80-81
Toubou (see also Tebu and Tibbu) 241-244
Toucouleur 236
Touggourt 199, 227
Tripoli 39, 42, 88, 95, 102, 104, 108, 134, 189, 205, 211, 212, 215, 218
Tripolitania, Tripolitanian 39, 43, 118, 119, 142, 215, 230
Troy 171
Tuareg 5, 15, 50, 74, 149, 186, 189, 195, 201, 218, 220, 221, 236, 237, 238-240
Tuat (also Twat) 216
Tunis 109
Tunisia, Tunisian(s) 8, 40, 51, 58, 65, 110, 113, 117, 137, 142, 147, 170, 183, 187, 195, 197, 206, 215, 223, 225, 227-228, 237
Turkey, Turk(s) 63, 111, 119, 215
Tyre 33

United States of America, American(s)
25, 88, 89, 97, 98, 102, 112, 115,
118, 135, 142, 166, 179, 190, 194,
197, 198, 207, 212, 213-216, 230,
235, 245
Upper Egypt 31, 32

Valley Forge 164
Valley of the Kings 30, 218
Valley of the Queens 30
Valley of the Whales (*see also* Wadi al-
Hitan) 3, 4
Vandals 44, 52, 55-57
Vatican City 99

Wadai 109
Wadi al-Hitan (*see also* Valley of the
Whales) 3, 4
Wadi Natrun 53
Wadi Telisaghé 13
Walata, (also Iwalatan, Oualata and
Wualata) 69
West Africa 40, 74, 78, 89, 110, 117,
243

Western Desert, Egypt 31, 32, 120,
121, 132, 194, 204, 206, 215
Western Sahara 24, 25, 114, 126, 142,
144-146, 150, 232, 242

Yugoslavia 138

Zanzibar 109, 187
Zawilah 68
Zerzura, and Club 206
Zinder 216
Zouar 25